Advance Praise for
Adrift: The Cuban Raft People

"**A compressed epic** of the suffering, heroism, and determination that evinced itself in the Cuban refugee crisis in the 1990s . . . . Carries heavy moral weight . . . . Fernández offers a terse but detailed narrative from within Cuba, capturing the desperate ingenuity of the Cuban people (both to build rafts, and merely to survive the post-1989 socialist privations), as well as the hoary treachery of the Castro regime . . . **Fernández also pulls back for the crucial global view,** examining Castro's long run, Cuba's contentious relationships with other Latin-American nations, and its perpetually worsening relations with the Clinton administration . . . . The author's portraits of these players and politicians, juxtaposed with details of the perpetually struggling Cubans, are **laced with mordant irony.** Fernández's passions, the immediacy of his reportage from the battered Communist redoubt, and his understanding of the Cuban people's willingness to risk all for better lives make this **a substantial contribution to a thorny international debate.**"

—*Kirkus Reviews*

ADRIFT
The Cuban Raft People

Alfredo A. Fernández

Translated by Susan Giersbach Rascón

Arte Público Press
Houston, Texas

This volume is made possible through grants from the City of Houston through The Cultural Arts Council of Houston, Harris County.

Recovering the past, creating the future

Arte Público Press
University of Houston
Houston, Texas 77204-2174

Cover photograph by Reuters/Archive Photos

Cover design by James F. Brisson

Fernández, Alfredo Antonio, 1945-
    [A la deriva. English]
    Adrift : The Cuban Raft People / by Alfredo A. Fernández ; translated from the Spanish by Susan Giersbach Rascón.
        p.   cm.
    ISBN 1-55885-300-6 (pbk. : alk. paper)
    I. Cubans—United States—History—20th century   2. Refugees— United States—History—20th century.   3. Refugees—Cuba—History— 20th century.   4. United States—Emigration and immigration— History—20th century.   6. United States—Relations—Cuba. 7. Cuba—Relations—United States.   8. United States—Foreign relations—1989-   I. Title.
E184.C97 F46 2000
973'.04687291—dc21   00-042006
                                                                          CIP

∞ The paper used in this publication meets the requirements of the American National Standard for Information Sciences—Permanence of Paper for Printed Library Materials, ANSI Z39.48-1984.

0 1 2 3 4 5 6 7 8 9   10 9 8 7 6 5 4 3 2 1

Contents

Harsh and bitter fate

Casts us toward foreign shores . . .

—José Agustín Quintero, *El banquete del destierro*

To the Cuban people, who deserve a better fate.

Acknowledgments

AT NOON ON FRIDAY, August 5, 1994, I was in Miami in the company of Lisandro Pérez, director of the Cuban Research Institute at Florida International University. He gave me a detailed explanation of the upcoming Rockefeller Fellowships Conference on Cuban affairs, to be held the following year. As I was a potential candidate, Lisandro asked what my interests might be. I responded with a very current topic: the exodus of the Cuban raft people and the rescue efforts carried out by Brothers to the Rescue.

That very afternoon, radio and television stations had aired news of the riots taking place on the Havana waterfront as an angry crowd, made desperate by the unbearable crisis their country was suffering, took to the streets in defiance of government authorities.

The events that followed further confirmed my sense that the topic I had chosen was the correct one. The U.S. government ordered its Coast Guard to interdict Cuban raft people at sea and send them immediately to the U.S. Naval Base at Guantánamo, ending an astounding maritime exodus that, in only a couple of weeks, had brought many thousands of people to U.S. shores and had left an appalling death toll as thousands more disappeared forever into the rough waters of the Florida Straits.

A year later, in August 1995, I returned to the United States to carry out my proposed activities under the Rockefeller Fellowship, awarded to me by a five-member jury. At that time I left my position as visiting professor at the Universidad Autónoma Estado México-Toluca and my master's in Latin-American Studies program at the Universidad Nacional Autónoma de México.

Here, then, are the people who became familiar with, helped in, and expressed solidarity with the development of this project:

In Mexico—Drs. Hernán Lara Zavala (UNAM), Enrique Balp (UNAM), and Jaime Collazo (UAEM); and writer Paco Taibo II.

In the United States—Drs. Lisandro Pérez (Florida International University), Rodolfo Cortina (University of Houston), Lynn Cortina (University of Houston), Uva de Aragón (Florida International University), Mark Rosenberg (Florida International University), Pedro Gutiérrez (University of Houston), and Nicolás Kanellos (University of Houston/Arte Público Press); Susie Penley, Teresita Marril, Humberto Tarafa, Tony Martínez, Ana Knatt, and Edwin Padilla; and my *simpático* editor at Arte Público, Clifford Crouch.

To all of them, to the uncounted raft people whose heroic odysseys are recounted in these pages, and to the Cuban people, many thanks.

Alfredo A. Fernández
Summer 2000

Chapter I

The Comandante, The Rafts, and International Diplomacy

THE REPORTER FROM THE FRENCH MAGAZINE *Elle* was giving up hope of interviewing Fidel Castro before leaving Havana. She had heard comments that the Cuban Communist leader, a man of incredible public impact whose speeches before hundreds of thousands of people often lasted several hours, was extremely reluctant to grant interviews to the press, especially foreign journalists. The *Elle* reporter believed she had taken all the appropriate steps: She had spoken with Cuban State Department officials, Communist Party officials, and Council of State employees. To all of them, she had reiterated her interest in interviewing Castro. More than once she had heard the anecdote about a reporter from the United States who, after waiting several months for the requested interview, was finally climbing the steps to the plane to return to his country. At that moment, Fidel Castro arrived at the airport in a jeep and took the reporter on a tour of the whole island, showing him agricultural development plans he had designed himself.

For that reason, on that afternoon in the early summer of 1994, when the *Elle* reporter received confirmation that she was being granted the long-awaited interview, she said to herself, "This is my chance." During the interview, she went so far as to tell the Cuban leader a joke she had heard on the streets of Havana.

"Comandante, do you know what the greatest achievements of the Cuban Revolution are?"

As in the joke, the Comandante responded immediately: "Education, public health, and sports."

1

"And the greatest failures, Comandante, do you know what they are?"

Faced with the silence of the Comandante at this point in the joke, the reporter herself was forced to respond: "Breakfast, lunch, and dinner."

That summer afternoon, Fidel Castro was evidently in a good mood; he laughed loudly. The *Elle* reporter, seeing that she had passed her "trial by fire" by telling the Comandante a joke of doubtful revolutionary color, decided it was an opportune moment to ask the Cuban leader: What will happen when you're gone?

Castro's tone of voice changed, and the smile disappeared from his face: "That, you'll have to ask the CIA." And immediately he added: "Honestly, I don't believe anything will happen."

When asked about U.S. President Bill Clinton, Castro stated that his opinion was favorable. He hurried to add, though, that he would love for his personal friend Ted Turner, owner of the multimillion-dollar television network CNN, to one day become president of the United States.

This interview was conducted in early June 1994, when the exchange of emissaries among Latin-American state departments was most intense, and the hotel complexes of the famous Caribbean resort of Cartagena de Indias, Colombia, were finalizing preparations for the Fourth Annual Summit of Latin-American Nations.

Neither Fidel Castro nor Bill Clinton would have guessed then that the differences between their countries prolonged for more than thirty years would place them only a couple of months later in a new situation: no longer distant rivals, but close opponents, intent on seeing which of the two could first deal the strongest blow to his adversary.

On this occasion, the fuse was lit not by the presence in Cuban territory—as occurred in October 1962 during the Kennedy Administration—of Soviet ballistic missiles capable of striking major U.S. cities with atomic warheads. Rather, it was lit by the presence in the waters of the Florida Straits of more than thirty thousand raft people who, on tiny rafts and vessels of primitive manufacture, in the little less than two weeks during which unrestricted departure was authorized, threatened to reach the coasts of the United States in uncontrollable numbers.

The economic situation of the Cuban people had begun to deteriorate distressingly beginning in the summer of 1989. Preceded by the destruction of the Berlin Wall by sledgehammer blows, one after another the various socialist states undertook the task of dismantling the Communist Party as the sole governing body of the social, economic, political, and ideological lives of their countries.

In economic terms, Cuba saw its gross domestic product (GDP) plummet terrifyingly between 1989 and 1994. A recent report presented by Carlos Lage, vice president of Cuba for economic affairs, at the World Economic Forum in Davos, Switzerland, indicates that in 1989—the last year before the crisis took hold in Cuban economic life—the national GDP had reached 19,589 million pesos. The following year, it fell to 19,008 million; in 1991, to 16,975 million; in 1992, to 15,022 million; and, finally, it crashed in 1993 and 1994 to 12,000 and 12,084 million, respectively.

On the streets of Havana, and in the towns in the interior of the island, there was a scarcity of products such as bath soap, laundry detergent, electricity, transportation, food, shoes, medicine, water, and gas. Housewives were forced to work miracles to stretch their already meager food rations, received through rationing coupons, enough to cover even the minimum of family consumption.

One of the most critical shortages was in the supply of petroleum that Cuba had been receiving from the Soviet Union in exchange for sugar. Over five years, from an amount of approximately thirteen and a half million tons of petroleum, the supply was drastically reduced to a little less than three million tons.

On the streets of Havana, tens of thousands of bicycles, hurriedly purchased by the Cuban government from China, were substituted overnight for gasoline-driven transportation.

Industrial activity in the country was suddenly semi-paralyzed by the lack of raw materials; during the early days of the crisis the entire responsibility for nonproductive salaries fell on the shoulders of the state.

The sudden reduction in supply in the domestic market caused the fiscal deficit to soar from 1,403 million pesos in 1989 to 5,050 million pesos in 1993.

The sugar harvest, the main source of convertible income for Cuba, became the focus of the economic catastrophe; in 1993-1994 it reached its lowest production level, with a harvest estimated at four million tons, a little less than half of what the country was producing during the late 1980s.

In the ruins of the state economic collapse, clandestine commerce flourished—the black market, the exchange of dollars for Cuban pesos. By April 1994, four months before thousands of people would abandon the country *en masse* on rafts, a dollar was worth 120 pesos. According to tentative figures by official Cuban economists, the excessive total of monetary circulation in May 1994 was nearly twelve thousand million pesos, almost four times what the Cuban economy usually required to function normally.

In Cuban cities and in the countryside, the unanimous clamor of the people bordered on despair, as they saw no sign on the horizon of an end to the so-called "special period" decreed by the government in response to the severe crisis.

For Noel Argüelles, goalie of the Cuban national soccer team, this was the moment, and the most appropriate place was the tiny international airport of the Grand Cayman Islands, a British territory south of Cuba. There, on the tiny islands devoted entirely to tourism, a colony of boat people had found safe refuge since 1989, when the crisis began to be felt.

Argüelles was participating in a friendship match with a local soccer team, and heard comments that Cuban raft people were living in a small camp composed of seven military tents surrounded by a tall fence topped with barbed wire. He did not give it a second thought. After kicking the ball hard during the last game of the series, he packed his bags and went to the airport with the rest of the team. While in line to board the plane that would take him back to Havana, he pretended stomach pain. Instead of going to the bathroom, he went to customs. In an improvised speech and through gestures, he requested political asylum in shouts that were at times unintelligible to the English-speaking Cayman guards.

≈ ≈ ≈

From Havana, in late May 1994, international news agencies reported the clandestine forced entry of 124 Cubans (sixty-eight men, thirty-two women, and twenty-four children) into the Belgian Embassy through a white iron gate.

Three weeks earlier, in early May, twenty-eight-year-old Rolando Martínez, one of the leaders of the group, had called his aunt and uncle in Miami. He told them that he was planning "to do something to get out of the situation." Before hanging up, he mentioned the word "Belgium."

His uncle Orlando Martínez later told the press: "When I finished talking to my nephew, I thought he was going to get on a Belgian ship at one of the wharves of Havana. As soon as I hung up the phone, I went to get a map to see where the hell Belgium was. When I saw that Belgium was over there by Europe, I said to myself, Well, they're going to end up far away, but anything is better than starving to death in Cuba." So on May 28, when Orlando Martínez heard on the radio what had just happened in Havana, he did not hesitate a second before calling his wife. "Melbi, they're there, in the Belgian Embassy!"

≈ ≈ ≈

But fate did not smile on all the refugees.

In Santo Domingo, capital of the Dominican Republic, a group of thirty-six Cubans was being threatened with forcible police eviction from the premises of the Hostel Víctor if they did not pay the rent. Fifteen months after leaving Cuba and arriving in Santo Domingo, the Cubans saw their fate still up in the air. They were becoming a familiar sight to the people of Quisqueya, who often saw them wandering through its streets and parks. Tired of the continuous back and forth and the endless bureaucratic procedures in hot government offices full of papers and flies, the Cubans went to President Joaquín Balaguer, asking to be confined in the Centro Vacacional de Haina. From there, they were forcibly evicted after a frustrated flight by sea to the neighboring island of Puerto Rico.

The Cubans had originally arrived at the Grand Cayman Islands in February 1993. Most of them accepted an offer by members of the anti-Castro organization PUND (Partido de Unidad Nacional Democratica, or Party of National Democratic Unity) to travel to Santo Domingo; from there, they were told, they would obtain entry into the United States.

PUND had assured the raft people that they would receive their visas in forty to fifty days, but nothing happened. Desperate, they burst violently into the Mexican Embassy in Santo Domingo in September 1993, and demanded visas to travel to the United States. A year and a half later they were still awaiting a response.

Jorge Martínez, a U.S. Army sergeant stationed at one of the U.S. bases in the Panama Canal Zone, liked to go dancing with his wife on weekends. In the wee hours of the morning on June 4, 1994, they were returning home after having danced *cumbias* and *vallenatos* to the point of exhaustion at one of the discotheques in the Canal Zone. Entering the house, he heard the unmistakable sound of an emergency call. He sat down at the receiver. To his astonishment, the message was from a Cuban boat adrift in international waters in the Florida Straits. It was a call for help; the boat was being fired on in the middle of the night by gunners and patrol boats.

Sergeant Jorge Martínez shouted to his wife to bring him a wet towel to wipe his face. The effects of the alcohol he had consumed that night disappeared rapidly. Martínez wrote down the information he had received thus far in a notebook he kept alongside the receiver. The Cuban-registered boat *René Heredia Morales,* with more than sixty people on board, among them women and children, was being closely pursued by four gunboats and one Cuban Navy patrol boat. Now fully awake, Sergeant Martínez maintained secret contact with the boat's crew. Seeing that the reports he was receiving indicated increasing distress, he sent S.O.S. signals to everyone he could: He alerted the Southern Army Command, the U.S. Embassy in Panama, the U.S. Coast Guard, and the pilots of Brothers to the Rescue.

Meanwhile, on board the *René Heredia Morales,* the sixty-four crew members threw themselves to the deck floor every time the Cuban patrol boats shot at the craft, shouting at them to stop their engines on the open sea: *Criminals! Sons-of-bitches!* The tenacious pursuit had begun practically the moment they set off from the port of Mariel, in western Cuba, at one o'clock in the morning. A half hour later, when they could still see the town's few lights in the distance, the hijackers watched in horror as Cuban Navy patrol boats moved quickly toward them, sweeping the choppy waters with their powerful searchlights. The shooting started moments later. The women's fearful screams, warning that there were children on board, fell on deaf ears. The patrol boats took turns in the chase; when some of them ran out of bullets, they shot screws and nuts, which fell and bounced on the deck of the *René Heredia Morales,* causing tremendous noise and panic.

It was then that Elio Díaz, one of four crew members wounded in the shooting, noticed that the sun was about to come up. Knowing that daylight meant capture of the fugitive ship, he decided to send an S.O.S. signal with a radio he found in the captain's cabin.

On the Isthmus of Panama, Sergeant Jorge Martínez picked up the distress signal, and did not leave his radio for the next four hours. At 8:45 A.M. on June 4, a Falcon aircraft belonging to the U.S. Coast Guard sighted the Cuban vessel and its distressed crew some sixty-seven miles southwest of Key West. "We're saved!" and "God heard our pleas!" chorused those on board the fleeing vessel when they saw the plane circling above them.

Elio Díaz and the three other men who were wounded during the spectacular escape were immediately transported by helicopter to a hospital in Stocks Islands. The rest of those on board were taken to Key West in a U.S. Coast Guard cutter.

Arturo Cobo, director of the Cuban Refugee Center in Key West, was accustomed to seeing people arrive with sunburn, dehydration, or fish bites on their arms and legs. However, this was the first time he had seen Cubans with gunshot wounds arrive at U.S. hospitals.

In Washington, a spokesman for the U.S. Cuban Interests Section termed the act a hijacking of a boat that was the property of the Cuban government, and justified the use of force by Cuban Navy troops in the attempt to capture the stolen vessel.

"For me it was a great honor to help all of you," declared Sergeant Martínez four months later when he traveled from Panama to Miami on October 16 to meet the men, women, and children he had helped to save. "I was fortunate to have been able to respond at an extremely critical moment," added Martínez, visibly moved. The meeting of savior and survivors took place in the Brothers to the Rescue hangar at Opa-Locka Air Force Base.

Sergeant Martínez was wearing a Panama Canal Amateur Radio Association sweater. Members of Brothers to the Rescue and Díaz's family presented Martínez with a plaque in gratitude for his meritorious work. Amidst hugs and applause, the sergeant heard from the mouths of the survivors words that moved him to tears: "We will never forget what you did for us," and "We owe you our lives."

☙ ☙ ☙

In Cartagena de Indias, Colombia, beneath a burning sun, in 104° temperatures even in the shade of the walls of ancient fortresses from the time of the pirate attacks of Francis Drake, the presidents of the Latin-American hemispheric community prepared to begin their fourth annual Ibero-American Summit. The topic of Cuba was not on the agenda as a separate point, but as the presidential planes arrived and an entourage of chancellors and diplomatic aides descended the red-carpeted stairways, reporters questioned the new arrivals about the "Cuban matter."

One of the first to offer his opinion was Uruguayan President Luis Alberto Lacalle, who declared: "President Castro is a dinosaur; let's think about Cuba, not about Castro."

Colombian Chancellor Noemí Sanín, hostess of the conference, stated that, although Cuba did not occupy a specific place on the meeting agenda, all those present should agree to contribute to the democratization of the island. In response to the reporters' inquiry as to whether the conference's final declaration would contain a condemnation of the U.S. embargo of Cuba, Sanín said that the document would condemn unilateral embargoes of any type.

Against this background, it was easy to suppose that the arrival of Comandante Fidel Castro, who for thirty-five consecutive years had controlled Cuba's destiny, would turn out to be a real time bomb.

Castro appeared on the scene on June 14. Before an audience of presidents, chancellors, diplomats, reporters, agents of various secret police services of the world, customs officials, and departing passengers, he arrived dressed in an unusual manner. For the first time in almost forty years, he was not wearing his traditional olive-green uniform and tall combat boots of the days of the guerrilla struggle in the Sierra Maestra, but rather the most typical of traditional Cuban garb: a *guayabera.*

Immediately the comments began to roll through the old polished-stone streets of the colonial city: Fidel Castro, the leader who had been in power longest as a result of an armed revolution, had decided to change his personal attire. Who knows, commented some, perhaps he was willing to moderate his habitual anti-imperialist expressions and his Marxist-Leninist ideological intransigence as well.

Wearing an elegant, white long-sleeved *guayabera,* khaki slacks, and black shoes, Fidel Castro arrived at the Conference Center at 8:20 A.M., and walked slowly toward President Gaviria through a double row of Colombian Navy cadets, while the military band played the theme from the film *Bridge on the River Kwai.* (Some of those in attendance wondered if British actor Alec Guinness was in the audience.)

Within the premises of the Conference Center, there was such a commotion that several of Castro's bodyguards hit Reuters reporters who were trying desperately to be the first to capture the Cuban leader's new look on film.

News of Castro's wardrobe change went around the world instantly. The reaction was immediate. Ramón Puig, owner of Miami's Casa de las Guayaberas, who for years had made those shirts for former Cuban presidents Carlos Prío and Fulgencio Batista, declared that in a matter of hours, he had received more than one hundred calls from some of his most exclusive clients in the United States and abroad, asking him if he had made Castro's new *guayabera.* "Never," commented Puig. "I would make him a custom-made straitjacket, not a *guayabera.*"

Unlike the other Latin-American heads of state, who used the time allotted for their opening addresses to talk about the realities and perspectives of their respective nations, Castro barely spoke of Cuba, but rather dedicated most of his seven-minute speech to attacking the United States. After praising the process of Latin-American integration, he emphasized that the United States government was concerned about that possibility and that, therefore, it was inviting the countries to another summit that would be held, coincidentally, in Miami.

"Cuba, besieged and blockaded for more than thirty years now, is prohibited by the supposed owners of the hemisphere from participating in that meeting. Cuba is not opposed to that summit. But if these subjects are debated in the Miami Summit, Cuba wishes them success." When Fidel Castro ended his speech, no head of state responded directly to his statements, although there were indeed strong calls for carrying out reforms in Cuba.

In the opinion of Venezuelan President Rafael Caldera, the time had come for Cuba to become fully incorporated into the Latin-American community—and its legal and social systems.

President Carlos Saúl Menem of Argentina in turn expressed his support for Caldera's comments regarding Cuba, and expressed hope that a true change toward democracy on the island would occur soon.

It appeared that "the Cuban matter," not included on the agenda of the summit debate, would be alluded to only by oblique references when, unexpectedly, the social situation on the island of Cuba established itself as a breaking news story on June 15, the day the fourth Ibero-American Summit was ending.

Nine more people had just secretly entered the Chilean Consulate in Havana, thereby raising to 151 the number of Cubans who, during the preceding three weeks, had forcibly entered the diplomatic headquarters in search of political asylum.

Chilean Chancellor Figueroa, who, together with President Eduardo Frei, was participating in the summit, said that Frei was very concerned about the recent news and hoped to meet with Castro prior to his return to Havana, to discuss the matter in detail.

Even before Frei spoke out, Spanish President Felipe González had expressed his concern for the fate of the Cubans sheltered in the embassies—there were now 121 at the Belgian Ambassador's office and twenty in the German Embassy. Castro reiterated only that Cuba's position was "to not permit that this type of conflict spread."

While arrangements for the imminent closing ceremony of the summit were being made, side comments were increasingly heard regarding supposed last-minute secret agreements, modifications to the event's final declaration, and the fate of the asylum-seekers in Cuba if Fidel Castro did not make new conciliatory pronouncements before his return to Havana.

The press took charge of refreshing public memory as to the series of recent illegal entries into the perimeters of Havana's foreign diplomatic headquarters. Before the latest entry into the Chilean Consulate, 124 Cubans had entered the Belgian Embassy by climbing over an iron gate. On June 13, the day before the opening of the summit, another twenty-one people had penetrated the German Embassy by ramming a filled garbage truck against the garage door.

The embassies are located in the elegant Miramar neighborhood. The most recent entry had occurred eighteen days after the Cuban government ordered strict security measures at the embassies in the Cuban capital.

It appeared that the Cuban authorities feared there would be a process similar to that of the summer of 1990, when five human-rights activists took refuge in Havana's Czechoslovakian Embassy, took four Czech diplomats hostage, and threatened to blow up the building if they were not given a plane to fly to the United States. In the following days, another seven people entered the Czechoslovakian Embassy, three the Spanish Embassy, four the Italian Embassy, three the Swiss Embassy, nine the Belgian Embassy, and one attempted to enter the U.S. Cuban Interests Section.

In the opinion of Dr. Luis Aguilar León, formerly a professor at Georgetown University and currently a political commentator on Radio Martí, the process of Cubans breaking into authorized foreign embassies in Havana was nothing less than "strike three." Speaking in baseball terms, he stated that the situation—the game—could get out of hand for the Cuban government. "If they don't control it—the game—next time, they're going to have to machine-gun people to prevent them from entering other embassies."

Coinciding with the closing ceremony of the summit, the U.S. Coast Guard was reporting: 145 Cubans rescued from desert islands; 102 shipwrecked persons adrift among the different islands of the atoll of Cay Sal Bank (Bahamas); two helicopters of the U.S. Navy that detected a raft adrift and taking on water with eighteen Cubans aboard some fifty miles from Key West; a commercial ship en route to the Bahamas that picked up seventeen Cubans lost at sea near Looe Key; a U.S. Navy Coast Guard vessel that in one busy day's work picked up four raft people near Key West Bay and another four near Isla Morada. One of those rescued, Javier Castilla, declared that he, two male friends, and one female friend who was six months pregnant, had been rowing for two and a half hours trying to reach the coast on a raft surrounded by inner tubes.

By June 17, 1994, the number of boat people who had reached the Florida coast had risen to 3,263, approaching the record figure of 3,656 of the previous year. In the face of the massive increase, Brothers to the Rescue began dropping packages of food, tents, and blankets for the hundreds of refugees who were being carried by the waves to the sands of Cay Sal Bank. Frustrated because the refugees beached there were not receiving prompt assistance through standard channels, Brothers to the Rescue said it would begin to send food to the refugees by boat if U.S. and Bahamian authorities did not cooperate in their rescue. "We are not going to allow the people to starve to death," said José Basulto, president of Brothers to the Rescue.

The fish and snack vendors on the colonial streets of Cartagena de Indias witnessed an unusual amount of vehicular traffic the afternoon of Wednesday, June 15, as the fourth annual Ibero-American Summit finally ended. Dozens of limousines, their tinted, bullet-proof windows covered by curtains, rushed by, casting onto the faces of the newspaper and lottery-ticket vendors the dust of centuries accumulated on curbs and drains. The luxury cars were speeding toward the airport. Their passage along the narrow streets and festooned avenues was backed by a cloud of motorcycle police, armed with helmets, bullet-proof vests, and Israeli machine guns.

Everyone seemed to be in a hurry to leave behind the arduous final discussion sessions of the event, such as the unusual closed-door meeting in which the leaders of Spain, Portugal, and Latin America had exhorted Castro to establish democracy in his country as an initial condition of reintegration into the Organization of American States (OAS). They had also said that once this requirement was met, they would ask the United States to lift the embargo against the island. According to Carlos Saúl Menem, no other possibility existed: "It is an indispensable requirement that Cuba democratize. . . ." The heads of state had rejected Fidel Castro's suggestion that Cuba enter the OAS before undertaking political reforms.

It was the first time since the annual meetings of Latin-American presidents began in 1991 (in Guadalajara) that Fidel Castro had faced such vigorous, direct appeals for reform and a promise that, if he undertook them, the Latin-American heads of state would argue for the end of the U.S. embargo. As was to be expected, there were many versions of what happened in the meeting. According to one source, the Latin-American leaders used the plainest language ever directed at Fidel Castro at a hemispheric summit. With an openly defiant attitude, Castro insisted that he was proud to be a Marxist-Leninist, and even joked that he was being subjected to a new Nuremberg trial.

According to the well-informed journalistic source, Castro, retreating, argued that he would abandon socialism only if Latin America united economically and politically, a concept that, according to him, excluded the United States.

Argentinian Chancellor Guido di Tella allowed himself this public comment: "To keep repeating that everything that happens to Cuba is provoked by U.S. persecution is to have one's head in the clouds. Castro's attitude does not contribute to encouraging anyone to talk about anything."

Seconds later, the Cubana de Aviación plane that had brought Fidel Castro and his delegation to the beach resort city of Cartagena de

Indias was taking off, destined for Havana, amidst a deafening roar of engines. The political analysts who had followed the summit watched it overfly the airport and head off toward the northwest above the silver mirror of the Caribbean Sea. They wondered in anguish if, as in the end of the best-known of Gabriel García Márquez's novels, there would be a second chance on earth for the Cuban people when, a month later, Fidel Castro would again cross the Caribbean to attend the meeting of the Association of Caribbean States (ACS), which would have as its setting, again, Cartagena de Indias.

Word spread among future raft people that with Castro's return to Havana, the Cuban government would intensify its vigilance at sea and try to prevent, through every means at its disposal, clandestine departures from the country. It was said that the full weight of the law would fall upon those who fled in vessels stolen from the Cuban government, or who forcibly entered the grounds of foreign embassies in Havana.

Among the first victims of the intensification of the maritime anti-exodus measures was a valiant group of Cubans who escaped from the island on a tugboat. The boat left at 1:15 A.M. Twenty minutes later, as had happened with others who tried to escape secretly, the gunboats of the Cuban Naval fleet began to follow the hijacked boat. There were moments when only fifty feet separated the two vessels. At first, the Cuban Navy fired blank cartridges, but then they commenced using real bullets, according to survivors' accounts.

On this occasion, the methods employed by the pursuers were extremely refined, precise, and drastic. As the stolen boat approached international waters and entered the Florida Straits after almost five hours of relentless pursuit, the pursuers tried to stop it by jamming the propeller. Then they attempted to cut it off; later, they shot over the prow, and, finally, they machine-gunned the hull, causing panic among the refugees. During the confusing fight going on in the midst of the sea and the night, an individual somehow boarded the hijacked tugboat and identified himself as a member of the Cuban Interior Ministry Police. To the refugees' astonishment, he took out his pistol and shot into the ship's command deck. Some of the men in the group managed to capture him and tie him up. After fifteen minutes of negotiations carried out in shouts across the open sea, they turned him over to the Cuban authorities on the condition that they be permitted to continue their voyage to the United States. However, the patrol boat stayed close to them, but held its fire. As a precaution against another assault, the fugitives hurried to communicate their position over the shortwave radio. At dawn, a Coast Guard plane sighted the eighty-foot-long *Mar Azul,* which had two enormous two-foot holes and was taking on water in the stormy sea. The pilot tossed them a spare motor so they could reduce the torrent of water gushing into the ship. A short while later, a Coast Guard helicopter transported seven of the refugees to Key West, where they were attended to.

Consistent with the announcement of greater severity for those who left the country in stolen state property, a spokesman for the Cuban Interests Section in Washington, D.C., placed blame for what had happened on U.S. immigration policies, which favor this type of incident. The Cuban spokesman alleged that the United States should authorize a larger number of visas so that the inhabitants of the island could emigrate legally; according to him, there existed a double standard when Cubans who arrive are immediately permitted to become U.S. residents while, at the same time, entry to the United States is denied to persons who come from other Third World countries.

The answer to the increase of severe measures against those who tried to emigrate illegally across the sea came immediately. This time it was expressed by Cuban writer Norberto Fuentes.

Fuentes stated: "The next time that Castro repeats his assertion that all Cubans can leave the country and that only the U.S. is to blame for having denied visas to those who want to leave, it would be good for someone to remind him about my case . . ." Fuentes had long been friends with the popular General Arnaldo Ochoa and Interior Ministry Colonels Antonio (Tony) and Patricio de la Guardia. The writer quickly suffered the consequences of the trial held in Havana in July 1989, in which two of his beloved friends were sentenced to death by firing squad and another to twenty years in prison because of their supposed connections to Colombian drug cartels. Fuentes remained confined to his apartment in Havana, prevented from traveling abroad, having been denied a visa by the Cuban authorities.

Shortly after making that statement, Norberto Fuentes, accompanied by relatives and some friends, joined the legion of anonymous raft people trying to leave Cuba clandestinely, evading existing vigilance on the coasts. Perhaps thinking that he would make a bit of history and that his flight deserved to be recorded in writing, among the few belongings that he carried with him was a diary in which he wrote on the night of October 10, 1993, the date when, paradoxically, a new anniversary of the beginning of the struggles for Cuban independence was being commemorated: ". . . calm seas, and no hint of a moon, and I entered the other fatherland of poet José Martí: the night. . . ."

A couple of miles off the Cuban coast, the inflatable rubber raft driven by a Johnson forty-horsepower engine broke down and floated adrift on the dark waters. Finally, it was discovered and captured by a Cuban Navy artillery boat. Norberto Fuentes spent approximately a month confined in a cell of Villa Maristas, as the general headquarters of state security in Havana is popularly called. He was again confined to his apartment, where he declared a hunger strike. Fifteen days after his impassioned strike pronouncement, he was hastily authorized to leave the country in a plane belonging to the Mexican Agriculture Department, thanks to the mediation of Nobel Prize-winning author Gabriel García Márquez and then-president of Mexico, Carlos Salinas de Gortari.

Chapter II

An Old Tugboat Sinks

THE MONTH OF JULY 1994 was beginning with alarming statistics regarding the growing number of Cuban raft people newly arrived on U.S. shores. According to the Immigration and Naturalization Service (INS), during the previous year of 1993, the record of raft people picked up was broken with a total of 3,656. Said José Basulto, president of Brothers to the Rescue, "The floodgates have been opened."

Basulto, and other individuals who participated on a daily basis in the task of searching for raft people, had predicted in early 1994 that the new year would bring an estimated seven to ten thousand refugees by the maritime escape route. This projection was based on statements made by newly arrived refugees who emphatically stated that the Cuban people could no longer stand the crisis the country was suffering.

For Arturo Cobo, director of the Center for Cuban Refugees in Key West, the figures on the numbers of raft people indicated an even more dramatic reality. According to him, for every two Cubans successfully arriving in Florida, three were captured or died at sea, devoured by sharks or swallowed by the waves. According to his estimate, the ten thousand new refugees predicted by Basulto for the current year 1994 would put the chilling figure at about fifteen thousand victims.

The day after the INS released its statistics on the number of clandestine arrivals of Cubans in 1993, Miami newspaper headlines reported the arrival of 107 people in a boat, which, spectacular in itself, set a new record. The new arrivals had taken with them spears and Molotov cocktails to protect themselves from the Cuban border guards who would surely have tried to stop them. The group had made the trip in a total of seven days, eight hours, and twelve minutes.

The crossing that Jesús García and his wife, Santa Reina Maza Oramas, would undertake a few days later broke all existing records for length of time at sea by raft people: No less than thirty-eight days! It was a difficult mark to surpass, given that the distance between the west coast of Cuba and Florida's Cay Peninsula varies from ninety to one hundred and fifty miles. Everything began suddenly; a friend who had tried to leave Cuba in a rowboat changed his mind in the midst of the sea and the night, when he saw the enormous height of the waves he would have to face to reach U.S. shores. He returned to his hometown of Caibarién, on the northern coast of Villa Clara Province, where he told his friends of his short odyssey. He asked them to keep his secret, since he feared that if the Cuban authorities found out, he would be sent to jail for two or three years.

As a token of his friendship, he gave the boat to the trusted couple. Jesús and his wife did not give it a moment's thought. Without even making any plans, Jesús explained later to reporters, they left that same night, June 4, at 8 P.M. Jesús, who had experience at sea as captain of a small fishing boat, assured his wife and six other relatives that they would arrive in Fort Lauderdale or another city on the Florida coast the next day with no problems. They never imagined that the crossing they had just begun, instead of taking a day, would span no less than thirty-eight days and take them to three countries before they would touch the Floridian soil where they had relatives and friends.

By the morning of the following day, June 5, they were adrift. Believing themselves lost, they noticed a boat on the horizon; it approached their location and turned out to be the *M/V Atlantic Sea*. The boat picked them up, since they were shipwrecked, but the captain explained that before taking them to Florida, he had to complete his assigned commercial circuit faithfully. Therefore, Jesús, his wife, their relatives, and nine others, would be guests on board for the rest of the boat's scheduled voyage. The boat that rescued them docked in Haiti, Venezuela, the Turkish and Caicos Islands, and passed very close to Aruba, Curaçao, the Dominican Republic, and Puerto Rico. At each place, when the refugees asked if they could go ashore and contact their relatives in Miami, or request asylum, the answer was the same: They were to remain on board in quarantine, and they did not have any international rights. At the end of the trip, exhausted but still in somewhat good humor, ex-fishing boat captain Jesús García commented: "Instead of going around the world in eighty days, we went around the Americas in forty. . . ."

The sad social misery and lack of civil rights suffered by Cubans on the island contrasted notably with the obvious opulence of the residential sectors of the various Miami beaches on which they came ashore.

A report published in Miami's *El Nuevo Herald* in the summer of 1994 made reference to the fifty most expensive homes built in Dade County, along the coast. In one of the top positions on the list was the luxurious residence of basketball superstar Rony Seikaly. In addition to seven bedrooms, Seikaly's home had a guesthouse, servants' quarters, basketball and tennis courts, a swimming pool, jacuzzi, indoor racquetball courts, and, of course, what every basketball player needs: high ceilings. Seikaly's house, located on Star Island, was only sixth on the list, being valued at more than five million dollars.

It is unlikely that a sharper social contrast exists in the world than that between the Cuban refugees—scorched by the sun, dehydrated, half-naked, bitten by marine creatures, starving, and depressed as they arrive on tiny rafts made of old, worn-out tires—and the row of magnificent and shimmering multi-million-dollar homes that marks the heavenly fairy-tale coast of Miami Beach.

July 1994 lurched along in this situation, burdened with bad omens for the future fate of Cuba, when a news item again captured the attention of both sides of the Florida Straits. On July 15 the papers ran the story of some forty Cubans who drowned at sea when four Cuban government boats first rammed the old *13 de marzo* tugboat, in which they were trying to flee, and then used high-pressure hoses to shoot streams of water onto the boat.

In the succeeding hours and days, as the magnitude of what had happened began to be known in detail, it was possible to begin piecing together the bits of initial information. It was calculated that in the disaster, Cuban border guards rescued only thirty-one survivors of an initial group of seventy-two people. One of the survivors, María Victoria García Suárez, told, amidst sobs, the story of the tragedy. According to the vivid description she offered, several children were wrenched from their mothers' arms and catapulted into the sea by the huge streams of water. Some men and women were thrown against the walls of the tugboat; others were thrown into the sea by the force of the water. Finally, one last blow succeeded in rolling the old tug over. According to witnesses of the unusual shipwreck, the old *13 de marzo* tugboat had set sail from the port of Havana at 3 A.M. on Wednesday, July 13, with thirty women, twenty children, and twenty-two men on board. The children's ages ranged from three to ten. One of them was a four-month-old baby. In moving testimony given in Havana, García Suárez told the press how she lost her husband, ten-year-old son, a brother, three uncles and aunts, and two cousins, all of them residents of Guanabacoa. García Suárez recounted in an interview with WSCV Channel 51 that when they had been traveling for about forty-five minutes and the boat was about seven miles from the coast of Cuba, two fireboats came alongside the *13 de marzo* and began to shoot water into it through high-pressure hoses. The attackers, she pointed out, were dressed in civilian clothes, some of them wearing no shirts. "We asked them not to harm us; we showed them the children, but they continued spraying water on us," said García.

For his part, the Cuban Interior Minister indicated on Saturday, July 18, that the shipwreck had occurred when the renegade vessel collided with another similar craft that was trying to catch up with it. The Interior Minister went on to say that the tugboat, which belonged to the Transportation Ministry's Maritime Services Enterprise, had been stolen from the pier where it was docked, and that those responsible disabled the means of communication at the office's installations at the site before taking the boat. He declared that the craft had a problem that caused it to take on water and that the authors of the plan knew this and had carried out their actions, irresponsibly, in spite of it. To try to prevent the hijacking, three Transportation Ministry craft attempted to intercept it, and in the maneuvers they executed to attain this objective, a lamentable accident occurred that caused the boat to sink. The statement given by the Cuban Interior Ministry ended by pointing out that near the area of the accident, there were two Cuban patrol boats, which immediately came to help, as well as the three aforementioned vessels.

On Monday, July 21, it was reported in Havana that four crew members of the government vessels that caused the sinking of the *13 de marzo* tugboat were arrested. This information came initially from the Spanish news agency EFE. According to the same source, the magistrate in the case against the survivors of the tragedy, a lieutenant colonel whose name is not known, declared that excesses had been committed in the attempt to stop the illegal departure of the tugboat with seventy-two people aboard. The four detainees were civilian employees of the Transportation Ministry. One of the survivors, seventeen-year-old José F. Valdés, was set free early Wednesday morning. Relatives in Miami of the victims and survivors, as well as numerous human rights activists, were skeptical of the arrests. The *13 de marzo* tugboat incident drew reactions of repudiation from the Cuban population on the island. Several dissidents were arrested at the entrance to the U.S. Cuban Interests Section in Havana; others received telephoned threats. Five dissidents were arrested on their way to the Havana Cathedral to attend a mass in honor of the dead. The mass was never held, but in Miami, about three thousand exiles met at the Chapel of la Caridad del Cobre to pray for the souls of those who died in the shipwreck and for the protection of the survivors. The Cuban Catholic Church, through Archbishop of Havana Jaime Ortega Alamino, asked for a full investigation of the tragedy.

As the days passed, more details of what occurred the early morning of July 13 became clear. Consequently, the opposing sides either played down its importance or made it an unquestionable tragic act. The newspaper *Granma,* official organ of the Cuban Communist Party, declared that sixty-two people had been on board the tugboat, out of which thirty-one were rescued by two border patrol boats and thirty-two drowned. According to *Granma,* the group set sail in the tug from the port of Havana shortly before dawn on July 13. *Granma* indicated

that the wooden tugboat was built in 1879, and that its use was restrict-
ed to the port of Havana, since safety inspections had revealed leaks.
Originally designed for four crew members, the seventeen-meter craft
had only four life preservers, and its emergency water pump was broken. The *Granma* report goes on to say that Port Subdirector Fidencio
Ramel Prieto Hernández, father of Daniel Prieto Suárez, one of the survivors, had drugged the night watchman and removed the chains that
tied the craft. Fidencio Ramel and the captain of another tug, Raúl
Muñoz García, boarded their friends and relatives and later headed for
the mouth of the port of Havana at 3:30 A.M. *Granma* points out that
the investigations indicate that in this lamentable accident there was no
hostile intent on behalf of any of the three tugboats that attempted to
stop the fugitives. According to *Granma,* the stolen tugboat was pursued from the port first by one, and then by an additional two tugs:
Polargo 5, Polargo 2, and *Polargo 3.* At one point in the chase, *Polargo
5,* whose hull was steel, took measures to avoid a collision when the
stolen tug tried to ram it to make it stop its pursuit, said Raúl Muñoz
García, a member of the group, in testimony quoted by the newspaper
Granma. Granma also quoted the statements of other survivors, who
suggested that the craft was in such terrible condition that it never
would have reached the United States: "It was overloaded; it was very
old and made of wood. What happened would have happened a few
miles on. When they discovered us, we should have turned back or
stopped our engines. So many deaths would have been avoided," said
survivor Alquímides Venancio Lebrigio.

Political commentator Carlos Alberto Montaner is one of the
Cuban exile voices that have strongly criticized the Cuban government
in recent years. In an article distributed through the Firmas Press news
agency, he provided unusual information and a controversial view on
the sinking of the *13 de marzo* tugboat. According to Montaner, the
Cuban Interior Ministry had learned of the escape plan through an
informant, and at the highest levels—according to a horrified high-
level source quoted by Montaner—made the decision to teach them a
terrible lesson. General Colomé Ibarra urgently informed Fidel Castro
of the preparations of those planning to flee the country, and Castro
personally issued the order to sink them, showing no mercy. Accord-

ing to Montaner, the matter of "personally" is a nuance behind which Colomé Ibarra, without saying so, dilutes his own responsibility for the crime. Montaner continues:

. . . as soon as the old *13 de marzo* tugboat left the Bay of Havana with its hopeful passengers at about 2:50 A.M., the three ships which had been given the task of sinking it were advised by radio. A fourth ship, a border guard Griffin patrol boat, was to wait a short distance from the chosen site. The three fireboats were all named *Polargo.* The *Polargo 2* was under the command of an Interior Ministry officer nicknamed David; the *Polargo 3* was under the authority of Arístides; the *Polargo 5,* nevertheless, had at its helm a very special person: Jesús Martínez. Jesusito was an officer filled with bitterness and a desire for vengeance because, not long before, due to circumstances beyond his control, the boat he was sailing had been diverted toward Florida without his being able to avoid it. Following that incident, he had returned in embarrassment to explain the matter to his superiors. This was his chance to show the Interior Ministry that he should not be judged by that episode. He was an iron combatant. An invincible revolutionary. A merciless man when the Commander-in-Chief so ordered. And so it was. Seven miles from the coast, still in Cuban territorial waters, the *Polargo 2* and *Polargo 3,* both of Dutch manufacture, began their macabre task of filling the deck of the *13 de marzo* with powerful streams of water paradoxically intended to save lives and put out fires. The passengers screamed and held up the children for them to see, begging for their lives. Fidelio Ramel, an officer of the fleeing craft and faded portrait of a Communist Party he once believed in, disappeared immediately in the swell. The *Polargo 2* and *Polargo 3* began to move in circles to increase the turbulence. Their orders were very clear during this phase of the operation: A good number of the victims were to drown quickly. The passengers still on board were trying to take refuge below deck in the engine room. Nearly all of them were women and children. That was brave Jesusito's star moment. The *Polargo 5* went into action. With its iron keel, and at great speed, it rammed the stern of the tugboat, which, at that moment, its engines down, was rocking wildly. The *Polargo 5* circled again and, rammed the prow, finishing the task: The *13 de marzo* capsized and began to sink. In its wooden belly, twenty children, now a mass of beaten flesh, drowned helplessly, many clinging to their mothers, others with no consolation other than the quickness of an incomprehensible, black death in a Caribbean sea stained with hatred. Once the crime had been committed, the alibi was arranged. A Revolutionary War Navy Griffin launch, stationed five hundred meters from the scene, approached the slaughter with its searchlights and powerful loudspeakers: What happened? How awful! So many dead! Maybe thirty-five. Maybe forty. With the utmost hypocrisy, they began to take some of the survivors on board. The lesson was complete. Jesusito, the hero, contemplated his accomplishment with satisfaction. They congratulated him . . .

After the *13 de marzo* tugboat tragedy outside the Bay of Havana, four big questions were left floating on the rough waters that separated Cuba from the United States: (1) Would the clandestine departures to the United States continue, or would future raft people be intimidated after the sinking of the tugboat that took the lives of more than thirty people? (2) What would Fidel Castro's reaction be: hardening or conciliation? (3) How would Cuban exiles in Miami and their most representative leaders react to the uncertain future that was approaching? (4) Would U.S. President Bill Clinton do nothing, initiate a dialogue, or intensify the measures of embargo and hostility against the Communist regime of Havana, in spite of the fact that history had turned the page on the Cold War as a political issue?

In the opinion of Jorge Mas Canosa, president of the Cuban American National Foundation, the most powerful of the Cuban exile political organizations, the time had come. The announcement that Fidel Castro would soon return to Cartagena de Indias, to participate in the incorporation of the new Association of American States, drove him to throw the first quick punches in the ring against his adversary.

"I support the idea," declared Mas Canosa, "and I have said this to several officials of the Castro government, that the next time Fidel Castro leaves Cuba, he should not be allowed to return. There are a thousand ways to eliminate Castro without bloodshed!"

The next month, the door of the Cubana de Aviación plane opened slowly on the runway of the Cartagena de Indias airport, and out came aides wearing *guayaberas* of different colors. Immediately, they lined up on both sides of the stairway to the plane. Seconds later, Fidel Castro appeared in the doorway—and the mystery was over. This time, Comandante Castro, as some reporters and diplomatic officials like to call him, provided no doubt whatsoever about his intentions. The best proof of that was his return to his shiny olive-green military uniform instead of the white *guayabera*. The reporters insisted on having an exclusive press conference with Castro just before midnight on Saturday, as he arrived at the Las Américas Hotel. When he was asked who was responsible for the tragedy that had occurred in the Bay of Havana, Castro angrily responded that the United States was to blame. The impromptu press conference ended abruptly with his answer. Ambrosio Hernández, a reporter from Channel 51 TV in Miami, tried to approach Castro to interview him and managed, in passing, to repeat the question about responsibility for the sinking of the tugboat. He immediately found himself roughly thrown against the wall by two of Castro's big bodyguards.

The violent reaction of Castro's personal security agents provoked a protest by some of the journalists in attendance, and Hernández tried to clarify to one of Castro's bodyguards the rights and duties of journalists at this type of international meeting. "As long as I'm here, you can't ask the *comandante* that kind of question," the bodyguard responded. Later, in an interview with *El Nuevo Herald,* Cuban Chancellor Roberto Robaina declared the sinking of the *13 de marzo* tugboat "an event that is too serious to be resolved in such a short time, and in which outsiders are much more implicated than insiders . . ." He declared that there were videotapes of the very authors of the plan, which said "more than any of our statements. In their own words, they make judgments about the stupid thing they did, and analyze the consequences they set themselves up for by doing something like that," Robaina declared emphatically.

Fidel Castro never mentioned the matter again. During the short duration of the conference, he wore only his heavy, olive-green military uniform, though the suffocating late-July heat in the colonial city of Cartagena de Indias reached hellish temperatures of one hundred degrees. In the opinion of many political observers, he left the same way he had come, without compromising at all, and blaming U.S. imperialism and the Cuban counter-revolutionary Mafia based in Florida for all the ills his country was experiencing. There was another opportunity to see him in action soon, when on August 7, Comandante Castro returned to Colombia for the third time in the space of one and a half months, for the inauguration of President Eduardo Samper in the capital city of Bogotá.

Another of the mysteries was still unresolved—whether Cubans would dare to continue their clandestine departures on rafts after the terrible experience suffered by the *13 de marzo*. The answer came immediately, as news agencies reported the arrival in U.S. territory of a ferro-cement boat that set sail from the port of Nuevitas in Camagüey Province with seventy-eight Cubans aboard. And part of this case seemed like something out of a Hollywood movie: The hijackers used none other than a plastic toy pistol to carry out their plan. The craft was sighted by tourists and summer guests of the Hotel Fontainbleau Hilton in the Miami Beach area when it was about two hundred meters from shore. Seeing the bare arms waving shirts and rags on deck and hearing the cries for help and freedom and finally that of "We made it!" they immediately informed the U.S. Coast Guard, which proceeded to pick up the travelers. It was the largest number of raft people that had escaped from Cuba since July 13 when the *13 de marzo* sank. According to statements made by Juan Carlos Arcalla, organizer of the group that brought the craft to Florida, several Cuban border guards followed them for about fifteen miles, warning them several times that they would sink due to the poor condition of the ferro-cement boat.

"That's why we did it now. They, the border guards, killed a lot of people in Havana Bay; they couldn't kill us, too." Their first night in Miami, the raft people offered a detailed account of their story as they consumed their first ham-and-cheese sandwiches and canned Coke, which, for the youngest ones, constituted little less than a true discovery. In all, the trip in the forty-foot-long ferro-cement boat took them six days. Their escape plans had taken a month to crystallize because they had to calculate carefully which was the best boat to take and the most opportune time to board. For four months, Arcalla had been working as a fisherman, getting to know the other fishermen and their respective schedules. Arcalla and four of his friends traveled in a small rowboat to where the ferro-cement boat was anchored. Another member of the group was Antonio Lorenzo, who carried with him an old plastic toy pistol that he zealously kept with other old mementos of his childhood. At the moment of boarding the boat, Lorenzo recalled for the five-hundredth time a scene from an old movie he had seen in the Campoamor Theater in Nuevitas. In the scene, Robert Mitchum held the guards of a boat at gunpoint, a toy pistol to their backs. Lorenzo did the same with the two men he saw on board the ferrocement boat, ordering them, in a dry, gruff voice like Humphrey Bogart's, to give themselves up without resisting the terrible weapon in his hands. Thrusting the barrel of the gun between the ribs of the guards, he swore that he would shoot to kill if they did not get off the vessel immediately. It all happened like in the movies, thought Lorenzo, since the guards, moviegoers like he, had certainly seen a similar film in which John Wayne asked his captors to tie his feet and hands to erase—for the purpose of the future investigation by the authorities—any trace of guilt and, yes, of course, happy to, Lorenzo assured them, and if you like, I'll punch you lightly on the chin like Alan Ladd did in another old American movie. Their hands and feet duly tied, the guards were left by Lorenzo and his friends in the small rowboat that had brought them. They dropped anchor and left the guards a few stale crackers and a bottle of water in case they got hungry or thirsty during the succeeding hours they would spend in solitary confinement.

As soon as they were out of sight of the guards, they changed course and headed for the lonely beach of El Bagá, where about seventy people awaited them. Many of the people were strangers to one another, but quickly climbed aboard anyway, willing to take whatever risks were necessary for the sake of reaching the United States. Among the last-minute arrivals was Alberto Otero, a former Armed Forces (FAR) pilot who had served in the war in Angola and during most of the trip to Florida acted as navigator, reading maps and nautical routes and deciding which route to take.

But there would be new and more surprising maritime adventures and odysseys before the hot month of July 1994 ended. One of the most traditional, economical, popular, and picturesque means of transportation in Havana are the wooden boats that travel between Havana and the small towns of Casablanca and Regla, on the other side of the bay. The trip, just under a mile, takes place against the backdrop of the impressive stone walls of the El Morro and La Cabaña fortresses. July 26, the anniversary of the assault on the Moncada Barracks in 1953 by Fidel Castro and a group of young revolutionaries, was used by a group of nine young friends as the appropriate moment to hijack the boat called *Baraguá* and take her on the longest voyage of her history. In the wee hours of the morning, the group of friends took control of the boat just as the ten-minute trip from Regla to Havana was about to end. The nine young men swept along on their adventure thirteen astonished passengers who couldn't believe their eyes. The fugitives finally arrived in Miami Wednesday afternoon, some thirty-six hours after having carried off the unexpected hijacking.

"I never thought we would be so lucky," said Adalberto Acosta Gato, one of the surprised passengers. "As soon as I realized what was happening, I started praying that they'd pull it off," added Adalberto, who, until that moment, had worked as a cook in a Havana hospital and every morning at 3 A.M. for twenty-seven years had taken that boat to work. He had often dreamed of the possibility that someone would divert the boat and they would end up in the United States. During the

difficult times of total economic shortages the country was experiencing, the United States was the longed-for destination of thousands of
Cubans. That early morning, July 26, 1994, the *Baraguá* was placidly
crossing the Bay of Havana, surrounded by eddies of dark water. One
of the passengers approached the prow, where the captain of the
Baraguá had a steady hand on the helm. The stranger took out a pistol
he had bought from a policeman two days before for thirty dollars and
stuck it into the captain's back. Then he turned to the sleepy passengers and announced in an excited voice that he had just hijacked the
boat and was forcing the skipper to set a course for the United States.
Hearing the announcement, four young men of the group of nine took
out knives and pretended to take their friends hostage. Taking advantage of the reigning confusion, during a momentary lapse in the hijackers' attention, the skipper dove into the deep, dark waters of the bay.
The group of conspirators, all of them between the ages of seventeen
and twenty, seeing that their golden opportunity to travel to the United
States could slip away, forced a skipper's apprentice who was on board
to take the helm and take them quickly out of the bay. Informed of
what was happening, the Cuban naval authorities soon intercepted
them; about two hundred meters from El Morro fortress, they found
themselves surrounded by two Cuban border-guard tugboats and a
patrol boat.

"But we kept going," said Ioami Torres Hernández, one of the
organizers of the escape. One of the passengers, realizing how difficult
the situation was, said that he was a Communist and refused to continue on to Miami. One of the hijackers shouted to the pursuers that if
they did not take the searchlights off and stop pursuing them, they
would throw the Communist into the water. And that is just what they
did. Moments later, the skipper and the Communist, soaking wet and
shivering with cold, were rescued by the Cuban border guards, who
stubbornly continued the chase until mid-morning, when they gave up.
A short time later, a Brothers to the Rescue plane sighted the little boat
about thirty miles north of Havana. An extraordinary operation was
carried out at sea, which consisted of finding out who truly desired to
continue on to Miami, and who wanted to return to Havana. The U.S.

Coast Guard cutter *Baranoff* picked up the thirteen who wanted to come to the United States; the nine remaining passengers returned to Cuba in the Regla boat, among them the mother of Bernardo Pérez Terry, one of the three passengers who joined the escape. "You can't imagine how sad it is to have your mother there, and have her leave you," declared Pérez, an engineer, who went on to say that his mother did not want to leave her four other children.

For María Carmona, the hijacking of the Regla boat was like coming home by an unexpected means of transportation. María had traveled to Havana from Miami on the Mar Azul ("Blue Sea") charter flight airline. It had been years since she had seen her relatives in Regla, and the first day of her visit was spent telling stories, remembering old times, and catching up on neighborhood gossip. She hardly slept that first night. Old friends and relatives had come to greet her. The next day she left early for Havana, to buy fresh food and canned goods at the store across from the old customs building. She didn't want her relatives to go hungry. During the two weeks she was permitted to stay in Cuba, she planned to buy, in dollars, everything that was necessary to maintain the household. How was she to imagine that instead of crossing the bay in ten minutes, she would cross the entire Florida Straits in just over thirty hours? When interviewed, María declared: "After this, anything is possible. I went to Havana on a Blue Sea travel agency flight and I returned to Miami in a boat across the blue sea."

The reaction to this remarkable occurrence even among those in Florida who are used to hearing of such happenings was one of genuine surprise. "Cubans no longer attach much importance to life," stated Arturo Cobo, director of the Center for Cuban Refugees in Key West. "They've shot others who did what these young people did, and they've defied them again." Arnaldo Iglesias, secretary of Brothers to the Rescue, said that it was to have been expected that it would happen again. "When they told me that the craft looked like an aquatic taxi, the Regla boat came to mind, and it seemed ridiculous to me. Now, every time you get into the Regla boat, you won't know if the trip will end in Miami."

Soon the astonished commentaries of the press found a new echo in a second and equally unusual hijacking of the little boat that regularly covers the Regla-Havana route. At 4 P.M. on August 3, 1994, before the astonished stares of hundreds of people who were waiting their turn in line to get on board, and of hundreds more who were traveling along the Havana Malecón, the Regla boat pushed off from the old pier and, instead of making its way toward the city, set a course for the mouth of the port, followed very closely by two Cuban patrol boats. People began to shout and wave their arms wildly when they saw two people swimming near the tiny craft. Their astonishment was mixed with doubt. No one could tell if the two were fugitives who had thrown themselves into the sea in order to return to Cuba or two passers-by who had been walking along the Malecón and, seeing the boat turning toward the entry to the port, without giving it a moment's thought, threw themselves into the sea and began to swim after the fugitive boat, catching up to it even with the rocky outcrop of El Morro.

The day before, Wednesday, August 2, during the busy noon hour, the boat that usually traveled from Luz Pier in Havana to the village of Casablanca was similarly hijacked before the astonished stares of hundreds of people who were waiting to change buses and boats in that busy area of the Havana coast, located a few blocks from the Plaza de Armas and Havana Cathedral. The hijacking occurred in a flash, due to the concerted action of fifteen passengers armed with one pistol, one revolver, one grenade, and machetes, who proceeded to divert the La Coubre motorboat, which had a hundred and ninety people on board. After several hours of uncertain struggles with the waves, two U.S. Navy ships intercepted the boat adrift some thirty miles northwest of Havana. A group of seventy-three people from the boat returned to Cuba. The remaining 117 passengers, including the boat's skipper, applied for political asylum upon arriving at Key West after an exhausting twenty-eight-hour trip. Most of the sixty-five men, forty women, and twelve children had boarded the ship in Casablanca with the intention of taking a five-minute trip to the other side of the Bay of Havana. A total of seven passengers who refused to join the escape threw themselves into the sea during the first moments of the unexpected trip and were picked up by Cuban border guards.

A dispatch from the Cuban news agency Prensa Latina reported that two Cuban Navy ships followed the boat, but, to avoid accidents, at no time did the border guard units attempt to intercept the hijacked craft. In interviews of the recent arrivals by the Miami press, new details of the trip surfaced. For example, Yeniley Barcía Tamayo, age sixteen, stated that she became involved in the adventure when she was on her way to Havana to take kerosene to her grandmother with her friend Lázara. When the boat changed course toward the mouth of the bay, hundreds of Havana residents waved to the fugitives, declared Barcía. "The Malecón was full. Monumental Avenue was full. People were afraid the same thing that happened with the tugboat would happen to us," said some of the newly arrived refugees.

During a press conference at the well-known Victor's Café, several of the refugees told how the hijacking of the boat took them by surprise, although they acknowledged that about half of the passengers knew that this could happen at any moment. Florentina Ochoa, cousin of the executed General Arnaldo Ochoa, said that on Thursday, while she was waiting for the boat to go to Havana, she observed that people were gathering in a group and whispering. "I decided to join them to see what would happen. I suspected that it had something to do with the boat and that they were going to take it." After the press conference, Víctor del Corral, owner of the restaurant, invited the refugees to have lunch. Seated at an elegant table, the fifteen guests were given menus. When she sat down to eat, the cousin of General Arnaldo Ochoa—hero of the Angolan war, shot by a firing squad a year before for supposed ties to Colombian drug cartels—looked around her. She saw silver platters with charcoal-grilled filets, lobster tails covered with melted butter and parsley, a platter replete with rice, black beans, and fried ripe plantains. That noon, in the soft half-light inside the restaurant, Florentina Ochoa sobbed, shaken. "It's that, you know, in Cuba I left my husband, my son, my grandson, and my mother . . ."

Surpassing all possible predictions, a third boat making its customary trip between Regla and Havana was hijacked on Thursday, August 4, about 7 P.M., according to a Reuters report from Havana. At 6 P.M. on Friday, August 5, the boat was listed as missing by the U.S.

Coast Guard since, in spite of an intense naval and air search, it had not yet been seen, and according to reports of several witnesses, it was followed out to sea from the mouth of the Bay of Havana by two Cuban Navy patrol boats. According to a report of the French news agency Agence France-Presse, thousands of people witnessed the scene from the Malecón; it was said that from various areas of Havana, such as Marianao, La Víbora, and El Cotorro, people were arriving continuously in hopes of being close by at the moment someone suddenly decided to hijack the fourth boat of the week.

News agencies reported that the third hijacked boat never reached its destination. The *Baraguá* was captured twelve miles off the coast of Cuba by Cuban border guards. During an impromptu press conference held Friday night in Havana, Fidel Castro said that the boat's hijackers had killed two police officers in the Regla area. The craft ran out of gas and was adrift on the waves for an hour and a half, until it was located and boarded by Cuban coast guards. No details were given regarding how the police officers died, nor were the names of the guilty parties released. By the next day, Monday, August 8, a demonstration had been organized in the Plaza de la Revolución to bury Police Officer Gabriel Lamoth Caballer, age nineteen, who was killed in the line of duty.

What was truly surprising was the dizzying speed with which events unfolded. According to news reports, on Friday, August 5, thousands of Cubans shouting anti-government slogans fought police with sticks and stones all along the Havana Malecón. Correspondents estimated at twenty thousand to thirty thousand the number of Cubans gathered along the four-kilometer-long Malecón before the incident erupted. They were apparently drawn there by rumors that a fleet had left the United States and was coming to pick up anyone who wanted to leave Cuba.

Some hours after the riots, Fidel Castro threatened to permit another Mariel if the United States did not punish those who fled the island by sea. "If the United States does not change its policy, we will be forced to not block any craft with those characteristics," declared Castro in a meeting with Cuban journalists, carried on Cuban radio and TV. Thousands of demonstrators attacked and threw stones at the windows of several stores that catered to foreign tourists and a hotel near the Bay of Havana. The police opened fire, and left several people seriously wounded. According to opposition sources on the island, "there were three dead, among them two police officers," although it was not possible to obtain independent confirmation of this last report. The demonstrators, shouting anti-government slogans, spread out over a four-kilometer area, between Antonio Maceo Park and the Alameda de Paula. It was stated that hundreds of persons came down Galiano and Neptuno Streets breaking store windows and shouting "Freedom! Freedom!" The incidents began shortly after midday, when the police attempted to clear the Malecón, which had been invaded by thousands of Cubans who arrived at the port from which several boats had been diverted to Miami. The acts of violence lasted about two hours; by 5 P.M. calm had been restored.

A diplomatic source stated that the crowd began to gather at the Malecón in response to rumors that a fleet of boats had left Miami for Havana to pick up those who might wish to leave the island. "No one knows exactly how that rumor started," said some reporters who were present during the demonstration. In the streets of Havana they were saying that a speedboat managed to enter the bay very near a line of Havana Malecón coral reefs, and immediately, a Griffin boat of the Cuban Navy gave chase after the intruder along the Havana shoreline. The crowd, out of control, began to throw stones and bottles at the windows of several stores that allowed purchases in dollars, including the special store for diplomats located where the Ultra department stores used to be. A human river had overflowed its banks and was running all along Galiano Street to the Malecón. Soon the Malecón was full of screaming people running up and down the avenue. Hundreds of men had climbed the Malecón wall to scan the horizon; women carrying their children stood on the coral reefs, the seawater licking their ankles. The crowd continued spilling onto the Malecón from Neptuno, Galiano, Infanta, San Rafael, San Lázaro, and Belascoaín Streets. Demonstrators threw stones at the windows of the Deauville Hotel, shouting "Freedom! Enough!" and "Down with Fidel!" According to the version offered by one political dissident who went out to the streets to protest, the first police officers who arrived on the scene compelled the citizens to join the Rapid Response Brigades of the Blas

Roca Contingent. But the demonstrators refused and shouted to the police officers' faces: "Down with Fidel!"

From its studios in Washington, D.C., Radio Martí, sponsored by the Cuban-American National Foundation, which since 1985 has broadcast news and a variety of programming to Cuba twenty-four hours a day, broadcast a special program on Friday, August 5, about 5 P.M. Each half hour it sent a message addressed to the Cuban people in which the U.S. State Department denied, by every possible means, the rumors that a fleet had set sail for Havana to pick up future refugees.

On the morning of Saturday, August 6, 1994, twelve hours after the violent riots, the Havana Malecón was flooded with a crowd—but this time of police officers. Police patrols and groups of civilians armed with pistols, clubs, and belaying pins were patrolling the entire Malecón area and neighboring streets as a precaution against further disturbances. Armed with batons, clubs, and lead pipes, the Blas Roca Brigade continued keeping watch, as they had done all night, at the scenes of the violent clashes between security forces and anti-Castro demonstrators who threw stones and bottles, and in response, met with gunshots that left several wounded. Downtown, in the area known as the historic quarter, with its palaces of the old Creole aristocracy, colonial fortresses, archbishops' monasteries, and many tenements with their collapsing roofs and ruined exteriors, old trucks and jeeps full of police and soldiers kept order in the streets of Old Havana. Some of the patrollers carried Cuban flags and red-and-black banderoles of the Movimiento 26 de julio, founded by Fidel Castro in the early 1950s. From the balconies of rundown houses that were shored up by old planks from foundation to roof, people responded to the exhortations of the revolutionary patrols with shouts of "Long live Fidel!" and "Long live the Revolution!"

On Saturday afternoon, August 6, Castro, who was about to leave for Bogotá where he was to attend the inauguration of President-Elect Eduardo Samper, in a televised appearance, blamed the United States for the recent events at the Havana Malecón. Comandante Castro, unusually irritated, pointed out: "If the United States does not change its policy, we will be forced to not stand in the way of the departure of any craft with those characteristics . . ."

Castro revealed details of a supposedly secret conversation that took place early Friday night between Principal Officer Sullivan, Joseph G., of the U.S. Interests Section in Havana and Cuban Vice-Minister of Foreign Relations Fernando Ramírez. According to Castro, in the meeting Sullivan warned the Cuban government of the serious consequences that the opening of another Mariel could have for future relations between the two countries. "It wasn't a warning," said Castro, "but an unacceptable threat." Finally, in closing, Castro again accused the United States of encouraging the incidents that had occurred Friday in Havana.

Within the Cuban exile community in the United States, mainly in Miami, the reaction to Fidel Castro's words came immediately. Jorge Mas Canosa declared emphatically: "Castro is trying to make this into an immigration problem, and it's not. It's an institutional problem, of the incompetence of the regime, which can be solved by Fidel Castro leaving power. Please, ladies and gentlemen, don't play along with Fidel Castro with another Mariel . . ."

On the popular Calle Ocho (8th Street) in Miami, there was unanimous agreement among the Cubans who had gathered to play dominoes: "What is happening means that Fidel Castro has to leave power . . ." Across from the Versailles Restaurant, located on Calle Ocho, a customary meeting place for old anti-Castro conspirators, pickup trucks full of exiles passed by and stopped for a few minutes to shout slogans. Andrés Vargas Gómez, an old anti-Castro leader who was a prisoner in Cuba for years and founded the Cuban Unity organization while in exile, pointed out: "We have been waiting for these things to happen and to intensify until there is a social explosion; we have been encouraging the people of Cuba to rebel because there is no other solution . . ." For many, the words of Andrés Vargas Gómez were a clear signal that members of his group on the island of Cuba had been involved in the riots that occurred on the Havana Malecón the afternoon of Friday, August 5.

Contrary to any notice, speculation, or judgment that perhaps it was best that Castro not leave Havana at such a critical moment, Fidel, again wearing his olive-green uniform, tall black boots, and guerrilla kepi, suddenly appeared at the Bogotá airport at 7:15 P.M. on Sunday, August 8, 1994, aboard a Cubana de Aviación jet. To the amazement of customs officials, State Department personnel, the ceremonial military group, and passengers who happened to be on the premises, as Comandante Fidel Castro came down the stairway from the plane, he was preceded by the quick, nervous steps of no less than *seventy* personal security agents, most of whom showed little interest in hiding the pistols and short-barreled submachine guns they carried under their shirts and coats.

Moments later, the marathon-like descent from the plane of some one hundred officials and personal guests began. Soon the slow-moving, corpulent figure of the commander-in-chief was being lost in the labyrinth of the protocol rooms of the Bogotá airport, surrounded by a cloud of plainclothes police officers and a few more in uniform who competed among themselves, trying to offer the most protection possible to the newly arrived and problematic Caribbean guest on his third visit to Colombia in little over a month.

Chapter III

The Malecón in Flames

AS THE OFFICIAL ACTIVITIES SURROUNDING Colombian president Eduardo Samper's inauguration were ending, Castro decided to call a press conference in which, reporters presumed, he would air his main viewpoints regarding the difficult situation in Cuba and possible future coordination of Latin-American countries in the interests of mutual economic benefit and political independence.

But prior to the expected press conference, Castro, nostalgic at the sight of Bogotá, felt a desire to recall old times of youthful revolutionary glory by taking a tour of familiar sites. On April 9, 1948, forty-six years earlier, he had been an unknown student leader of the University of Havana recently arrived in Colombia to participate as a delegate in an International Student Conference. The 1948 Conference sessions were interrupted suddenly when thousands of people, infuriated at the death of leader Jorge Eliecer Gaitán, took to the streets to loot businesses, burn buses, and shoot at soldiers in the world-famous El Bogotazo riots. According to reports, among the most impassioned of the demonstrators was a young law student named Fidel Castro. And the riots that day, in which he participated extensively, began for Colombia one of the bloodiest chapters of contemporary Latin-American history, known as "*la violencia*" (the violence).

Might Comandante Castro have meditated, during his trip through the streets of Bogotá, on the recent acts of violence on the Havana Malecón?

Shortly after his tour of Bogotá ended with a visit to the statue of Bolívar the Liberator, Castro faced the international press and explained: "If there is not a speedy and efficient solution, we are going to suspend all obstacles so that those who may wish to leave Cuba illegally can do so once and for all. . . . We cannot continue guarding the borders of the United States, because that is when incidents occur and we have to pay the price and they call us cruel and inhuman." Through a long and rambling explanation filled with quotes, personal references, and abundant anecdotes, Fidel Castro attempted to convince reporters that after half a century in international politics, he did not feel the loneliness of power that his friend Gabriel García Márquez describes repeatedly in his novel *The Autumn of the Patriarch.* "I have never felt the solitude of power," Castro almost swore, "because I have always had the habit of sharing responsibilities whenever possible . . ." That solitude, Fidel Castro continued, is attributed by García Márquez to *autocratic* leaders. According to reports of journalists present, Comandante Castro gazed again and again through the wide window of the Tequendama Hotel meeting room. From there, he could see the peak of Monserrate overshadowing the Colombian city he had not visited since 1948, in the midst of the bloody "Bogotazo," and whose enormous increase in traffic now barely allowed him to sleep at night.

Leaving Bogotá on the evening of Monday, August 8, Fidel Castro reiterated, in an unequivocal reference to the "raft people crisis" that was about to explode, that his government "would authorize Cuban border guards to permit the entry into territorial waters of boats of anyone who wished to pick up their relatives in Cuba . . ."

Apparently unconcerned by Castro's intransigence or the prohibitive measures the U.S. government could take against them, a large number of Cuban residents of Miami were preparing to go to Cuba to pick up their friends and relatives once the results of the August 5 Malecón riots were made public.

A woman residing in the Hialeah area, considered by many to have the second-largest Cuban population outside Cuba, declared to the press: "Even knowing that it's illegal, I would do anything to bring my son, whom I haven't seen since 1980 . . ." She stated that her son had married and that she had several grandchildren she had never met. The woman and her relatives pooled their resources with another Hialeah family to purchase a twenty-foot boat that they considered adequate for the round trip to the island. "Once we reach Key West," she declared emphatically, "there is no one who can make us return to the Hell of Cuba."

Other Cubans residing in Miami stated that their relatives on the island were calling constantly, announcing their departure for the upcoming weekend. It seemed they expected that at any moment the Cuban government would give the green light for free emigration through one of the ports on the western coast. They imagined something similar to the Mariel exodus in 1980, which brought a record 125,000 Cubans to the United States in only four months. Nevertheless, the question remained whether the U.S. government, seeing a green light from Cuba, would maintain its own red light, which still made any attempt to get relatives or friends off the island illegal.

Meanwhile, in the beautiful and peaceful town of Key West, only ninety miles from Havana, prices among boatmen were shooting up tremendously in the face of the imminent growth in demand. On Monday, August 8, seventy-two hours after the violent riots on the Malecón, a clandestine trip to Cuba to pick up relatives was priced at between eight and ten thousand dollars.

Ramón Sánchez pushed his single-wheeled wagon down the streets of Hialeah, a red-and-white beach umbrella protecting his merchandise from the hot sun. He passed by the homes offering tasty hot dogs with mayonnaise, mustard, and catsup. Not stopping for a moment, he listened carefully to his customers' conversations on the topic of clandestine voyages to Cuba to pick up relatives. Ramón drew numbers in the air, calculating whether the money he had saved in two years of selling hot dogs door-to-door would be enough to rent a boat in Key West, Isla Morada, or Cape Marathon, the most common points of illegal departures to Cuba. Two days later, Ramón sold his hot-dog wagon, his permit, and all that went with it. He spent five thousand dollars on an old boat anchored in Biscayne Bay. Ramón heard that in Cuba the only possible means of transportation were bicycles, so he placed one on deck and headed out to sea, telling his friends and customers that he was going on a weekend fishing trip. Twenty-six hours later, he went ashore on the northern coast of Oriente Province, near his hometown of Gibara. Before disembarking, he put on a blue denim shirt, olive-green pants and black boots, like the members of the Cuban militia wear. Leaving the boat hidden in a cove covered by mangroves, he pedaled his bicycle along the crab-infested sandy road. Ramón greeted all the militiamen and soldiers on their Chinese bicycles who were on their way to work at that early hour. When he reached his home, he begged his wife, daughter, mother, and sister to be quiet, and they spoke not a word in the short time it took to reach the coast and board the boat. One day later, penniless but jubilant, the reunited family celebrated in their small apartment near downtown Miami, with a succulent meal of rice with chicken, fried plantains, and plenty of beer.

The week of August 8, 1994, marked not only the unleashing of rampant market speculation in the prices of clandestine trips to Cuba. It also marked the first reports by participants in the Malecón incident, newly arrived in Miami after crossing the tempestuous Florida Straits on tiny rafts.

All Alberto Martínez wanted to do on Friday, August 5, was to get a little gas for his boat. His best-kept secret was that he and most of his relatives would head out to sea that very night. But according to his calculations, he figured that, to achieve his objective, he needed to get a tank with thirty extra gallons of gas. In a country like Cuba, lacking Soviet petroleum supplies for the last four years, getting thirty gallons of gas was an incredible feat; nevertheless, with the best good will in the world, a cousin of Alberto, a resident of the Miramar district, had told him that if he paid in dollars, he could get them through a Cuban employee of a Swiss diplomat.

Alberto did not hesitate. On Friday afternoon, he left Guanabo, located on the east coast, for Miramar. He drove his old Ford station wagon through the Bay of Havana tunnel. He had just turned on to the four-lane Malecón when a human sea flooded the Malecón and began to shout anti-government slogans. Meanwhile, in the surrounding areas, the windows of the stores at the entrance to the Deauville Hotel were being shattered by thrown stones. The Cuban people, a frenzied crowd, clashed with police and paramilitary forces loyal to Fidel Castro. Alberto Martínez, against his will, ended up trapped in the crowds, in the midst of the greatest mass disturbance that had occurred in Cuba since Fidel Castro had risen to power thirty-five years before. Alberto watched through his windshield as the crowd, infuriated, turned over the police patrol cars that had responded immediately to the emergency call. The police officers, trapped in the crowd, fired perilously into the air and crashed into each other in the feverish confusion. "People couldn't take it anymore," declared Martínez, a diving instructor, when he told his story in the Center for Cuban Refugees. Martínez and eight members of his family, among them a son who had deserted from the Cuban army a few hours before the Malecón riot, left Cuba that same night on an inflatable rubber raft.

When Alberto Martínez was finally able to extricate his vehicle from the crowd and continue his trip, he had a better view of what was happening on the Malecón. In response to questions by reporters after his arrival in Key West, Martínez stated that there was a riot on every street corner along the almost ten kilometers between Avenida del Puerto and the National Hotel. The windows of the stores frequented by tourists were destroyed by thrown stones; the stores were then looted. The violent, uncontrollable crowd spilled over into the surrounding streets, and hundreds congregated on the beachfront in Maceo Park, where they chanted: "Down with Fidel!" "We're tired of this!" and "This is too much!"

"I had never seen anything like it," said Marcel Martínez, Alberto's eighteen-year-old son, who had accompanied his father in the search for gasoline that afternoon. He added that the police proceeded to surround the neighborhoods near the Malecón as a precaution against new outbreaks of violence. Then a human wave exploded from the end of a narrow street and attacked the police officers with stones and bottles. The police, surprised by the sudden assault, opened fire, as dozens of military vehicles and patrol cars rushed to the scene of the new clash, horns and sirens sounding.

A few blocks away from where Alberto Martínez and his son Marcel were trapped, another Martínez son, nineteen-year-old Douglas, was about to go into combat in the riot area. Unaware that his own father and brother were in the danger zone, he and other young soldiers had just received from their superiors assault rifles and 150 bullets each. Incredibly, none of the officers gave orders or even explained in detail how the troops should carry out the containment operation. Even so, Douglas Martínez was aware that the rifle in his hands and the clips of bullets in the side pockets of his uniform had not been issued on a whim. "I was dying to get out of there," Douglas would declare later. "None of my friends, myself included, wanted to do anything. It was like turning against my brothers, my mother."

Meanwhile, Alberto Martínez and his son Marcel were desperate to escape the new bottleneck in which they were trapped. Time was passing quickly, and it seemed ever more unlikely that they would be able to obtain the gasoline for the clandestine voyage. In front of them, a mob armed with baseball bats and rocks marched toward the long Malecón wall, covering it almost completely. Uniformed police armed with assault rifles closed off the area and prepared to fire on the crowd. Looking out over the Malecón wall, they could see a vessel loaded with people attempting to leave the Bay of Havana for the United States. Immediately, a Cuban Navy border patrol-boat cut it off and gave chase. The crowd began to scream "Bullies! Let them go!" The mob moved against the police, shoving them up against the Malecón wall. Several security agents clashed with the angry demonstrators. Two of them either jumped or were literally catapulted over the Malecón wall into the dark waters of the bay. Other security agents took out their pistols and began to fire over the demonstrators' heads. "It was like a war," said the Martínez family later. "It was like Fidel had fallen from power. We thought it was the end. People were screaming 'Enough, enough!'"

At the end of that unforgettable, hot afternoon, Alberto Martínez and his son Marcel arrived at the gates of the military base where Douglas was stationed, to pick him up. Sergeant Douglas Martínez had previously informed his superiors that his father had just suffered a heart attack and that he needed to go home right away. As soon as night fell, the riots spread from downtown Havana to the periphery of the city. In ever-expanding waves, they spread to the town of Guanabo, where the Martínez family lived. In Guanabo, sporadic outbreaks of violence were shaking the ordinarily sleepy seaside village. The townspeople, taking advantage of the almost absolute darkness of the night, a result of one of the many blackouts characteristic of the "special period," threw stones from hiding places at the soldiers who patrolled the streets. From time to time a shout of "Down with Fidel!" burst from a dark street corner.

At the Martínez home, the family began to get the boat ready as secretly as possible, as they pretended to watch closely the televised speech of Fidel Castro condemning those who left the country illegally. The family's youngest daughter slept peacefully on an improvised cot set up in the middle of the living room, very close to the television. Fidel, visibly upset, reiterated revolutionary phrases and slogans.

> If in that afternoon's demonstration there were some stones thrown and some shots fired, I wanted to have my share of stones and shots, too. You want to be there where the combatants are. It's a habit. . . . The imperialists want there to be a shooting, want there to be dead, to utilize them as instruments of propaganda, subversion, and, finally, intervention in our country. The imperialist strategy is to create the maximum of discontent in our country, divide the population and drive the country to a bloodbath. What happened today is related to that, to those stimuli, increasing the boldness and the audacity of those members of the underclass who carried out today's provocation. The United States has not complied with its migratory accords with Cuba, yet they take in any Cuban that gets onto a raft or anything. They don't care about those who may drown on the way. There is nothing more that Cuba can do with a view to facilitating the departures of those who may wish to leave. What more can they ask of us?

Peering through the blinds of one of the side rooms, two members of the Martínez family kept watch over the neighborhood as Fidel orated and the fourteen-month-old child slept placidly in front of the television. They saw the domino players in the doorway of a neighboring house finish their game; a young couple stopped kissing and went to bed; the pair of drunk night-owls who usually wandered the beach were returning to town, zigzagging slowly along the asphalt.

"Now!" said the elder Martínez, spreading the word. The Martínez family quietly left their house at exactly midnight. "With no shame, as if we were going out to buy cigars at the corner store," said Douglas Martínez. Watching the blinking lights of Guanabo get progressively smaller, they rowed in silence for two hours. Then, convinced that no patrol boats were following them, they started the motor and set a course north. The greatest danger for the Martínez family was that they were using an enormous, bright orange inflatable raft that shone like a brilliant sun in the midst of the sea and the night. Ten hours later, at noon on Saturday, August 6, the end of their odyssey was in sight. A Brothers to the Rescue plane had located them among a group of raft people adrift in the midst of the turbulent waters of the Florida Straits. In a gathering with the rest of the group of newly arrived survivors, the Martínez family hears comments being muttered around them: "This is nothing compared with what is to come." "Everyone wants to leave." "It's over."

The day after the Martínez family's arrival in the United States, the U.S. and Cuban press were contradicting each other with regard to estimates related to the August 5 riots. According to U.S. papers, the riots left a total of more than five hundred arrested, five dead, and almost one hundred wounded, including anti-Castro demonstrators, police, and government supporters. According to the same source, at least ten thousand people demonstrated, openly shouting anti-government slogans. The Havana newspaper *Juventud Rebelde* stated that there were seven hundred demonstrators.

White House spokeswoman Dee Dee Myers communicated President Bill Clinton's reaction to the statements made by Fidel Castro on Monday, August 8, in Bogotá during Eduardo Samper's inauguration. In the presence of reporters, Comandante Castro had reiterated his threat to permit a new exodus of thousands of Cubans to the United States, as he had in 1980. "Our policy is very, very clear. No, I do not agree with Fidel Castro. He will not dictate our immigration policy," declared Myers.

In the opinion of many political analysts, a new crisis with unpredictable consequences was about to explode between Cuba and the United States. Diplomats and specialists understood recent Castro statements as the prelude to a new phase of the prolonged secret war that the Cuban leader had waged for years against eight U.S. administrations. ("Cuba is not going to guard the United States' borders; if there is not diligence and efficiency on the part of the immigration authorities of that country, we will open the floodgates so that any Cubans who wish to leave can do so, and let the U.S. respond . . .")

For colonial Caribbean historians, the Florida Peninsula has always held a unique fascination, in part due to the large number of expeditions and Spanish conquistadors, such as Ponce de León, Hernán de Soto, Pánfilo de Narvaez, and Vázquez de Ayllón, who tirelessly pursued ghosts and illusions such as the Fountain of Youth and hidden treasures. That was if they weren't killed by rheumatic fever on the banks of the Mississippi River, drowned in one of the many boggy swamps of the Everglades, or swept away by the Gulf Stream. Literature is full of some of these myths; witness *La Florida,* a classic of Hispanic letters by the Peruvian Garcilaso de la Vega, and the extraordinary account *Los Naufragios* by repentant Spanish conquistador Cabeza de Vaca.

As a natural environment, the Florida Straits count among their main attractions the bottomless Gulf Stream—one of the most powerful forces of nature, whose devastating effects have been compared to the torrential force of a thousand Mississippi Rivers. The Gulf Stream moves thirty million cubic meters of water per second at any point of its estuary along the Florida coast. Those turbulent waters have also been the object of countless contemporary novels, mainly the works of Ernest Hemingway. The reader will remember with pleasure *The Old Man and the Sea, To Have and Have Not,* and *Islands in the Stream,* with their liquor smugglers, obsessed fishermen, and alcoholic painters who faithfully follow the Key West-Bimini-Havana route.

The Gulf Stream comes from the Gulf of Mexico, approaches Cuba, and turns toward Florida. During the summer it carries an even greater quantity of water and reaches closer to the coast of Cuba. Raft people who take the risk of leaving during that time of year can catch the current and its beneficial effect much sooner. The best place to catch the Gulf Stream is the north coast of Cuba, on either side of Havana, from El Mariel to Matanzas. This explains the predilection of Cubans who plan clandestine departures from one of those beautiful beaches. But even when the winds are calm and the weather is good, the navigation can be dangerous. The Gulf Stream moves with such strength and speed—from two to four knots per hour on average—that it can carry a raft beyond the Florida Keys. In the winter, when the winds that blow across the rough sea reach speeds of twenty knots per hour, the enormity of the waves makes it almost impossible for the Cuban Navy Coast Guard to detect the rafts. But, consequently, the risk faced by the raft people of being buried by the impetus of the swell is greater, and the risks in traveling by raft to the United States reach suicidal proportions.

At midnight on Thursday, August 11, 1994, the eve of the day when hostilities were expected to break out between the Cuban and U.S. governments over the matter of the probable exodus of thousands of people, the National Weather Service of the United States was issuing its forecast. It was predicting winds of up to twenty knots in the Florida Straits, with the possibility of ten-foot waves, an unusual forecast for that time of year. Dr. Tom Lee of the Rosenstiel School of Marine and Atmospheric Sciences of the University of Miami declared worriedly, "I would not want to be out there in a rowboat, much less in a raft . . . As weak as the vessels that have been arriving are, they are not going to be able to even reach the twelve-mile limit, where the Coast Guard could sight them . . ." As if in an urgent warning to future victims, Dr. Lee added, visibly distressed, "The rafts will break! They will have no way out!" Would the bottomless and majestic Gulf Stream turn out to be the tomb fate had reserved for thousands of fugitive immigrants who in a few hours would head out to sea and probably to the most desperate adventure of their lives? The imminent crisis was reflected in a variety of admonishing statements made by important figures in the Cuban exile community who had wrestled with the problem of clandestine immigration since it first appeared. The various directors of the agencies in charge of rescuing and processing raft people stated on Monday that their resources were about to run out, due to the large number of Cubans setting sail.

On Saturday, August 6, José Basulto of Brothers to the Rescue declared that his organization had sighted the largest one-day total of vessels since it had begun to search for raft people in the Florida Straits on May 15, 1991. The pilots of the voluntary organization sighted eleven groups with a total of seventy-two people aboard, and three empty rafts, stated Basulto in a press conference.

Near Key West, the Center for Cuban Refugees, which receives the raft people after they are rescued, was expecting approximately eighty people on Monday, August 8. So far that year the Center had processed a total of 4,442 raft people, almost double the 2,981 it had helped the previous year, stated Arturo Cobo. Due to this increase, the Center was running out of clothes, shoes, toothbrushes, toothpaste, and many other necessities generally given to new arrivals. "Our reserves are going down. Care of the raft people is costing us ten times more than it did last year," said Cobo.

The approaching crisis was also becoming evident in the state-ments of U.S. government officials, who spoke of putting into practice what they called "Operation Distant Coast." According to several gov-ernment agencies, this plan had been designed in great secrecy starting at the time of the Mariel Cuban Refugee Crisis, which brought 125,000 Cubans to the United States during the first half of 1980. According to information leaked from the offices of the various agencies to editors of Miami newspapers, the most relevant goals of "Operation Distant Coast" were: (1) to interdict boats carrying refugees; (2) to detain peo-ple who tried to enter the United States illegally until immigration pro-ceedings could be carried out and a decision reached with regard to admitting, relocating, or returning those who left the island; (3) to prosecute owners of vessels that attempted to bring in refugees, and to confiscate their boats.

The emergency plan in development since the Mariel Crisis was ready to be implemented if necessary, Democratic Senator Bob Gra-ham of Florida said from Washington on August 6, 1994: "We are much better prepared today than we were in 1980 to respond to an ini-tiative by Castro to convert his internal problems into a mass exodus toward Florida . . ." Among the offices coordinating the plan were the U.S. Attorney General's Office, together with Lawton Chiles, governor of Florida, and about forty federal agents specializing in the subject. One final clause in the "Operation Distant Coast" plan indicated that Cubans living in Miami would be arrested if they traveled by boat to the island to pick up their relatives, as they had done during the Mariel Crisis. This last, of course, sounded to the U.S. Cuban community like little less than a grave threat.

Asked about the origin of the anti-exodus measures, a State Department official indicated that the exodus was caused by the "inability of Cuba to provide freedom or economic security to its people." Meanwhile, the Havana government insisted that the United States had agreed to receive up to twenty thousand Cuban immigrants annually and was not complying with the agreement. For its part, the U.S. government responded that "Cuba has always misinterpreted the 1984 agreement, which does not guarantee a certain number of visas per year but rather includes only close relatives of Cuban-Americans . . ."

On Thursday, August 12, 1994, Bill Clinton ordered twelve U.S. Navy and Coast Guard vessels to patrol the Florida Straits in readiness to repatriate Cuban refugees forcibly in case of a new mass exodus.

The U.S. plan aimed to show the Cuban government that the United States was determined not to permit another mass exodus. It was also designed to dissuade Cuban-Americans from setting sail for Cuba to pick up their relatives. The orders issued by Clinton seemed categorical: U.S. ships were prepared to intercept any refugees and return them to Cuba.

Wayne Smith, former head of the U.S. Interests Section in Cuba during the time of the Mariel Crisis, pointed out similarities between that emergency and the one on the horizon. The Cuban government could be calculating that, if it permitted a mass exodus, it would be reorienting that discontent toward the mechanics of escape. The Cuban government's conclusion could be: "There is instability, but if we open the doors, [the disaffected] will focus their discontent on how to leave and not on protesting . . ."

Smith's opinions were not shared by Vladimiro Roca, leader of the dissident group Corriente Socialista Democrática, who indicated that manifestations of discontent would continue to occur even if Fidel Castro opened the doors to emigration. Roca, son of Blas Roca, head of the old Cuban Communist Party for decades, indicated that for all the would-be emigres, there were many others who wanted to resolve the country's situation once and for all. "The level of violence that exists here is so great, that if this explodes, not even God will be able to stop it. When this explodes, it's going to be as terrible as Bosnia-Herzegovina . . ."

Jorge Mas Canosa seemed to favor Roca's doomsday scenario actively imploring, "We must not allow Castro to make this into an immigration crisis when in reality it is a political crisis . . ." And to his fellow Cuban-Americans, he added: "Don't play along with Fidel Castro and head for Cuba on boats; that does not serve the interests of a free Cuba . . ." Mas Canosa said that Attorney General Janet Reno had told him on Thursday that the United States would take the next step and begin a total blockade of the island; it had not yet been done only because so many resources were devoted to the Haitian blockade (against the regime of Raoul Cedras).

Miami Mayor Steve Clark declared to the press: "The Mariel [exodus] of 1980 helped Castro remain in power fourteen more years, and if there is another Mariel, he will exist for fourteen more. We must stop it now!"

Meanwhile, in Havana, the Cuban government had no intention of allowing the genie of public protest to escape its bottle. Foreign journalists in Havana reported that the Cuban military was patrolling the Malecón day and night as a precaution against further rioting. Thousands of soldiers had been mobilized from the interior to Havana, according to passengers arriving at Miami International Airport. From Saturday, August 6, on, troops were patrolling the Malecón to keep order in the port, the streets, and train and bus stations. "Things are more or less calm now, but you should see the number of police they have on the street," one Cuban woman told a reporter. "If Fidel opens another Mariel, and the United States lets him do it, he's going to be left all alone. Even the cat is leaving!" declared another.

With hostilities about to break out, a team of camera people and reporters from CNN rushed to Havana for the purpose of interviewing

Castro. U.S. viewers watching at midnight on Thursday, August 11, 1994, suddenly saw the bearded Cuban leader appear on their screens. As soon as he began to speak, Comandante Castro mentioned the problem of illegal departures from his country and again blamed the United States for the consequences that could arise from a new mass exodus. According to political analysts, during the televised appearance, Fidel appeared erratic and hesitant. Two days later, August 13, Fidel Castro would celebrate his sixty-eighth birthday.

On Castro's birthday, the newspaper *Granma* circulated through the streets of Havana with a great call on the front page: FOR LIFE, WITH FIDEL.

Raft person Carlos Babastro Batista arrived in Key West on the night of Friday, August 12, and was immediately settled in a room at the Center for Cuban Refugees. Among its furnishings, the room had a television set, and soon Babastro saw Fidel Castro's bearded face appear on the screen in a repeat of the CNN interview. Noting the abundance of channels on U.S. television, he said, amazed: "Oh, all I've done since I arrived is watch TV. It's amazing. In Cuba we only had two channels: Sports and Fidel. And now, I get here, and all you see is . . . Fidel."

The first craft that dared to leave Cuba immediately after Fidel Castro's televised appearance was sighted on Friday, August 12, about 4 P.M. some six miles east of Miami Beach. Aboard the gray-and-yellow, twenty-three-foot, Florida-registered boat were a total of eight men, seven women, two children, and a black dog. It was the harbinger of a legion of vessels: with or without Fidel Castro's official authorization, a new mass exodus of incalculable proportions had begun. Foreign journalists in Havana mobilized to the east-coast beaches (Cojímar, Alamar, Bacuranao, Tarara, Santa María del Mar, Boca Ciega, Guanabo, and Brisas del Mar) to report what promised to be an unusual spectacle.

On the gray sands of Cojímar Beach, immortalized in 1952 by Hemingway in *The Old Man and the Sea,* hundreds of people were looking for a chance to board a boat. They watched with growing envy as the first raft people headed out to sea on tiny inflated rubber rafts that were cast about on the waves like lost life preservers after a shipwreck. The majority of the daring crew members of the rafts were young men between the ages of twenty and thirty, who carried their rafts on their shoulders to the beach. As they passed through the narrow streets of town, people cheered them on. The police and militia members feigned indifference and looked away.

"As long as they don't steal boats, and have permission from the owners, anyone who wants to leave can go ahead," a police officer interviewed in the doorway of the La Terraza restaurant on Cojímar Beach told a Spanish journalist from the news agency EFE.

Inside the houses in town, everything was feverish activity. Until the wee hours of the morning, one could hear the dull pounding of hammers. Though it may seem incredible, at 3 A.M. on the second day of authorized maritime departures, hardly anyone was sleeping in the neighborhoods of the beach town of Cojímar, east of Havana. All were gazing in one direction: toward the dark, turbulent waters of the Florida Straits.

Suddenly, the squealing of brakes was heard. In the instant that the young people approached the old car, two men took down from its roof a black rubber raft four feet long, reinforced with a few poles. In the pale ashen light of dawn, the group ran with the young men to the shore, shouting "Good luck!" At the last minute, one of their friends ran thigh-deep into the water and handed them two plastic containers full of gasoline—to repel sharks during the crossing. "Thank you!" the young men shouted to them, and the crowd burst into applause. "May God protect them!" sobbed an elderly women, never taking her eyes off the departing raft.

About twenty rafts had set sail from the coast of Cojímar since Fidel Castro, in his televised appearance the previous night, had indicated his acceptance of a mass exodus to the United States. During the "rush hour" of the maritime traffic, about 2 A.M., a raft was leaving every twenty minutes, accompanied by happy shouts from the crowd. "In almost every family there's someone who has gone," explained a dark, middle-aged woman who lived in a modest little concrete-block house near the sea. At 4 A.M. the woman and her family, four women and two men, were still awake, all of them praying a collective rosary asking the Virgin to protect the young people of the family who had left on rafts just hours before.

With each passing day, there were more and more reporters and camera crews wandering the dark, narrow streets of Cojímar in search of new images. They waded into the water to film close up the faces of the young people carrying rafts on their shoulders at the instant they proceeded to put them into the water. Nearby, there was an enormous red raft, blown up like a balloon, with ten men aboard. "Freedom! Freedom!" one of them screamed toward the cameras in a hoarse voice, without stopping his rowing for an instant. Another young man, carrying his inner tube, wore a sweatshirt bearing an enormous picture of Madonna in a tight bikini.

Not all the rafts that left made it out to sea. At dawn, four men who had left at midnight returned, soaking wet and disheartened. Their raft, made of tires and wood, had taken on water when they were only a couple of kilometers from the coast. As they carried the raft to a nearby home to repair it, the disappointed raft people joked with the crowd that surrounded them, laughingly saying that they had been fishing. "We're revolutionaries, not sea worms." They shouted the official slogan of "Long live the Revolution!" as the crowd around them burst into uproarious laughter.

The next morning, on other beaches on the east coast of Cuba, the scenario of swimmers and probable raft people getting ready to leave was being repeated with slight variations when a speedboat, equipped with powerful outboard motors, approached the coast and, seconds later, pulled away briefly, staying parallel to them. "It's here to pick people up!" shouted a man already in the water. As soon as they heard him shout, a dozen swimmers ran up onto the coral reef, trying to guess the next movement of the craft. "If you're going, leave me your bikes; I'll sell them," shouted the man, now submerged up to his neck. But the boat left the would-be refugees in suspense. After cruising back and forth for a few minutes along Bacuranao beach, it withdrew at great speed, disappearing from sight. "Everyone on this island is waiting for a boat to come and pick him up," commented the man sarcastically, still swimming. "If a sailboat appeared on the horizon, everyone would jump into the water trying to reach it."

The atmosphere of expectation had been even greater the previous day, when someone claimed to have seen a craft signaling with reflectors to people standing on the beach at night. Tati, a young homosexual who frequented the beaches day and night, commented on the incident. "The reason I didn't jump in is because I was too far away to swim to it; I didn't want to take the chance without knowing for sure what it was." For want of a motorboat to take him to the United States, Tati wandered the beaches of Havana like a sleepwalker, in search of a Colombian, or any other foreigner, who might send him a letter of invitation that would permit him to apply for a visa and stay for a time in any Latin-American country. "I can't stand it anymore. My God! Someone has to take me away! The situation here is desperate!"

A short time after the speedboat approached the coast and then left again at high speed, a man passed by in front of the group of swimmers, rowing like crazy on a homemade raft. "Are you practicing for going to Miami, honey?" asked Tati sarcastically, and immediately declared to the group of swimmers: "I'll bet my ass that guy's leaving tonight."

A half hour later, in front of the Tritón Hotel, a young Canadian tourist was gracefully riding the waves on his surfboard. A look of envy came over the swimmers' faces, as they wished they had a similar instrument with which to travel to the United States. Again, Tati's voice interrupted the other comments of the group: "Nobody wants to stay here. If a big enough boat comes, everyone in Cuba will get on and leave."

For many Havana residents, lacking electricity, food, and transportation, going to see the raft people off and stopping to watch how they were building their rafts in broad daylight was nothing short of the greatest entertainment available. The city, feeling the effects of the "special period" and the lack of supplies from the former Communist bloc, was day by day becoming a land devastated by an invisible war. At one time, clandestine departures by raft were prohibited, and brought jail sentences and stiff fines. But after August 13, 1994, the sixty-eighth birthday of Maximum Leader Fidel Castro, departures in boats, or in whatever was available, had become a national festival, a party, a carnival without costumes, in which everyone declared their opinions. In short, it was a true popular celebration, a festival of the people, by the people, and for the people, as many in the crowds in the town squares and along the avenues and the Malecón insisted on calling it.

On Monday, August 15, on one of the many beaches of the Miramar neighborhood, Rogelio, a young mason, was hurriedly preparing a wooden raft. He seemed completely relaxed even while all around him crowded fun-loving people, peanut vendors, and U.S. television camera crews, calmly filming the scene. Parents put their children on their shoulders so they could have a better view of the construction of the raft. Passers-by on First Street, riding Chinese-made bicycles, stopped and discussed construction details with Rogelio, at the same time offering advice for his trip. One of the passers-by shouted to Rogelio, without getting off his bike, "Hey, partner, if I pay you in dollars, will you give me a seat there?"

There was no doubt that the authorities were turning a blind eye. Thousands of young people were building their rafts in parks, town squares, and out on the streets. At the end of the day, the rafts were put into the water right from the Malecón wall, the scene of the violent riots one week earlier, on August 5. The police, who on that occasion had directed repression against the thousands of demonstrators, now stood with arms crossed, cynically contemplating the departures. Again, a group of curious bystanders milled around the fragile vessels, offering toasts of rum to the future raft people, wishing them good luck during the long night that awaited them at sea. "Hey, partner, when you get there, to Yuma City, remember me, and send me a pair of size eight shoes." Laughter came from the crowd. The reference, like much of present-day Cuba, reaches back to the pre-Castro era—to the 1957 Hollywood western *3:10 to Yuma,* in which the town represents the distant beacon of civilization.

Rogelio was not at all intimidated by the close presence of police in the streets. In fact, he had gone so far as to choose as his departure point none other than the rocky cove in front of the enormous Russian Embassy. "As long as you don't shout 'Down with Fidel!'" Rogelio explained to a reporter, "the police don't intervene; they leave you alone."

Rogelio deemed it prudent to depart in the late afternoon of that Monday, August 15, 1994, accompanied by his wife, their five-year-old son, and five friends. He was firmly convinced that in Cuba there was no future for him or his family, and at no time during the conversation he had with reporters from the international press did he appear hesitant or fearful about the U.S. government's decision not to offer asylum to future raft people, and its plan to detain refugees at the Guantánamo naval base. Like Rogelio, most of the young raft people neither expressed nor felt any fear. For many of them, the voyage was an exciting adventure; for others, it was their only chance to escape the enormous crisis in Cuba. Like almost the entire Cuban population, they complained of hunger, unemployment, and a lack of future prospects.

In La Terraza, which specializes in paella and seafood from the beach of Cojímar, a waiter serving cocktails to tourists stated that business, already good, had improved in recent days. This was due to the enormous number of foreigners arriving to see the raft people off. They would then go to La Terraza to eat lobster Thermidor or breaded shrimp in garlic sauce. It was clear to everyone, nationals and foreigners, tourists, journalists, and local townspeople that, in the midst of the crisis, Cojímar had become Raft People Central. Just a few yards from the terrace of La Terraza people crowded onto the coral reefs to see the raft people set sail. Under an enormous multi-colored beach umbrella, a vendor was selling *chambelonas,* roasted peanuts, and corn fritters to tourists and Cubans. Meanwhile, a BBC film crew was waist-deep in the dark water of the inlet of Cojímar to film the latest scenes of the departure of a group of rafts. "This is better than TV," said a woman watching the rafts being tossed onto the waves. "This is live and in living color!" she exclaimed, hurrying to say farewell to the next raft.

If a small, poorly constructed raft, or one that was insufficiently supplied, began to spin in circles in front of them, unable to maintain its course, the crowd made fun of the navigators. But when a craft took off with good speed and wind in its sails, it received applause and cheers from the audience.

What awaited the raft people beyond the three-mile limit that they supposedly could reach in their tiny vessels? No one knew. And for the moment no one dared answer the question. The political climate, the announced maritime blockade, the forecasts of the experts regarding the fearsome Gulf Stream, as well as the predictions of the Miami Meteorological Service, did not bode well.

Nevertheless, the raft people, daring all that might befall them, advanced slowly across the waves, on tiny rafts, believing, with the highest hopes in the world, that they would arrive safe on the coast of the new Promised Land of the United States of America.

Chapter IV

On the High Seas

THE BROCHURES OF THE CRUISE LINES that travel the Caribbean include a brief description of the area where the conflict between the United States and Cuba over the raft people was about to unfold, such as the fact that the islands and sea that extend from south of Florida to Surinam include a total of about two thousand miles in length and are composed of sixteen independent nations and numerous island territories under foreign control.

It is unlikely that the promotional publications, directed at future customers of the cruise lines, include any story like that of Daniel Bussot, an eight-year-old child, who was left orphaned and alone in the waters of the Florida Straits. Daniel Bussot never imagined that the peaceful life he led in the town of El Mariel, located on the north coast of Havana Province, would be abruptly interrupted by his family's departure by boat for the United States. From that moment on, the peaceful sea of an immense blue that he had seen every morning when he awoke turned, suddenly, into a hell of whirlpools and opposing currents, in which his parents and everything that had meant anything to him in his short life died.

The story of the solitary child Daniel Bussot moved everyone at the Center for Cuban Refugees in Key West, when Mrs. Ivis Rivero, an eyewitness in the case, told the story through her tears.

Mrs. Rivero, like many others, had left Cuba on Saturday, August 13, 1994, encouraged by Fidel Castro's statement that the Cuban Navy Coast Guard would not interfere with departures for the United States. Ivis Rivero traveled in the company of her husband, her two children, and two other men, friends of the family. The Bussot family, their friends, and the Valdés family traveled close behind them, in an even smaller boat. When they left, the sea was calm, and it seemed to them, as they talked to each other across the water, that the voyage would turn out to be as happy and enjoyable as those of the big cruise ships that cross the Florida Straits. At dusk a strong storm came up; its huge waves and strong winds began to pound the rafts, tossing them about. The Bussots' boat did not last long under the violence of the waves; it capsized in the stormy sea that dark night, amid heavy thunderclaps and enormous bolts of lightning.

Julia, Danielito's mother, put the only lifejacket they had on her son. Then his father, holding him up by the shoulders, swam through the heavy waves until he reached the Riveros' boat. With his last bit of strength, he managed to get Danielito on board. "Mommy, Daddy," murmured the child, nearly unconscious, "be careful; don't drown." A short time later, Danielito Bussot's mother and father, along with a ten-year-old boy and his parents, were dying as the sea swallowed them up.

The Rivero and Bussot families had been good friends for years. The Riveros' group spent most of Sunday and Monday, August 14-15, adrift, tossed about by the waves in the midst of a storm that seemed endless and pushed them from side to side, constantly throwing them off course. To make matters worse, their boat's engine died, and they were unable to restart it. A sudden crash of the waves tore the compass from the hands of Ivis's husband, and they were left at the mercy of the waves. Ivis reproached her husband for having insisted that they make the trip. He reminded her, on the brink of despair, that their children deserved a better life. Crouched in a corner of the boat with Danielito Bussot, Ivis' youngest son sobbed inconsolably, repeating "Mommy, I don't want to die; I'm only ten years old." Ivis was thinking she never should have risked her son's life. It would have been better to stay in Cuba, with fewer comforts, but not bring him to his death. Late Monday morning, a French boat sighted them and called the U.S. Coast Guard. Danielito Bussot was immediately transferred to Jackson Memorial Hospital, where he was listed in serious condition due to emotional trauma and chemical burns from the gasoline his parents had poured on him to protect him from sharks. His relatives in Miami remained with him, doing their utmost to help him get over the terrible trauma. The boy now knows that his parents died at sea. Cuban physician Manuel Rico Pérez, age 53 and father of six himself, offered to pay for Danielito's education, including college.

One of the greatest attractions of the Caribbean Basin are the old redoubts, hidden in the coves of the islands, where pirates went ashore. Such a tourist attraction does not go unnoticed by those in charge of advertising for the transatlantic cruise lines. Among the many promotions they offer their customers, at the top of the list is the opportunity to find treasure buried by John Hawkins, Olonés, or Sir Francis Drake, in the sand on a lonely beach.

The stories of shipwrecks told by surviving raft people would put those of the pirates to shame, especially in view of the defenselessness of the raft people compared with the sturdy frigates, cannons, and seamanship possessed by the pirates.

The lifeless body of Rafael Gámez Rodríguez arrived at the Miami Beach Coast Guard Station. Rafael was one of two brothers who had fled hurriedly on a precarious raft, spurred on by the fear that the United States would soon prevent raft people from entering the country. Traveling on a raft made of only two old inner tubes, with insufficient drinking water, was a mortal voyage for one of the Gámez brothers. According to statements by Pedro Gámez Rodríguez, age thirty-two, on the night of Tuesday, August 16, his brother Rafael lost consciousness and fell into the sea. Pedro, exhausted, with a supreme effort, managed to pull him halfway onto the raft. They remained in that position until they were finally found on Wednesday, August 17. "We had to ration the water we drank, and that had to affect him," stated Pedro from his bed in Miami Beach's South Shore Hospital, where he was admitted for dehydration and burns.

In another group that reached Miami, a young girl named Indra Lemus Castellanos was admitted to Jackson Memorial Hospital in critical condition, suffering from severe dehydration and burns over her entire body. Pummeled by four storms, her group had lost its food and water, and survived by drinking urine and eating vitamin pills while navigating precariously aboard a raft made of planks and inner tubes.

Alexis Moreno, age twenty-five, and three friends left for the United States on Saturday, August 13, from the Alamar neighborhood on the coastal area east of Havana. Shortly after setting out, they were battered by strong storms. The violent waves soaked their provisions. On Monday, August 15, after two days adrift, the four ate their last hamburgers, which were totally soaked with saltwater. Shortly after eating, Moreno began to complain of severe stomach pain and a fever that made him hallucinate, as chills and convulsions made his body tremble and shake. Moreno threw himself into the sea, but his traveling companions rescued him, put a life preserver on him, and tied him to the raft. That night, they saw lights on the horizon. Believing it was the coast of Cuba, they began to row in that direction. "Let's try to get back," said one of the men. "Alexis' life is in danger." Exhausted after almost three days lost at sea, the four friends fell asleep. When they woke up in the middle of the night, they realized that Moreno had disappeared into the darkness. One of the victim's friends, Mario Franquis, age twenty-four, swears they heard Alexis shouting incoherently in the distance. "I'm going to Cuba!" his friends heard him say. "My house is near that corner." That was when they heard horrifying screams: "Let me go! Let me go!" The three survivors now believe that Alexis Moreno was screaming at sharks that had him surrounded. "Let me go! Let me go!" Those screams cannot be erased from their memories. Finally, on Tuesday, August 16, the three survivors were spotted by a Brothers to the Rescue plane, which immediately notified the Coast Guard of their position.

If you dream of becoming one of the eight million people who visit the Caribbean Islands each year, the tourism brochures recommend that you do so in late summer. This is off-peak time, as tourists from the northern United States do not yet feel the urgent need to escape the terrible blizzards. The only foreseeable danger is that the Caribbean region may be lashed by a cyclone or hurricane. The August 1994 announcement of such a disturbance and its devastating consequences for the waters of the Caribbean made the cruise lines, with their fabulous three- and four-story vessels, free cocktails, exercise equipment, sauna, Olympic pool, and multiple enormous dining rooms, immediately suspend their scheduled departures.

But such was not the case with the voyage scheduled by Cecilio Rojo, age fifty-five; Inti Rojo, age twenty-three; and Yulina Rico, age nineteen. Against all the odds and with a hurricane blowing across the Caribbean, they never hesitated in their decision to escape Cuba on Tuesday, August 16, 1994. At that point, the predictions regarding the path of the hurricane were nothing more than speculation. Cecilio Rojo worked as the director of a small circus; he traveled with his old patched and mended tent through the tiny towns on the north coast of Havana Province. His son Inti Rojo was the circus magician; he made doves appear and disappear, swallowed fire, and made eggs appear in the palm of his hand. Yulina Rico, Inti's wife, was the tightrope walker. She performed incredible feats on a unicycle, and also managed to read a book while seated on a stool balanced precariously on a high wire.

Father, son, and daughter-in-law set out to sea from the Alamar neighborhood the night of August 16. With the money they had saved from the sale of their tent and other circus equipment, they had purchased a small sailboat. As they sailed under cover of darkness, the border patrol fired shots into the air from the coast. They were leaving behind the sad memories of recent days: a circus in ruins that no longer performed because, due to the lack of fuel, it could not travel from place to place as before. The last pair of doves from Inti's prestidigitation act were sacrificed and eaten with rice. Because of the same lack of fuel, he could no longer breathe fire for the audience. The Beautiful Yulina, high-wire artist, had to cancel her two sensational acts. In the first, called "Crossing Niagara," the unicycle she used had a flat tire, and they had no spare. In the second, known as "Tightrope," for want of the umbrella she needed to maintain her balance, she fell and broke her arm. She had to have it placed in a sling because the hospitals had no plaster to cast it.

As they moved away from the Cuban coast, they were leaving behind the best times of their lives, the happy times when they had visited the provinces of Matanzas and Pinar del Río, contiguous to Havana Province, and in the small town of Las Calaveritas had set up their patched, mended tent among fragrant meadows of tobacco. Young and old alike had descended joyfully from the El Rosario Mountains, lighting their way with candles and flashlights, to see a one-night-only performance. Well-practiced, they had delighted the crowd with their spectacular juggling. Blindfolded, they had juggled knives and plates, and removed long tablecloths without upsetting even one of the many crystal goblets that rested on the table. Everything had seemed to be going very well for them despite the terrible "special period" that the entire country was experiencing.

But in May 1994, frightening things happened, such as a robbery and the progressive loss of almost all the crystal they used in their juggling acts. And the pair of monkeys they exhibited, caged, somehow connived to stone and beat to death the old toothless lioness that was the relic of the Rojo Circus. Before the family's astonished eyes, the monkeys devoured the lioness; this occurred after a week of intense hunger during which the owners had not been able to offer the monkeys even a banana. That day, the Rojo family agreed that it was better to emigrate secretly than to wait for the phantom of cannibalism to be unleashed among them. If they stayed in Cuba, they might devour each other in the end, like the old family of the Cuban aristocracy in the film *The Survivors,* directed by Tomás Gutiérrez Alea.

After midnight, they turned on the small transistor radio they carried on board. Under a faintly starry sky, as the current pushed them across the calm sea, they heard on a Radio Martí broadcast that Hurricane Chris was entering the area of the Bahamas. Reports of scattered showers, thunderstorms, and wind gusts of up to seventy miles per hour sent shivers of fear down the backs of the Rojo family. Yulina began to pray quietly. Very soon, her husband Inti and father-in-law Cecilio joined her. At dawn, the waves began to crash around them, and the sky filled with huge gray clouds, while the wind began to gust, making their worn canvas sail tremble, an insignificant leaf. Spontaneously, the Rojo family began to pray for a miracle, that a boat or plane would rescue them before it was too late.

The Caribbean, of course, has its magic. As a result of the fusion and mixture of native peoples, Europeans and Africans, various religious syncretisms abound. There are Christians, Hindus, and Muslims in the Caribbean, but many residents of the Caribbean profess religions of African extraction. Among other beliefs, voodoo is one of the most common in Haiti. Obeah still exists in some of the British colonies, while *santería,* a mix of Catholicism and African beliefs, is one of the most popular forms of religious worship in Cuba.

For a person adrift at sea between immense walls of saltwater many times higher than the tiny dot that is the raft on which he or she sails, believing, praying, imploring, are ways of clinging to the last and only life preserver.

Among the thousands of raft people who undertook the enterprise of reaching the United States in what were little more than floating corks, the mixture of magic and tragedy abounds. Hallucinations at sea, in which exhausted raft people are awakened from their sleep by the warm hand of Santa Bárbara, who then takes the helm and guides the raft to its destination; or the miraculous apparition of the Virgin of la Caridad del Cobre, with her mantle of gold that shines like a thousand suns in the midst of the darkest night imaginable; or the dolphins, sent at the last minute by Providence, which are able to push lost rafts with their noses to beaches of calm waters and white sands; or the angels belonging to the celestial brigade of Saint Gabriel who, up above in the sky, fly Cessnas and are able to sight rafts in the middle of the ocean. These are just some of the most common beliefs that attempt to alleviate, with their innocent beneficial effect, the harsh reality seen in U.S. Coast Guard statistics.

During 1993, one of every four raft people who departed Cuba was lost at sea. Hence the prayers; hence the stories; hence the hope sustained beyond the horizon.

Whether it was owing to the intervention of Almighty God, or more prosaically, the Coast Guard, the Rojo family survived. Before quite reaching the Bahamas, Hurricane Chris did a few zigzags, then reversed its course, eventually petering out in the north Atlantic.

There have been times when the true miracles of raft people have surpassed even the wildest imagination.

In their rush to leave Cuba, six raft people forgot to take a flashlight with which to scan the horizon or signal for help during the terrible nights that awaited them. Their first night at sea, tossed about by the waves, they had no way of reading the tiny compass they carried on board, and they could only guess, looking at the stars, where north was. One of them, on the brink of despair, rummaged in a bottle he had hidden in a bag and brought out a tiny companion he had picked up at the last minute when he realized their dilemma of having forgotten the flashlight: A firefly! To the astonishment of his traveling companions, the man placed the insect upon the compass and exclaimed excitedly, "No, we're going the wrong way. North is over there!" The salvation of these raft people is attributed to the miraculous firefly, who, after effectively carrying out his task, died at dawn the following day at the precise instant that a providential U.S. Coast Guard ship sighted their raft. The firefly's body rests peacefully in a tiny white box on display in the Center for Cuban Refugees in Key West.

It is almost certain that the firefly has been the smallest creature that raft people have brought with them, but it was not the only one. On a blackboard at the Center, director Arturo Cobo allocated an entire section for a list of the various passengers from the animal kingdom. A glance at the board reveals that, as of August 1994, the Center had welcomed thirty-two dogs, three parrots, fifteen mockingbirds, and three parakeets.

But there are even more extraordinary cases in the exodus of the Cuban raft people that would require a new edition of *Ripley's Believe It or Not*. The unusual experience at sea of Arturo Méndez and Rosa Carvajales, husband and wife, is one of those. As residents of Cojímar suspected, "La Tiburona" (The Shark Woman) and her husband, a well-known local raft builder, set out to sea and managed to arrive alive. Arturo Méndez, a fisherman, always swore that he was not afraid of sharks. In the years he had been fishing, he had seen them close up many times and was used to dealing with them. Among the proudest accomplishments of Arturo's life was having built three rafts that reached their destination without any problem. Arturo Méndez now believed the time had come to build a raft for himself and his family. Accompanied by his wife, Rosa Carvajales, alias Shark Woman, his thirteen-year-old daughter, Yelenys, and three other relatives and close family friends, he left Cojímar Beach, like so many hundreds of others, on Tuesday, August 16, at 8:30 P.M., after having suffered two initial defeats in his attempt to reach U.S. territory. The first two times they had been stopped by Cuban border-guard boats and had all their supplies confiscated: bottles of water; cans of condensed milk; bread; hard-boiled eggs; lemons; and *guayaba* candy.

Each time that this happened, they had to go out and buy their supplies again, spending more than the thirty dollars sent by their relatives in the United States. With great effort, they managed to save their raft, which measured two and a half meters long by a meter and a half wide, and consisted of two tractor tires joined by a canvas and a yellow wooden frame. Since the raft was so brightly colored that every time they took it out everyone on the beach noticed it, they told them they used it to fish for sharks. The night of their escape, they walked the four hundred meters to the beach, carrying their supplies, without being detected by the police. They got on the raft, and it was then that Méndez discovered, to his horror, that two of the four men accompanying them did not know how to row properly. To make matters worse, one of his daughter's friends, Irvenis Mederos, no sooner climbed aboard than she began to vomit. With no other solution, Méndez and Miguel Valdés, an old childhood friend, took the oars and began to row hard in a northerly direction.

Soon after they lost sight of the city lights, which told old sea dog Méndez that they were approximately twenty miles from the coast in international waters, they saw with growing horror that a Cuban Navy patrol boat was approaching them. "Lie down and don't move," said Méndez. Luckily for them, but unfortunately for others, the Cuban border guards instead intercepted other groups they found close by. About 4 A.M. Méndez, who was rowing in front, spied a new danger: An enormous shark was swimming along with them, right in front of their raft, and two more huge sharks flanked the craft. One of the sharks bit one of the oars, breaking it in two. Old salt Méndez changed his strategy and decided they should stop rowing, to avoid attracting the sharks' attention.

According to the testimony of Méndez's wife, Rosa Carvajales, during the hazardous crossing they counted ten gigantic sharks that approached the raft, swam lazily around it, struck it with their tails, showed their sharp teeth, and swam away, only to return a short time later. Carvajales states that in Cojímar, they had called her Shark Woman after their three oldest sons left Cuba on rafts built by her husband. All their neighbors thought that they possessed a magic formula, a divine mandate from providence that caused everything they attempted to go well for them. But once at sea, finding themselves surrounded by those enormous predators that harassed them constantly, Rosa and her husband began to wonder whether luck was on their side. The sharks were so large that from nose to tail they were as long as the raft on which the family floated.

On one occasion they were accompanied by a group of sharks from 4 A.M. until 7 A.M., when a southerly wind drove them away from the raft. Méndez commented to Rosa that the sharks they had seen were certainly "addicted to eating human flesh," since in the area in which they were traveling many raft people must have died. Tears in her eyes, Rosa embraced her daughter and prayed for their souls and those of the disappeared. At the front of the raft, plunging the oar into the water again and again, to get away from that place as quickly as possible, Méndez commented to his companions, "Sharks go where there is food."

At mid-morning they sighted a raft consisting of an inner tube with a sail placed in its center. They began to signal. There was no reply. They approached the raft, rowing as fast as they could, only to find, to their horror, that it was empty. The southerly wind that took them away from the sharks in the early morning took them into strong currents in the afternoon. Later, at sunset, with night upon them, a huge storm began. Waves more than two meters high swept the raft and swung it up and down like a toy. They spent almost all night being lifted by the waves and then dropping into the emptiness; they were unable to row. Méndez decided they should all tie themselves to the raft. It was then that the anguished sailor considered the possibility of giving up and returning to Cuba, although he thought, "At this point, who knows if that is even still possible . . ."

His daughter Yelenys, who until that moment had remained calm and spoken only to ask for water from time to time, began to cry, saying that it was better to die at sea than to return. Inasmuch as his young daughter was insistent, Méndez tried to steer the raft north, though the wind and waves were pulling it west. Instead of diminishing in intensity, the storm intensified. The waves made the raft fly and fall roughly. It was filling with water, and they could not bail fast enough. And each time a long lightning bolt tore the darkness of the night, looking around, they could see sharks' fins and heads peering out of the foamy edges of the waves like a bizarre funeral procession.

At dawn, after a night of anguish, the travelers were extremely hungry, but all their provisions had been soaked with sea water. However, they did not throw them away for fear of attracting the sharks again. They continued on, their hunger burning. The five liters of water they had brought were almost gone. In their rush to leave, they had not found any more water containers. At 6 A.M. they sighted some boats traveling slowly along the horizon. They waved and shouted, but no one came to their aid. They also saw a small plane fly over, but it did not see them either. In the afternoon, they saw a white dot in the distance, and began to row toward it desperately. They soon realized that it was a U.S. Coast Guard ship. His hands bloody from rowing, Méndez tied his orange T-shirt to the tip of the oar and held it high. As they were happily boarding the Coast Guard ship, Méndez was horrified when he turned and saw an enormous ten-foot-long shark swim slowly out from under their raft. It raised its head, gleaming back, and fins out of the water, revealing its full length to the astonished Coast Guard sailors gathered on deck. The shark had remained in the shade of the raft all day. Only then did Méndez and his family realize the enormous danger they had been in each time they thrust their hands into the water, trying to hurry to reach the Coast Guard ship.

Some of the world's most popular musical rhythms have their origins in the Caribbean. Their melodies and orchestrations have traveled around the world. Salsa has its roots in the Caribbean, the home of Tito

Puente, Willie Colón, and Rubén Blades. The mambo, made popular by Pérez Prado; the rumba, immortalized in the swinging hips of María Antonieta Pons y Tongolele; and the cha-cha-cha, harmonized by the Aragón orchestra and the magic flute of Maestro Jorrín, are some of Cuba's principle musical contributions to the cultural mix of the Caribbean.

For the Cuban raft people, risking the journey to the United States is like dancing the mambo on the high seas. An hour after President Clinton warned that the U.S. government would forcibly detain them, a flotilla of fragile rafts was leaving the sunny bay east of Havana, moving north to the rhythm of the Gulf Stream. On the beach, the most common opinion was that, although asylum-seekers might be detained at sea, sooner or later they would be released from the Guantánamo camps. This was the reasoning of Félix, a young man who leaned his bike against the small seawall of Cojímar and prepared to cheer on a group of future refugees heading for Florida on four rafts.

In the opinion of political observers in Havana, U.S. authorities were deluding themselves if they believed that the warnings issued on Friday, August 12, would stop raft people from leaving the economically paralyzed island. In Cojímar, some twenty rafts set sail within two hours after Clinton's announcement.

Residents of Cojímar, suddenly catapulted onto the front pages of international newspapers by the large number of reporters arriving every day to cover the departures, spent their afternoons discussing the latest anecdotes related to the exodus: who reached Florida; who they suspected had died in the attempt. On Wednesday, August 17, one of the most popular people in raft construction set sail. The Engineer—as we shall call him—is disabled, and so as to not spoil his departure, the day he decided to leave for the United States on a raft, he did so seated in a wheelchair, accompanied by his father and two neighbors. The Engineer was very popular, not only in Cojímar but also in the neighborhoods of El Vedado and faraway Miramar. People were able to see U.S. satellite television broadcasts at night because there was no one in the world like the Engineer. He was able to capture signals by simply twisting coathangers, tying wires, and making satellite dishes for many customers in Havana and the interior provinces, who were ever grateful for his services.

The night the Engineer left, the people of Cojímar said that a star had gone out in the sky. And with good reason. When he departed, seated in his wheelchair on the raft, the Engineer announced to his followers that they should be sure to watch Miami channels 23 and 51 the following evening. He assured them that in greeting reporters on his arrival in Florida, he would greet all the friends who had been kind enough to see him off at that critical moment in his life. That said, the Engineer ordered that his crew hoist anchor (a gesture more symbolic than real) and raise the sail, which consisted of a pair of patched sheets sewn together. And then they were gone.

In spite of the threat of Hurricane Chris in the Florida Straits, the Miami cruise lines' advertisements continued to encourage their customers to join the August vacation crowd. At the end of their ads, fearing the sea might become too rough as the hurricane approached, the cruise lines recommended that customers consult the travel agent of their choice to make sure the prices were still in effect for their desired travel date.

Luis Soler, age thirty-three, was one of the few who did not have time to call his travel agent to cancel his travel reservations when the hurricane approached. Soler and the two friends who accompanied him on his extraordinary late summer adventure had been at sea two days when one of their inner tubes burst. They were forced to cling to the two remaining tubes, their bodies half-submerged in the water. They were picked up the following day. As one of Luis Soler's legs was badly sunburned and blistered, it was bitten by sea creatures during the rest of the journey. "There came a moment when I disconnected mentally, put myself in God's hands, and felt nothing. I scared the fish away by slapping my hands on the water by pure instinct," Soler later told reporters.

There are other stories, odysseys, that do not generally receive a great deal of space on the front pages of the papers, but which will always be remembered by those who experienced them. There are those who went bak to Cuba, frustrated after having suffered countless obstacles at sea. Some returned frightened, still shaken by the hell they lived through at sea.

Ivonne Rodríguez Barroso, age twenty-two, was a student of English language and literature. Whenever she remembers how much she suffered, she begins to cry. For a day and a night she was aboard a fragile raft, with her brother and sister, a cousin, a neighbor, and a nephew only six months old. She remembers with horror the storm that came up; the waves were four meters in height. She recalls the terrible spectacle of many empty boats.

But the nightmare did not end there, according to Ivonne. What finally convinced them to turn back was something they never thought could happen to a group of refugees at sea. They were suddenly attacked by another group of raft people. Five big, strong young men approached the raft on which Ivonne was riding along with her sister and her small child. The men were desperate, their eyes wide, as they screamed for water, a pair of oars, and a compass with which to continue their journey. Their raft was weaker than Ivonne's, and barely floated. Ivonne and her sister were so afraid of the men that they decided to head back toward Cuba immediately, and began to row as hard as they could. Their strength was almost gone; they had lost a pair of oars to the assailants, and were rowing against the wind. It took them hours and hours to reach the Cuban coast. Ivonne and her sister, Diana, swear they will never forget the huge number of empty rafts they saw. "Everyone thinks that after twelve miles they'll be picked up. What they don't know is that there are many people risking their lives at sea," said Ivonne, still crying and repeating, "At sea, at sea . . ."

Chapter V

The Craziest Month Ever

THE MONTH OF AUGUST 1994 will surely go down as one of the most disturbing and craziest imaginable in Cuban history. In the course of that month, President Clinton reversed the "open arms" policy that the three preceding administrations (of Reagan and Bush) had maintained toward Cuban immigrants. That policy had been a tradition initiated in the early 1960s by John F. Kennedy and later ratified during Lyndon B. Johnson's presidency with the signing of the Cuban Adjustment Act.

One of the first measures taken by Clinton to penalize Fidel Castro for his renewed massive exports of Cubans to the United States was to prohibit the charter flights that had been permitted since 1979 to Cuban residents of the United States, to visit their relatives on the island. According to conservative estimates, that escape valve of family reunions allowed the Castro government to receive approximately two hundred million dollars per year.

The same day the accord went into effect, a bomb threat occurred on a Carnival Airlines charter carrying 144 passengers. The plane was only ten minutes from landing in Havana when it was forced to return to Miami. There, the plane was duly inspected, and no explosive device was found on board. "The atmosphere we are creating in Miami is terrible" stated Francisco Aruca, manager of Marazul Airline, involved in charter flights to the island. "Many people want to go to Cuba to help their relatives. We have observed a polarization in the Cuban community of Miami, and this matter is going to deepen that division." Both Francisco Aruca and John Cabañas, manager of C & T Charters, owner of the plane that suffered the bomb threat, describe themselves as moderate Cubans in opposition to those they consider the hard-line political leaders of the exile community.

If anyone thought that the hijackings of three insignificant little wooden boats that usually travel the Regla-Casablanca-Havana route, in the middle of the bay, would turn out to be an unbeatable record in the registry of clandestine trips to the United States, what happened on Sunday, August 14, 1994, surely made them reconsider their opinions. That Sunday afternoon, between two hundred fifty and seven hundred people—almost a whole town!—chorusing "Let's go!" assaulted a petroleum ship anchored at the port of Mariel, west of Havana. Upon learning of the assault, the Mariel Municipal Police fired several times into the air, to try to stop the multitude that was milling around the pier, preparing to board the vessel, but the shots were in vain. The gangplank was finally raised. Realizing they could miss the opportunity of their lives, a dozen young men managed to get onto the ship's deck by climbing the thick ropes that held the *Jussara* to the dock, while several police or paramilitary officers dressed in civilian clothes pulled on their clothing, trying to hold them back.

The incident began at approximately 2 P.M., and the news that the ship was carrying refugees spread like wildfire through town. The situation of conflict in the pier area continued at 6 P.M., when journalists were forced to leave. And on Sunday night the result was still unknown, and speculation abounded. At 6 P.M., well-armed Cuban Army units were controlling the entrance to the town and all entering vehicles, while inside Mariel, police put up barricades in the streets leading to the docks. As they withdrew, reporters saw at least six truckloads of special police troops speeding toward the port area.

The unusual act of taking over a foreign ship anchored at Mariel had its most immediate, local precedent in the hijacking of a fifty-foot boat belonging to the Cuban Navy. That event had occurred just a week before, on Monday, August 8, also in the tiny town of Mariel. The Cuban government reported that during the takeover, one officer was killed and four other sailors from the crew were forced to jump off the boat. Once in the hands of the hijackers, the ship immediately set a course north toward the United States. It was sighted, adrift, the following day, sixty miles southwest of Key West, by the U.S. Navy cutter *Monhegan*. The hijackers were immediately transferred to the U.S. ship, since theirs had suffered serious damage, rendering it practically useless. According to a statement by a State Department official, "those who participated in the violence will probably be detained while a detailed investigation is carried out." The same State Department spokesman stated that he viewed with great concern the increase in the use of force by Cubans who want to escape from the island. "It is an alarming tendency if more and more people become hijackers; we have to discourage the use of violence," he concluded.

According to all indications, the hijacking of the Cuban Navy vessel and the still unexplained death of an officer on board had all the necessary ingredients to become an international problem. As soon as the Cuban government learned of the case, it demanded the immediate return of the hijackers from the United States. State Department officials rejected the Cuban proposal for their return. As versions of the events were scarce and contradictory, both governments paid a good deal of attention to what the newly arrived hijackers told reporters in Key West.

In the version offered by Anaisa Bravo, it all started the afternoon of Monday, August 8, when her husband, Oliver Marzo, invited her to spend a few hours with their two-year-old daughter, Zoila, on a beach near Mariel. Once at the beach, watching little Zoila running through the sand, Anaisa received the surprise of her life when she saw a fifty-foot boat appear, with people on board shouting. One of those was her husband, who shouted loudly, so the coastal wind would not carry away his words, "Get on the boat; we're going to Miami!" In her statement to the press, Anaisa denied that a Cuban Navy officer had died and that four other crew members had been thrown into the water. Other passengers, however, said that the mate of the hijacked vessel, Leonel Macías, became involved in an exchange of gunfire with a navy officer, although they did not specify if the latter had died.

Anaisa Bravo, her daughter, her husband, mother-in-law, and two brothers-in-law, with their wives and children, joined seventeen others and boarded the ship that had been stolen by its mechanic Leonel Macías. In the midst of the Florida Straits, at the mercy of the waves and in the darkness of night, Anaisa Bravo and her little Zoila were taken from the hijacked boat onto a U.S. Coast Guard launch after the child's head was injured. According to Anaisa's testimony, at the moment when the Cuban Navy ship reached the Mariel beach on Monday afternoon, many people took off running, in their bathing suits, and jumped into the water, trying to swim to the ship. But Macías, the mechanic, managed to start the vessel and head out to sea before the crowd could board. A few minutes after they left the beach, they were spotted by several Cuban Coast Guard Griffin launches. One of them rammed them, breaking the ferro-cement hull, while the other one struck the stern with its side, terrorizing the passengers. "I threw myself down on the deck and began to scream," stated the anguished Anaisa Bravo. The Griffin patrol boats desisted from their assault when the fugitives called out to them that there were four children aboard. Once at sea, the ship began to take on water, until about 3 A.M. on Tuesday, when the engines stopped completely and the boat became a fragile toy tossed about by the huge waves. "The waves tossed us in every direction," continued the still-distressed Anaisa Bravo. The refugees believed they were lost, but finally they were spotted by the U.S. Navy cutter *Monhegan*. During the press conference held in Key West, Anaisa Bravo said that after the August 5 riots at the Malecón, the Cuban people thought only of escaping any way possible. "Everyone is in the same situation," said Anaisa. "People are going crazy; they're willing to try anything . . ."

On Thursday, August 11, Attorney General Janet Reno declared the matter of returning the hijackers closed. In a public appearance, she said that she opposed returning the alleged hijacker of a Cuban government boat to be tried on the island, but that she did not rule out the possibility of trying him in the United States.

From a remote cell in a county jail in Florida, Leonel Macías, who had been immediately separated from the rest of the hijackers and sent to prison, where he would spend long months in detention, wrote a letter to anyone who would listen to his laments: "I have committed no crime. I have acted in self-defense, and I trust in the U.S. laws, for which I risked my life, because I am a Cuban who wants to live in freedom. If they return me to Cuba, Castro will execute me. I prefer to live locked up in a U.S. jail, where at least I can dream and sleep in peace. This is preferable to participating in the Cuban Armed Forces, serving a tyrant named Fidel Castro. Please, help me. My only relatives in the U.S. are the Cubans . . ."

On the afternoon of Monday, August 15, 1994, after nearly twenty-four hours of hermetic silence, the curtain around the petroleum tanker *Jussara* was opened. The *Jussara* had been taken over by a crowd of hundreds the previous day, and was immediately surrounded by Cuban police and army troops. In what appeared to be the first success recorded by the Cuban government's mediation policy throughout the long "raft people crisis," more than five hundred people abandoned the ship voluntarily. A long line of entire families, with children and grandchildren, came ashore, while some of the youngest occupants of the ship got off the same way they had gotten on—by using the thick ropes that held the ship to the dock. The crowd immediately headed toward the exit of the port area, where busses awaited to take them to their homes. Others, seeing the general demobilization that occurred, did not wait on deck a minute more, but chose to dive into the water and swim ashore. Many of those who abandoned ship told reporters that they felt frustrated at the government's refusal to permit the boat to leave the port.

The Cuban Interior Ministry praised the efficient work of the personnel of the tugboats that kept the *Jussara* at the pier. The police had promised the people aboard the ship that they would not be prosecuted. The Interior Ministry also stated that the Greek captain of the ship and some of the crew were under investigation. In spite of the prompt and effective resolution of the crisis—less than twenty-four hours—experts on Cuban matters indicated that the Castro government was showing signs of progressive weakening of authority and lack of control when it came to stopping the protests and the massive attempts of Cubans to escape from the island. In a final communique, the Interior Ministry reported that several hundred "antisocial elements" from various areas of the Havana provinces occupied the tanker immediately after the burial of (Corvette) Captain Roberto Aguilar Reyes, who had died a week earlier on Monday, August 8, during the hijacking, at that same port of Mariel, of a ferro-cement ship belonging to the Cuban

Navy. In collusion with the Greek captain of the tanker, which typically carried out tasks of trading and transfer of fuel at various Cuban ports, the hijackers boarded the ship *en masse* with the purpose of traveling to the United States. According to the Interior Ministry communique, as soon as word of the events reached the government, rapid response brigades were mobilized, but it was already too late to stop the massive boarding of the ship. Therefore, the next step was to prevent the tanker from leaving port.

Analysts were of the opinion that Fidel Castro was astonished at the situation and could no longer sense how much more the populace would stand. "He is at a crossroads," analysts and Cuban experts proclaimed unanimously. On Monday, August 15, Fidel Castro himself—wearing, of course, his military uniform and accompanied by his personal security team—visited the area where the *Jussara* was docked, and ordered that water and food be supplied to the women and children on board. All day Monday, journalists were prohibited from entering the scene, and had to be content with the rumors that emanated from beyond the police cordon around the imprisoned ship. Two Cuban Navy ships remained constantly at a distance of one hundred meters from the tanker. Behind the police lines, groups of pro-government demonstrators shouted revolutionary slogans. Near the ship, another pro-government group was singing the National Anthem, which, amazingly, was answered loudly from the deck of the *Jussara* by a group of hijackers still on board. In the town of Mariel, many were saying that it was the captain of the *Jussara* himself who had promised to get the refugees out of Cuba and take them to the United States. The Mexican news agency Notimex reported that the would-be hijackers of the petroleum tanker took maximum advantage of a loosening in local security measures when police who usually patrolled the docks and ships attended the ceremony in honor of the officer who had died on August 8.

A week after the attempted hijacking of the *Jussara,* a "first-hand account" reached the press of the situation on board while the boat was surrounded by troops. Osvaldo Pérez was on the boat for thirty-six hours. According to his testimony, it was through a day and a half of threats and coercion that Cuban government agents managed to persuade the almost seven hundred occupants of the ship to desist from the idea of leaving Cuba and traveling to the United States. "They even brought psychologists to work on our minds. They tried to scare us; they cut off our food and water," Pérez told reporters. The thirty-three-year-old Pérez and eleven others arrived Wednesday at the Center for Cuban Refugees located in Key West. He stated that he left the island on a raft the day after he got off the tanker anchored at Mariel. "I had the raft half-built since before what happened with the boat," insisted Pérez. "I decided to leave before they put me in jail." In spite of government assurances that the Cubans who had boarded the *Jussara* would not suffer reprisals, Pérez pointed out, many of them were immediately fired from their jobs. According to Pérez, the Cuban authorities used their relatives who were on the pier to convince those aboard the *Jussara* that they should come ashore . He also stated that relatives of the people on the ship gathered at the entrance to the port. "All the Cubans on the ship began to sing the National Anthem. They couldn't do anything, because they knew that the people were going to attack the police if the police touched us."

When Pérez reached Key West, he reacted with tears when informed of the Clinton administration's new policy toward Cuban refugees. "It would be wrong to say I feel fine, because my soul is aching." Still barefoot, his clothing in tatters after the desperate two-day maritime escape accompanied by his wife and her parents, Pérez, staring out at the immense Florida Straits, meditated aloud, oblivious to the group of people surrounding him: "There will be mass suicide; there will be great bloodshed in my country."

Someone else who reacted with visible anger to Clinton's decision to cut off the maritime exodus of refugees and send them to Guantánamo was Carlos Solís. When he learned that the border had just been closed, he immediately thought of his son, whom he had not seen for fourteen years. His son had not been able to obtain a visa to come to the United States, and had made several attempts at clandestine crossings. When Janet Reno announced on Thursday that Cubans reaching the south Florida coast would be detained, Solís said, "I almost had a heart attack!" The news, of course, shocked not only Solís but all of those gathered around the television in the Center for Cuban Refugees near Stock Island, where Solís is vice coordinator.

Solís had expected that at any moment his twenty-three-year-old son would appear among the hundreds of Cubans welcomed at the shelter every day. That was what had happened on Monday, when his daughter arrived. Solís was resting for a few minutes when someone tapped him on the shoulder and whispered, "Your daughter is here!" First, he thought it was a bad joke. Almost everyone involved with the Cubans who came to Key West knew that Solís was waiting for his son and daughter. But when he went back to the Center, there was his twenty-two-year-old Yoana! It had been so long since they had seen each other that Solís barely recognized her. She had grown so much and was so beautiful! They embraced and cried tears of joy.

Solís's two children had been born while he was in jail accused of participating in a counterrevolutionary conspiracy. During the ten years he spent in prison, he was able to see them only on the days when political prisoners were permitted to receive visits. When Solís was finally released from jail and came to the United States fourteen years ago, his children remained behind on the island with their mother. Yoana left Cuba with sixteen others on an enormous raft made of ten tractor tires; it floated on the sea like an inflated whale. Halfway to the United States, the group sighted a Panamanian cargo ship. When they approached the Panamanian ship, they found that it already had guests; on each side of the vessel there was a raft with ten people aboard. That very day, Solís spent six hours flying with groups of volunteers in search of lost rafts and refugees. Each time he saw a raft with people on board, he threw them a cellular phone to ask where they were coming from, in hopes of finding his daughter. When he saw the cargo ship and the three rafts, he had no phones left. He did not find out until later that Yoana had indeed been on one of those rafts.

Trying to find an solution to his family's problems, Mario García Palacios was wracking his brain, conscious that in the end, whether the application of the idea was good or bad, the goal would be the same: to reach the United States! García Palacios, a resident of Sagüa la Grande in Villa Clara province, had attempted the crossing twice and both times the result had been the same: border-guard troops had arrested him as he attempted to climb aboard a raft. Thanks to his innate ability to smooth-talk and a certain natural astuteness, García Palacios had spent only four days in the municipal jail. He managed to convince his captors that it was a mistake, that he would never leave his native land to live in that repugnant U.S. capitalist world.

Incredibly, the local police chief believed that he was only intending to go fishing and released him. At night Mario did not sleep, trying to find the solution that would allow him to escape with his whole family. He thought that if Cuba had a border with another country, he would be willing to dig a one hundred-kilometer tunnel to get out on the other side, but here one could only leave by water or—or—or, Mario stammered aloud, *by air!* Why hadn't he thought of this before? Mario began the task of establishing friendships with the young pilots from a nearby air base devoted to crop-dusting. Mario discussed the matter with pilot Jorge Luis López, and when López said no, Mario's blood went cold. "Now," he thought, "I will surely go to prison for a long time if this guy squeals on me to the police." Mario spent the next nine months trembling in fear every time he left his house to go to work. He thought each day would be the last time he would walk freely through the streets of Sagüa la Grande since surely the pilot would report him and the police would come for him. And Mario already knew what he was risking: at least two years in prison!

To Mario's great surprise, in mid-June of 1994, Jorge Luis López approached him and whispered, "We're leaving on a trip soon." Mario immediately began to prepare. Hidden in the bushes of an abandoned sugarcane field, three men, four women, and six children waited for two hours in darkness for Jorge Luis López to pick them up on an abandoned airstrip. One of the women in the group was pregnant, and her baby was kicking so hard that they could hear its movements in the dark silence of that early morning. "We got up very early and got on a tractor," said one of García Palacios' children. "We went to the landing strip and hid near there in the bushes." When the green-and-yellow biplane arrived, flying low, they feared it might be a military plane and did not come out of hiding until García Palacios signaled to them that it was López. Then they knocked down a fence and boarded the plane.

Pilot López picked them up at 8:35 A.M., and they arrived in Cape Marathon, Florida, at 10:35 A.M. "We didn't have a radio. We were flying without guidance or anything," said García Palacios upon arrival. "You get into a storm with no visibility, and it always scares you. Everyone was afraid," said López.

After almost two hours of traveling through cloud cover, López arrived at a chain of islands that he recognized as the Florida Keys from the highways connecting them. According to witnesses, the plane flew over the airport buildings and then landed. "We could not see what type of plane it was in the distance," said María Ballejos, a receptionist for the Flight Department, the first agency that detected the plane. "We realized that it was a Cuban plane when we saw the CU on the tail." The passengers got out and Ballejo took them into her office to protect them from the rain. "They were hugging me and crying," added Ballejos. "They were so excited."

A few hours later, the recently arrived refugees from the crop-dusting plane, as well as the fugitive raft people from the *Jussara,* and any other Cuban survivors who reached the Florida coast, even floating on a board, were all immediately sent to the INS's Krome Detention Center for processing. Among the usual questions that were becoming common to the successive waves of raft people were:

(1) Were you ever imprisoned for committing a crime?
(2) Did you work for the Cuban government?
(3) Are you in good health; do you have any contagious diseases?
(4) What are people in Cuba saying? Will they come in spite of the new detention policy?
(5) Have you served in the military and, if so, how?
(6) Do you have relatives here?
(7) Is it true that everyone has rafts or are buying or building them?

The orders issued by President Clinton during the week of August 15-19 were definite: those coming ashore in the United States went directly to Krome Detention Center; those rescued at sea went to Guantánamo. Hearing the news, crowds spilled into the streets of Miami. "Miami, yes, Guantánamo, no!" was the chorus of the Cuban protesters in front of the Manuel Artime Community Center on Friday, August 19, in Little Havana. "We are upset, because the Cubans should be brought here, to Miami," said Bárbara Rodríguez. "Anywhere but back to Cuba." The measure, announced Friday by Clinton, provoked angry outbursts from the crowds traveling the streets of Miami awaiting the liberation of their relatives recently arrived from Cuba on rafts.

"Clinton and his policy aren't worth a penny," said protestor Fernando González. The group vigorously waved a banner bearing the slogan: "Cubans in exile, in unity is strength!" Anguished and disillusioned, a Bay of Pigs veteran stated to the press amidst the din of voices: "How can Clinton do this to the Cuban people after thirty-five years? We Cubans do not deserve this kind of disappointment."

For analysts in the Cuban exile community, sending Cubans to Guantánamo not only meant an abrupt change in the most recent immigration policy but also in past policy: the Cuban Adjustment Act. Although President Clinton had said that the law continued in effect, many doubted that such would be the case after the deportation of Cubans to Guantánamo began. In the opinion of many observers, U.S. immigration policy toward Cuba had been a bundle of contradictions, and the Cuban Adjustment Act, decreed in 1966 during the Johnson administration, one of its most debated and controversial parts. In accord with the Cuban Adjustment Act, nearly all Cubans who reach U.S. shores are accepted. But, at the same time, Washington was limiting the number of visitors' visas it granted to Cubans, because many decided to stay in the country. On several occasions, bills were introduced by different members of Congress to abolish the Cuban Adjustment Act, but none ever passed. On the opposing side, the law had many sympathizers, especially in the Cuban-American community.

That sympathy was not shared, however, by Immigration and Naturalization Service (INS) Commissioner Doris Meissner, a key figure in the discussion of whether the law should remain in effect or not. In Meissner's opinion, any preferential treatment of Cuban refugees "is a national shame, and it is time to correct the error." She made this statement in an article published in the *Miami Herald* in 1993.

So, the fate of the first group of 322 Cuban raft people who arrived on the U.S. coast that Thursday night was decided. They were transferred on Friday, August 19, to Krome Detention Center in Miami, located in southwestern Dade County. Within a week, Krome became part of the popular commentaries and street folklore of Miami. It was, undoubtedly, a painful moment in the history of the Cuban diaspora, for exiles to see their closest friends and relatives separated from them by fences and barbed wire. A clue to the identity of the refugees previously held at Krome resided in a sign written in Creole—vernacular language of the Haitian raft people—that hung from the door of the detention facility warning people against violating the law. Inside the Center, getting acclimated to jail conditions, were 336 Cubans dressed in the bright orange uniforms of prisoners.

The Cubans were assured that they would not be returned to Cuba, but not even the guards knew anything more about their future. Democratic Senator Bob Graham, a member of the Senate Intelligence Committee, arrived at Krome on Saturday, August 20, and spoke with some of the Cuban detainees. "It remains to be seen if this decision to send them to Guantánamo will prevent more Cubans from attempting the trip. And if they keep coming, we don't know what will happen when Guantánamo and Krome are full. Those are some of the questions that have yet to be answered," Senator Graham said to the press. He immediately pointed out that the new measures were a step toward achieving some U.S. control of the situation. Whatever questions remained, one thing was very clear: The change in policy regarding Cuban immigration had, in less than twenty-four hours, raised a barrier between the Cuban exile community—traditionally very pro-American—and the Clinton administration.

For the moment, all was complaints and laments in the exile community in Miami. Thirty-three-year-old computer programmer Juana Rodríguez had spent several hours in the hot August sun, her face pressed against the fence, hoping to receive news of her twin sister and other relatives. Rodríguez, many others anxiously waited for an officer at Krome to read a list, so they could find out if their relatives were among the detained. "I came during Mariel, and none of this happened," Rodríguez said to reporters. "I studied, I worked, I paid taxes,

I'm a good mother. I took advantage of the opportunities of the system, and my relatives will certainly do the same. The government will not have to take care of my family. I will take care of them. But first I need to know if they're alive."

But Juana Rodríguez seemed to be the exception to the rule on that turbulent August afternoon when a crowd gathered outside the bars of Krome. The group of demonstrators, after several hours of unbearable waiting in the hot sun, blocked the narrow access road to Krome and complained loudly to the INS guards. To the astonishment of the officers, the crowd then began to sing the Cuban National Anthem.

Paradoxically, the Cuban detainees, in their bright orange prison uniforms, seemed much calmer than the crowd outside. In spite of the fact that the new political circumstances created by the presidential decision were completely unfavorable to them, they were not worried and seemed satisfied with having been able to shower, put on clean clothes, drink Coke, and eat chopped meat, rice, and tomato salad. These were things that, in an imperceptible accounting, made them forget the prolonged time of deprivation they had suffered in Cuba and the many dangers they had been forced to face at sea.

In the days and weeks that followed, thousands of Cuban residents of the Miami area stoically withstood the scorching late-summer sun, oppressive heat, sudden downpours, and endless lines in order to have even short visits with their relatives detained at Krome. The long wait began at dawn. Entire families, some with babies in strollers, others with elderly relatives, arrived continuously in hopes of seeing their loved ones. The authorities blocked access to the center to prevent people from crowding into the entrance; the visitors were forced to wait some distance away at the corner of Krome Avenue and Calle Ocho. In their hands they held tickets that allowed them to board school busses and travel the mile of highway that led to the center, where they would see their loved ones, many of whom they had not seen in decades. For the highway patrol officers, the crowd became a habitual part of the landscape, and on Sundays the number of visitors was estimated at ten thousand.

The massive exodus of Cubans was not the only one that concerned U.S. immigration authorities; in Haiti, the dictatorship of Raoul Cedras had encouraged thousands of Haitians to set sail on precarious rafts toward Florida in search of better job opportunities and civil rights. Many of them, shipwrecked, had ended up at the U.S. Naval Base at Guantánamo, in southeastern Cuba, where they had preceded the Cubans in that huge tent city. On another front, there was the Mexican exodus toward the United States across an extended border more than two thousand miles long; its principal motivation was not political, as it was for many of the people who risked their lives to cross the sea from Haiti or Cuba. On the U.S.-Mexico border, an average of thirty-two thousand people are arrested every day trying to enter the United States illegally. Nevertheless, neither the White House nor the Congress treats the situation on the Mexican border as a crisis *per se,* in spite of the fact that every year about 1.1 million people who try to enter the United States illegally are returned to their countries of origin.

The new policy initiated by President Clinton toward illegal Cuban immigration was also a response to other criticism from within the United States, especially that of the Black Caucus of the U.S. Congress. On several occasions, black leaders in Congress had accused the U.S. government of open discrimination against Haitian refugees in favor of Cuban refugees. After mid-August 1994, both groups of refugees from the neighboring islands of Haiti and Cuba would be treated in a similar manner, and the territorial meeting point of both would be the U.S. Naval Base at Guantánamo.

Meanwhile, news had reached the northwestern coast of the Cuban provinces of Pinar del Río, La Habana, and Matanzas that U.S. naval patrols of the Cuban coasts would be substantially increased in the coming hours, with a total of eighty-four boats and cutters, thirty planes on permanent patrol, and eight thousand troops. Twelve young Cubans about to depart on tiny rafts threw coins into the air and knelt on the hot sands of Bacuranao Beach to invoke the aid of Yemayá, goddess of the Afro-Cuban pantheon and protector of the sea and the waves. They prayed that the journey they were about to undertake would end happily and that they would not be interdicted at sea by the U.S. Coast Guard, which, according to what they had heard on Radio Martí, instead of taking them to Key West would transfer them to the only part of Cuban territory under U.S. control: the naval base at Guantánamo.

A trip along the eastern coast of the La Habana beaches offered a spectacle of hope and disappointment among the future raft people.

In Guanabo, six citizens, who had traveled in a pickup truck from Pinar del Río and the distant province of Ciego del Avila, waited patiently on the beach for someone to appear who could sell them materials to finish building their raft.

On Cojímar Beach, the most important center of clandestine manufacture and sale of rafts, the latest novelty being offered to future sailors was an ingenious artifact made of tanks with a brass prow painted red and a guaranteed capacity of four oarsmen and one steersman.

The University of Miami scientists and academics at the School of Marine and Atmospheric Sciences did not feel as confident as the Cuban raft people who awaited nightfall on Cojímar Beach to set sail. Every time a raft person set off in the swirling waters of the Florida Straits, it was as if he were playing Russian roulette. Knowing the dangers that lay in wait for the people determined to break through the double maritime blockade imposed by Clinton and Castro, these researchers undertook the urgent task of plotting the logical path of rafts lost at sea, in accord with the patterns of the winds and marine current in the Straits.

On August 24, Dr. Bruce Rosendahl, of the School of Marine and Atmospheric Sciences of the University of Miami, presented the completed study: "Cuban Roulette: Crossing the Florida Straits." Receiving word of the research project carried out by oceanologists at the University of Miami, José Basulto, director of Brothers to the Rescue, commented enthusiastically, "Often we locate a raft and the Coast Guard cannot find it, but now we can calculate its possible path."

A new wave of raft people set sail on Tuesday, August 23, 1994, in spite of the recent prohibitions by the Clinton administration. After four days of relative atmospheric calm, the U.S. Coast Guard rescued 1,234 raft people during the night, almost six times more than the 294 picked up the previous day. The flotilla of new Cuban raft people was sighted at dawn on Tuesday by Coast Guard pilots flying twelve miles from the Cuban coast. They saw twenty rafts heading slowly north; most of them carried six to ten people, some of them children, clearly indicating defiance of Fidel Castro's prohibition against setting sail with minors aboard. With twenty-mile visibility and nine Coast Guard planes making radio reports on the vessels to a total of thirty Coast Guard and ten Navy ships, those who worked on the rescue said they were able to locate and rescue nearly all of the refugees. For the first time in long months and years of incessant searching for raft people in the Florida Straits, a miracle occurred: a day in which there were no victims to report.

What happened to Hildelisa Betancourt was very unusual. Like many women residing in Miami, she was awaiting, at any moment, the arrival of her husband on a raft. The news she received a few hours later submerged her in a sea of confusion. Her husband, Pepe, a refugee who left a Havana beach in the late afternoon on Friday, August 19, was forced to return when his raft began to deflate at sea. Hildelisa could not contain her sobs on the morning of Monday, August 22, when she saw a newspaper photo of a raft person found dead on Cojímar Beach. And yes, without a doubt, it was Pepe in the picture, his height, physical appearance, and even the blue shorts she had given him. When she calmed down a bit, she began to call Havana. The family would probably know if he had been found dead.

It took Pepe forever to get to the phone, or perhaps it was Hildelisa's desperation and anguish that made the seconds seem like hours. "He's fine; he's alive. We had to pick him up in the morning," shouted the grandmother, sounding very far away. Hildelisa could not believe what she was hearing; then she heard a voice that put her mind at ease. "Hi, *mi vida,*" was the first thing Pepe said, using his favorite term of endearment. Pepe told his wife the incredible story, worthy of equalling or surpassing Gabriel García Márquez's *Story of a Ship-wreck.*

Pepe and three others had set sail from Tarará Beach at 11 P.M. on Friday, rowing steadily north, in an inflatable rubber boat that was a wonder and had cost six hundred dollars. They had been at sea almost forty-five hours, and were about twenty-five miles from the coast of Cuba. "I was going to see you," said Pepe. Seconds later, Pepe told Hildelisa, he saw hundreds of Cubans floating in the middle of the ocean! Not all were on rafts. Solitary freedom seekers floated on simple rubber inner tubes. There were heads and shoulders gripping pieces of polyfoam, wood, inner tubes—anything that floated—with the rest of the bodies submerged in the water. Alongside Pepe's raft, one person was simply swimming. "Imagine that, *swimming!*" Three cargo ships passed Pepe's raft. People crowded on deck, staring. None of them stopped to offer help. Pepe could not believe it. It also surprised him that he saw not even one plane. "There was nothing out there, not even a little fish. Just raft people," declared Pepe. They spent all day Saturday without seeing even one U.S. rescue ship. Early Sunday morning, they saw the lights of one that was very far away. They rowed as hard as they could toward where it was. Halfway there, they launched a flare into the night sky. But the boat did not see them. Exhausted, they decided to wait for another ship, to see if they would have better luck. At dawn, a storm came up; the wind and water nearly sank their raft. The rubber boat was tossed about by gigantic waves of fifteen feet or more. The waves raised them up into the air, and when the water withdrew from beneath them, they were thrown onto the bed of the sea with such force that they felt their bones cracking. "It felt like we were being thrown off a skyscraper," commented Pepe.

In one of these violent crashes, the safety valve of the boat came out and was lost. The air began to escape and water began to come over the sides. They took turns trying to cover the valve with their hands, to keep it from deflating completely. In the midst of the most violent waves, they voted to decide what to do next. Pepe remembers that discussion as the only act of true democracy of his existence. By unanimous vote, they decided to turn back. Exhausted, thirsty, and scorched by the sun, they rowed all day Sunday. Their hands were so blistered they could barely hold the oars. The raft was becoming ever more flimsy as the air leaked out. When they were about five hundred meters from shore, Pepe jumped into the water. An athlete who for most of his life had been a swimmer and water polo player, Pepe tied a rope to his ankle and swam steadily toward the shore, pulling the raft with his friends on board. Miraculously, they arrived at Guanabo Beach, where hundreds of Cuban swimmers helped them reach the shore. Many of them were making their own rafts, while others were getting ready to depart and asking the returning refugees advice. "People were asking us if we were the ones who shot off the flare," Pepe said later. No one on Guanabo Beach asked them their names. There were not even any police there. "If there were, they ignored us completely," said Pepe. Others had returned before them, their inner tubes punctured or their rafts destroyed. While they lay on the sand resting, waiting for their relatives to come and pick them up, another six rafts set sail.

Hildelisa stated that seconds before they hung up, Pepe told her that very soon he would have another safe, fast opportunity. Hildelisa could not believe what she was hearing. Her beloved Pepe had not yet recovered from his first attempt, and already he wanted to try again. "Don't even think about it," his dear Hildelisa advised him. "Don't worry about me; I'll be there soon," responded Pepe, determined.

The incredible testimony given by Pepe to Hildelisa over the telephone confirmed the terrible scenes witnessed by sailors and reporters from boats, helicopters, and planes. The Cubans looked like shipwreck survivors in search of land, the witnesses agreed. Men, women, and children, most of them almost naked and blistered by the sun, at the mercy of the waves on the most pitiful floating objects. The men, with several days' beard, raised their arms imploringly, begging for help. Their ribs were clearly visible. The weakest ones lay semi-conscious on the rafts, able only to gesture to request water. Women clung to their exhausted children, who lay on top of them. And those were the survivors. Humberto Sánchez, a Brothers to the Rescue pilot, estimated that hundreds were dying every day. "You don't have to be a scientist to know that they're dying out there." On at least two occasions on Tuesday, the planes sighted rafts with dead or dying people aboard. "They didn't make the slightest movement; they were in very bad shape or dead," stated Sánchez.

In Havana, the rumored mass deaths of raft people spread daily through different areas of the city. At the central morgue, the rumors were dismissed as unfounded. "I haven't seen hundreds of cadavers here," said one Cuban with access to the morgue, who asked to remain anonymous.

Another of the rumors was that many cadavers were carried far from the Havana coasts by the waves, in which case they were carried to another city. Or they were devoured by sharks. Undoubtedly, the lack of information regarding deaths among raft people continued raising suspicions. Every time cadavers came to the morgue, a small yellow building discreetly hidden behind a shrub-lined fence, they were accompanied by flashing lights and sirens from police cars. The bodies were identified and then turned over to relatives. "It's possible that there are more, but this is where they bring them," declared a morgue employee.

Several men who were rescued by the Cuban Coast Guard as their raft began to sink said they had heard the sailors say that they had picked up seven bodies, and had to go back to pick up five more. One woman told a foreign correspondent that her brother-in-law, who worked with the Cuban Coast Guard patrol, had told her that the Cuban military used a net to find bodies lost at sea. On one of his patrols he had picked up two—a man and a child—and parts of the dismembered body of another person. Each alarming story generated a multitude of rumors that ended up becoming myths: someone on Santa Fe Beach swore he saw ten bodies; others said that twenty-five raft people from the town of Regla had also died. In Cojímar, one of the most popular places for departures, many of the residents had heard of bodies brought in by the current that no one had seen. Others insisted that the Cuban authorities were piling up cadavers in the morgue. "Anything is possible in this country," declared a forensic doctor.

Information appearing in *The Washington Post* indicated that an employee of a Havana hospital, with access to data on the number of cadavers, declared that the Cuban authorities had picked up a large number of human remains near the coast, presumably those of raft people who died trying to escape. Some of the bodies, according to the same source, were bloated, and other had been dismembered by sharks. Similarly, remains of empty rafts appeared on Cuban beaches; it is believed that they belonged to refugees who did not survive the crossing. "And if the Cuban Coast Guard rescues the people, it immediately shoots the raft to pieces so no one can use it again," said a Havana resident who identified himself only as "Guillermo."

In early September, the Cuban Interior Ministry broke its usual silence about the shipwrecks and disappearances occurring during the "raft people crisis." It stated that during the days of massive exodus, border-guard troops picked up along the coast and in Cuban territorial waters, a total of six bodies of drowning victims. Of them, four were in a condition to be accurately identified and turned over to their relatives; two were unidentifiable and were simply buried. The Interior Ministry added that another raft person was the victim of an accidental drowning off Bacanao Beach (Santiago de Cuba), where he jumped into the water to help the crew of a raft that was returning to shore. The communique from the Cuban Interior Ministry indicated that in the month beginning August 5, 1994, Cuban patrol boats assisted and brought back a total of 3,398 people who were in some type of danger. According to the same communique: ". . . that explains why the number of verifiable victims in our territorial waters has been minimal . . ."

Will it ever be possible to know the number of victims generated by the exodus of raft people during these years, particularly in August 1994, when thousands set sail following the tacit authorization of free emigration?

Not even the most severe censorship in the world can silence the rumors that still drift quietly through the streets of Havana regarding raft people who have disappeared at sea. Meanwhile, the bottomless Gulf Stream continues its voracious underwater journey; for many, its silent waters were the only witnesses to the tragedies that occurred.

Chapter VI

The Sea of Lost Rafts

IN EARLY SEPTEMBER 1994, the U.S. Naval Base at Guantánamo, Cuba, was a combination of a military fortress (inhabited by officers and soldiers of the U.S. Army) and a calm and orderly place featuring a multitude of shopping centers, restaurants, and bars open to the public. Among the most popular restaurants were one that served Jamaican-style roasted chicken and barbecued ribs, a McDonald's, and a shopping center. A taxi service also functioned on the base. This haven was destroyed when the first groups of Cuban refugees began to arrive, transported on the *USS South Carolina.* Shortly before the arrival at Guantánamo of the armored *South Carolina,* there arrived at the port a group of INS officials who, finding all possible housing facilities occupied, were provisionally housed on a luxurious cruise ship anchored in the middle of the bay. The INS officials had a specific function to fulfill: to proceed to the questioning and filing of the principal data of the Cuban refugees.

How long were the Cubans going to remain at Guantánamo? That was a question that could not be answered by General Mike Williams, military chief of the base, nor by the INS officers rushed to Guantánamo to process the Cubans, nor even Bill Clinton—much less, of course, by the newly arrived Cuban raft people.

They had barely begun to descend the gangplank from the cruiser when, instead of receiving the food they anxiously awaited, or blankets with which to cover themselves at night, or a pail full of fresh water to splash over themselves, the new refugees were subjected to a thorough inspection. Their hosts confiscated from Polo, an elderly *santero* from

Guanabacoa, a pair of little dolls dressed in the colors typical of the *santería* ritual, three long necklaces made of peony seeds, and a slice of dry coconut that he used in his fortune telling. Disappointment, doubt, and skepticism reigned among the Cubans arriving at Guantá-namo as they disembarked from the U.S. Navy ships.

And it was warranted. They had set sail risking their lives, with or without Fidel Castro's authorization, in order to reach the United States, with the dream of becoming political refugees. Instead, they had been interdicted at sea and immediately classified as illegal immi-grants and forcibly sent to Guantánamo.

Surgeons, university professors, attorneys, architects, soldiers, bus drivers, office workers, house painters, artists, pregnant women, elder-ly people near retirement age, and primary school children all received the same coded bracelets—a sort of plastic watch that does not keep time—from the hands of INS officials, with the strict order to wear them at all times during their confinement. This new luxury item given them by the INS Regional Office very soon became known among the Cuban refugees as "the watch of bitterness," since the hours of the time of despair were kept within its sphere.

During the first week of confinement, there were two severe out-breaks of violence among the Haitians who had been at the base since prior to the Cubans' arrival. A considerably representative group of the 14,600 Haitians held at the base threw stones, bottles, bedsprings, and parts of tents at the U.S. guards. When interviewed after the revolt was quelled, the Haitians declared that if the U.S. government did not improve living conditions in the camps, the situation would turn violent again, for the Haitians as well as for the Cubans. "We cannot remain here eating only rice twice a day, with nothing to do, no contact with the outside world, and no hope of being released," declared Jacques, a Haitian who had been at the detention center for two months.

According to initial statements by the U.S. commanders of the base, facilities for the newly arrived Cubans would probably be simi-lar to those in the Haitian camps. But the Haitians, at every turn, did not miss the opportunity to express their dissatisfaction to the few reporters permitted to enter the base. They were not allowed to receive letters or phone calls. Each one wore a plastic wristband with a microfiche on which was engraved the photograph of its wearer, his or her fingerprints, date of arrival, and other information.

Whenever the newly arrived Cubans caught sight of a reporter armed with camera and microphone and wearing a safari vest, they immediately jumped up from their cots and headed toward the fences. For most of the raft people, the reporters were the first people from Miami with whom they had contact outside of the military and civilian personnel on the base. In the midst of the confusion, a gigantic cloud of dust rose in the middle of the camp while the raft people, immutable, gathered behind the barbed wire in hopes of appearing in the photo that the U.S. reporter would take. In the distance, the repeated and unanimous cries of "Freedom! Freedom!" were heard. The shouts came from the refugees standing behind the fence, as tons of dust hung in the air and floated across the rocky, arid expanse of the base, pushed along crazily by the gusts of wind.

At Guantánamo, water is a luxury. Thirty years ago, in 1964, the Cuban government decided to reinforce its military garrison around the base in response to isolated shootings that wounded and killed soldiers. Among the punitive measures adopted was that of cutting off the water supply by damming the river from which water was normally drawn and pumped to the base through an aqueduct located on the Cuban side of the fence. Since that time, the water used within the perimeter of the base has come from a gigantic desalination plant built by the United States.

Once ashore, the Cuban women began to wash their families' clothing in pails of water, while the men gathered at the fence to receive information. Come what might, the refugees lived in hope that when their relatives and the Cuban exiles in Miami learned of their sad situation, they would do everything possible to get them out of Guantánamo. Meanwhile, they took advantage of the occasional visits of reporters to make public their opinions about the uncomfortable detention to which they were being subjected. "This is not another Mariel," repeated Nancy Alvarez, trying to dispel for the reporters the image disseminated by the Castro government that the refugees were delinquents and criminals. "There are professionals, doctors, and engineers here. We are not criminals; we are not scum; we are not low-class," the refugees chorused, their hands gripping the barbed-wire fence.

In the opinion of the journalists who visited the base, Guantánamo was not composed of people of all one color, social class, or political opinion. Guantánamo was a a mosaic of cultures, ages, and attitudes. Guantánamo was truly a tiny Cuba sheltered in tents, whose inhabitants came from every corner of the fourteen provinces and municipalities of the country, from all possible social strata and political and religious persuasions. Men and women, lazy and hard-working, military and civilians, activists and non-activists. But, above all, young people—great numbers of young people who protested in unison and waved their arms and shouted furiously whenever anyone happened to ask if they were economic refugees. "We wouldn't go back even if they gave us ham to eat, something people haven't seen or eaten for more than thirty years," declared Arturo Morales, a thirty-two-year-old baker.

For the young Cuban raft people, their two worst enemies in the world were Fidel Castro and Bill Clinton. Seven members of the U.S. Congress, including Cuban-Americans, who returned from the base on Thursday, September 1, said in Miami that within three days at the most a crisis could occur at Guantánamo due to the constant arrival of more refugees. The Congressional representatives agreed that there would be an overcrowding crisis if three thousand more refugees arrived at the base in the next three days. The bipartisan delegation was made up of New Jersey Democrats Robert Torricelli and Bob Menéndez and Florida Republicans Lincoln Díaz-Balart and Ileana Ros-Lehtinen.

Barely a few hours had passed since the seven representatives' visit to Guantánamo and their warning about the explosive situation there when a true explosion occurred. This time it was not rioting Haitians throwing bottles or Cubans trying to break down the fences. Rather, it was the explosion of one of the thousands of mines laid around the base, in what is considered by the U.S. military as well as by the Cubans, the largest field of explosives in a defined area in the world.

When they tried to sneak onto the base, three Cubans were seriously wounded by the explosion of several mines at noon on September 1. The wounded, part of a group of twenty-eight, were part of the constant stream of illegal immigrants who had been arriving directly at the U.S. base by land or sea at a rate of fifty per day for more than a week, reported Senator Bob Graham of Florida. Of the two Cubans who underwent surgery at Guantánamo, one had a leg amputated. The less seriously wounded man was taken to the Opa-Locka Airport on Wednesday night in a Coast Guard plane and admitted to Jackson Memorial Hospital to undergo eye surgery. There, he asked from his hospital bed to be allowed to live in the United States. "Don't send me back to Guantánamo, I beg you; I came to this country seeking freedom, not to be put in jail."

The young man was wounded, along with two others at one of the entrances to the base, when they were turned away by U.S. soldiers. One of them lost a leg immediately; the other suffered serious chest wounds. "We were being careful not to step on the mines. You could see some of them through little holes, threads, or sticks, but my friend stepped on one that was well hidden."

The refugees had left Santiago de Cuba Bay on a raft. They built the craft with the help of a naval engineer in Santiago de Cuba, who followed instructions from a magazine on foreign ships that he had happened to find in the periodicals section of the municipal library. "I cannot reveal his name for security reasons, but it was thanks to him that we didn't drown," declared one of the wounded. The three victims could not comprehend why U.S. soldiers turned them away knowing the field was mined. "It was incredible. First, some Americans came and pointed their guns at us," said one of the wounded men. "Then another one came, who seemed to be the boss, and he shouted something at us in English that we didn't understand." When the mine exploded, the raft people ran to the fence. "The Americans opened the fence and let us in."

The new measure for containing Cuban refugees at sea adopted by the Clinton government, in a reversal of the "open arms" policy of previous Republican administrations, in practice turned out to be contradictory and led to enormous problems. The old dispute between conservatism and liberalism in U.S. foreign policy seemed to reach its highest point in the new "crisis in the Caribbean," unleashed with the sending of thousands of Cuban refugees to Guantánamo, where they would join thousands of Haitian refugees previously detained at the military installation. It was a return to "the good old days" of expansionist politics, which provided more than sufficient motives for U.S. writer Ambrose Bierce—the same one whom Mexican writer Carlos Fuentes exhumed in his novel *The Old Gringo* to define in his *Devil's Dictionary,* the word *liberal* as "a conservative who aspires to create new problems without having first solved the old ones."

Not a week had passed since the mine explosion when the military command ordered an emergency mobilization of more than two hundred infantry troops armed with helmets, shields, and clubs, in case events like those of recent days were repeated among Cubans and Haitians. There were protest marches, shouts, thrown stones, and bottles. Within the perimeter of the base, marines dressed in civilian clothes carried out interviews and took down information on possible criminals or Cuban government infiltrators among the refugees. A group of fifty-five members of the Community Relations Service lifted the tent canopies and tried to counteract the generalized psychological depression by listening to complaints, advising the refugees on medical services, giving English classes, and organizing competitive sports. Meanwhile, outside the tents, in the midst of the permanent dust cloud that enveloped the gigantic circus that was the Cuban and Haitian refugee area, about six thousand troops from the U.S. Army, Navy, and Air Force kept watch day and night, trying to keep order among the more than forty thousand refugees from the two Caribbean islands.

In spite of the severity of the military measures adopted, Brigadier General Michael J. Williams did not consider the situation to be at the point of exploding, although he believed that potential existed. "Not much is required for a frustrated crowd to become a furious mob," stated Williams.

The complaints most commonly heard by the U.S. soldiers were: (a) insufficient water for showers, resulting in people being forced to use drinking water, which also ran out quickly; (b) given that the prisoners were people seeking freedom, there was no reason for them to be locked up behind barbed-wire fences with guards watching them day and night from observation towers.

When these demands were presented to General Williams, he declared to the press, "We have to be very sensitive; we do not want to create the impression that we are running a prison . . ." For that reason, the Task Force, under military orders, was working to try to obtain basic necessities such as medicine, as well as bats and balls and VCRs, to reduce the boredom and forced paralysis of the camps, which caused so much harm among the refugees who anxiously awaited the ever more imprecise moment of their liberation. Another problem of greatest concern to the soldiers was the lack of hygiene and the possibility of epidemics among the ever-changing population at the base. One statistic is particularly revealing of the situation: There were only three thousand portable latrines to handle the waste of more than twenty thousand people. In addition, the system of pickup and delivery of the latrines was insufficient. The result was that, among the hundreds of problems affecting daily life in the camps, that of the gigantic accumulation and penetrating stench of piles of human waste was the one causing the greatest number of complaints and demanding a rapid solution.

In the midst of their uncertainty and confinement, the Cuban refugees finally received the first indication that something was happening with regard to their situation. Press reports declared that an informal colloquy had been held in William Styron's house during a dinner, and although the guests might deny it, one of the main topics of conversation was the "raft people crisis." The participants were Colombian writer Gabriel García Márquez (author of, among other works, the novel *One Hundred Years of Solitude*), Mexican writer Carlos Fuentes (author of, among other works, *The Death of Artemio Cruz*), U.S. writer William Styron (author of, among other works, *Sophie's Choice*) and President Bill Clinton (author of, among other works, the measure that ended the Cuban raft people's presence in the Florida Straits).

The longstanding close friendship, in spite of certain conflicts, between Gabriel García Márquez and Fidel Castro is no secret. The reporters who cover the political world did not waste a second in declaring that the Colombian writer-turned-Florentine diplomat, as in the glory days of the Médicis family, had accepted Castro's assignment of exploring the possibilities of a meeting on immigration matters between the Cuban and U.S. governments, to be held in New York before the end of September 1994.

Another hopeful sign that perhaps things would improve for the detainees at Guantánamo was the comment, also filtered in through news reports, that a civilian director of the camps would soon be named to replace the rigid presence of the U.S. military. Cuban-American Guarioné Díaz was the leading candidate for the position. The executive director of the Cuban-American National Council would be in charge of the camps, with the goal of improving the living conditions of the approximately thirty thousand Cubans there.

Finally, the expected but nonetheless disconcerting news broke. The Cuban and U.S. governments had signed an agreement on Friday, September 9, in New York. It required Fidel Castro to end the exodus of raft people within seventy-two hours, in exchange for the United States' permitting the legal entry of at least twenty thousand Cubans per year. After a week of difficult negotiations that on several occasions appeared to be in jeopardy due to Cuba's insistence on discussion of political topics, the accord came after the return to New York of the head of the Cuban delegation, Ricardo Alarcón, who spent just a day in Havana to hold consultations. Included among the main agreements were:

(1) The United States would permit the legal immigration of at least twenty thousand Cubans per year in exchange for Cuba stopping the exodus of raft people.

(2) Both sides would take action to prevent the traffic of illegal immigrants to the United States and sanction those who hijack planes or boats to reach the United States.

(3) Through diplomatic means, both sides would arrange for the voluntary return to Cuba of the detainees in the camps.

(4) There would be future conversations regarding the deportation of excludable detainees in U.S. jails.

As soon as the news of the recently signed accord reached Guantánamo, a furious mob of more than two thousand refugees began to race through the tent camp shouting anti-accord slogans. This incident occurred at midday on Saturday, September 10. In its frenetic advance, the crowd of raft people traveled approximately one kilometer to a point very near the offices and buildings of the U.S. military personnel stationed at the base. A little after 1 P.M., the Cubans began to withdraw voluntarily, except a group of six hundred, which was then addressed by Brigadier General Mike Williams.

After a thirty-minute discussion in which the detainees protested the accord that, according to them, forced them to repatriate or remain indefinitely in the U.S. camps, the group returned to its original position. At one moment during the argument, a confrontation occurred ending with one detainee wounded by a bayonet. There was never a clear explanation of how it happened. But that night, after the tense calm of the afternoon spent under the protective canvas of the tents, the atmosphere among the refugees heated up. Shortly before midnight, some refugees snuck out of Camp Bulkeley in small groups, crawled to the fence, and, with the greatest care in the world, jumped over. They headed north, toward the center of the base, located about three miles from the point where they carried out their clandestine entry. Their destination was the same place where, at noon, several thousand of them had heatedly protested the recently signed Cuba-U.S. agreement.

The U.S. troops mobilized in large groups to try to keep the angry refugees from reaching their destination and creating further disturbances, at an early-morning hour when they were difficult to control. "We cannot stop two thousand people if they want to leave," stated Commander Rick Thomas on learning of the massive flight of the Cubans. In the darkness of the night, Herminio Salas, a thirty-year-old black Cuban, a truck driver, smiled silently when he heard the base commander's words. "We Cubans and Haitians know very well that all you have to do to get over the wire is put a canvas cot on top of the fence . . . and jump!" he told reporters several days after the first nocturnal escape.

Television and newspapers alike carried the news of the recently signed accords between the Cuban and U.S. governments to other Cuban refugee camps that had been established near the Panama Canal. The reaction, as at Guantánamo, came immediately. Not one of the Cuban refugees in Panama was able to sleep the night of Friday, September 9, after seeing the news of the agreement on television. The news flashed through the camp. At midnight the shouting mass of refugees, on the verge of revolt, demanded that all camp lights be turned on and that they be provided all kinds of typewriters, computers, and fax machines. They planned to write a unanimous protest letter addressed not just to the representatives of Cuba and the United States who had signed what they considered a disgraceful agreement, but to the whole world!

In the midst of shouts, arguments, and a chorus of chanted slogans, just before dawn on Saturday, September 10, 1994, on the banks of the Panama Canal, the grand Association of Cuban Raft People for Democracy was duly formed. As its first measure that Saturday morning, it held an international press conference and welcomed reporters with a loud and enthusiastic protest march along the streets of the camp.

To add to the dramatic character of the organized act of solidarity, that afternoon there was a tremendous tropical downpour, accompanied by endless thunder and lightning, causing those in attendance to flinch with every flash. The main representatives of the newly formed association appeared on an improvised wooden stage with a roof made of palm leaves. Their heated speeches contrasted notably with the cold rain that fell upon them. They furiously attacked the accord and shouted their demands that the Cuban-American National Foundation represent their interests in exile. "In the New York negotiations, neither the Cuban government nor the U.S. government took into account our principles, which will never be negotiable as long as there is no place in Cuban politics for the opposition," the association leaders read from the protest letter. Their audience of raft people stoically endured the streams of rain falling upon them. A short distance away, from improvised bleachers, a group of raft people chanted "Long live Panama! Down with Fidel Castro!" as they held up several banners bearing slogans protesting the Cuba-U.S. accord. Flordelisa, a twenty-two-year-old Cuban woman wearing tight red shorts and a white T-shirt, ran barefoot through the groups of refugees, cheering them on in a lively voice. Under the pouring rain, water streamed from her T-shirt, revealing her large breasts. Between them, written on the wet cloth, were these words: "I'll return to Cuba when all my dead brothers and sisters, all the raft people, come back to life."

~~~~~~~~~

As of Monday, September 12, there were very few raft people to be found on the eastern Havana beaches, which in preceding weeks had been the scene of the maritime exodus. Now, only police officers traveled the deserted sands, patrolling the coasts, since once again the Cuban authorities were preventing illegal departures. In Cojímar, the scene was similar to that in Guanabo, Alamar, Tarará, and Bacuranao, all of them points of intense activity when the Cuban government gave the green light for leaving the island on rafts. Within hours of the signing of the immigration accord in New York, the Cuban government had announced that as of noon on Tuesday, September 13, the police would take action against prospective raft people, fundamentally through persuasion, but using violence if necessary. Residents of Cojímar indicated that the last five authorized raft people set off at 7:30 P.M. on Monday, September 12, 1994, under a downpour and aboard a bright green raft constructed out of a pair of barrels, which, from a distance, floating on the ocean, looked like torpedoes.

On Tuesday, September 13, the sands of the beach contained a collection of strange objects: pieces of twisted metal, abandoned barrels, torn canvas that was going to be used as sails in what a month before was the incredible "raft fever." Very young men, just like those who had set sail for the United States in an incredible adventure, but in this case uniformed, constantly patrolled the coves and shorelines, searching cars and trucks that approached the beaches to make sure they were not carrying rafts. In the early morning, an Interior Ministry tow truck proceeded to remove raft skeletons and other garbage from Guanabo Beach. At dawn the next day, on Brisas del Mar Beach, not far from Guanabo, two young border patrol officers kept watch while, very close to them, lying on the sandy reefs like a pair of sluggish lizards, two half-naked tourists toasted their bodies under the burning tropical sun.

Late at night, when police vigilance was lessened, some of the residents who witnessed the clandestine departure of rafts would enter the deserted houses of those they knew had left for good. The looting would begin: televisions, washing machines, refrigerators, radios, beds, sofas, clothing, paintings, books, tables, chairs, eyeglasses, knives, forks, spoons, glasses. Anything could be useful or necessary at any moment in a country where everything was scarce. Several days later, the government might go into action, if someone reported that the house was abandoned; this was one more reason for the crafty neighbors to hurry to enter the abandoned dwelling.

If a house was reported abandoned, due to the obvious absence of a family of raft people, the government proceeded to place a seal on the door of the house, claiming it as property of the state. Then, the family and friends of the raft people entered a true labyrinth of nightmares: they would have countless sleepless nights, assailed by doubts, surrounded by memories, wondering over and over if their children, spouses, grandchildren, nieces, nephews, or cousins had survived, or if, as so many had heard, they had been swallowed up by the sea or hungry sharks. These were days of anguish and despair, when Cubans struggled constantly with the harsh reality of having lost their families, and existing with less money to buy necessary things, less food each day in the state-owned stores, more suspicions by the police and the Committees in Defense of the Revolution, and less hope of survival.

"How many marriages have been destroyed?" wondered Mayda, whose husband left on a boat. "How many more wives will have to be left alone before this changes?"

Mayda's story is similar to those of many Cubans trapped in the labyrinth of familial separation. She had no job nor any income. She and her husband had sold many of their belongings, even their refrigerator, to get together the necessary money to build the boat they christened "The Last Shark." They wanted to make a strong boat of welded metal and empty metal cylinders, which would carry them safely to other shores. "I want to leave, really I do," she stated. "But I can't, not with the children."

Mayda stayed alone in her home in the village of Regla, on Havana Bay, with two children and no idea how she would get the money she would need to feed them. Before her husband's departure, she took tranquilizers for her nerves. Her hands shook every time the truck her husband drove was stopped for any reason. She would cry silently in the back seat, her head bowed. Her eight-year-old son shouted

"Daddy! Daddy!" She told him, "He can't hear you now, but you'll be able to say goodbye to him, I promise."

On the beach, she embraced her Miguel tightly and cried a little more. Her son cried, too. Then, they waved goodbye. That night, they would return home to pray, with the hope that the Virgin of Regla, patron saint of sailors, would protect him at sea. "He is all I have. I have no other family left. My mother died last year. I honestly have no idea how I am going to survive. It won't be easy, but I'll have to do it," Mayda concluded.

A physician living in a coastal town near Havana frequented by raft people suffered severe consequences as a result of a failed attempt to escape to the United States on a raft. A couple of weeks before the signing of the accord between the U.S. and Cuban governments, the boat in which he, his wife and son were traveling had to return to Cuba when it began to take on water seventeen miles from shore. The boat docked in a Cuban port near his home. Part of the group repaired the boat and set sail again, but the doctor and his family decided to stay behind, fearing that the boat would not survive the trip. The authorities took down their names and other information and told them they were free to go. Two days later, however, the authorities showed up at their home, where the doctor had a small neighborhood office. They confiscated the house and took his equipment. "They said I was a traitor to the Revolution. They took most of our belongings. They took our refrigerator, air conditioner, and clothing. Everything I have worked for is gone." Now he, his wife and son live in a tiny house that belonged to his mother-in-law. They have no money. They sold many of their belongings, including his mother's house, to pay for the trip; they never thought they would end up back in Cuba. When interviewed, they were living on a hundred pesos that someone lent them. The government permits him to work in a polyclinic for three hundred or so pesos per month; the equivalent in dollars is $3.50. The doctor suffers from a persecution complex. He feels the noose tightening around his neck. He assumes that they are watching him constantly. "They've ruined my life. No one has given me a piece of paper or shown me a law that says they can do this to me. But they do it anyway," he told a reporter very quietly, constantly looking around him.

Many residents of Havana, where the housing shortage has been critical for years, broke the government seals and moved into the raft people's homes in search of better lodging. Some of them kept the houses until they were thrown out by a government inspector.

Perhaps because they knew that times would be even harder, prayers along with laments and memories, were increasing, too. Regla, along with Cojímar and Santa Fe, supplied the greatest number of raft people to the odyssey of the Cuban people. The same weekend that news of the Cuba-U.S. accord became known, a crowd headed toward the old church in Regla to commemorate the three-hundredth anniversary of the appearance of the Virgin to a poor hermit who lived near the bay. From her gold-plated metal platform held by eight men, the Virgin of Regla, dressed in a blue robe and adorned with silver roses, would travel the church grounds as was the traditional custom based on the religious pact established between priests and parishioners. The idea was for the Virgin to come out into the sun and fresh air. Her traditional procession through the city streets was not approved by the local Communist Party official. For many devotees, accustomed to throwing coins and flowers in the Virgin's path, the restricting of the procession to the church grounds was a repressive act by the political authorities. "Bring her out! Out! She's not a prisoner!" shouted one devotee, glaring defiantly at a group of government sympathizers who were watching from the street. "Long live the Virgin of Regla, the Virgin of the Sea! May her mercy rain down on our country!"

Had he shouted those words out in the street, the man surely would have been arrested. But his physical presence within the church grounds saved him. The Cuban church, silenced for decades by the Marxist-Leninist orthodoxy, had become one sphere in which, with limitations, national and international events are discussed from perspectives not necessarily typical of Marxist orthodoxy. Other factors pushing people to the churches were the grave economic and social crises and the total despair and helplessness of many sectors of the population who have gone through the drama of family separation, growing unemployment, and the lack of personal and social motivation of daily life in Cuba. And it is not exclusively the elderly, but also adults, young people, and children who attend the various religious services frequently and in large numbers. In addition, the Catholic Church has shown itself to be tolerant of the different types of religious syncretism practiced, especially by the ever-increasing Afro-Cuban population, such as *santería.*

And the strongest evidence that faith still exists even in the worst of circumstances can be found in the fact that many of the refugees reaching the Florida coast, rather than carrying necessary personal belongings, have chosen to bring religious items with them on their tiny rafts. These include cards bearing illustrations of virgins and martyred saints, paintings of Jesus on the cross, little candles, rosaries, scapularies, magic stones, *santería* necklaces and bracelets sanctified by the Holy Spirit. On reaching Miami, they immediately make a pilgrimage to the Chapel of the Virgin of la Caridad del Cobre, patron saint of Cuba, at times in profound gratitude for having survived the trip and at others, searching for relatives of whom they have had no news since setting sail on their rafts.

In Cuba, the roles of the Catholic Church during the crisis were many. The main task was posting on church doors and walls lists of the people detained on Guantánamo; this information had been previously published in Miami newspapers. It was astonishing to see great numbers of people arriving on bikes, motorcycles, cars, and any other transportation they find, from all over the island. After checking the lists to confirm whether their relatives were in the tent camps of Guantánamo, these travelers would enter the churches to pray and listen to the priests speak. "It is as if the faith unites them, even in distant places," stated Monsignor Román.

The new religious fervor in Cuba was a frequent topic of conversation among the Miami religious community. "What I find particularly noteworthy," said Father José Luis Méndez of Corpus Christi Church, "is that after thirty-six years of systematic atheism, the religion not only refuses to die but comes alive with more strength than ever. And not only in Cuba but also in Czechoslovakia, Poland, and everywhere else where the boot of Communism has stomped on beliefs."

But some Cubans who experienced the new fervor in Cuba and then came to Miami, observe that the Church in the United States is different. "In Cuba, the Church is less obsessed with money than here," explained Ana Vázquez. When her raft person son got married in the Catholic church in Miami a year ago, Vázquez noted that she was required to pay for the ritual. "Over there, people attend with greater fervor. Maybe it's the system?"

In the small town of Regla, on the banks of Havana Bay, the invocations to the Virgin are carried out in a syncretic manner, mixing Catholicism with Afro-Cuban rituals. Cuban women, kneeling at the altar, hold up black dolls dressed in blue, which represent Yemayá, the Orisha owner of the sea who has reported so much pain, hope, and death to Cubans in recent times. During 1994, prayers to the Virgin were raised with greater urgency. "For all who have headed out to sea! For all who have died!" a shaken woman cried at the church door. Some cried for relatives from whom they had never heard again; other prayed for an end to people risking their lives in a crossing they described as true insanity. "I know so many mothers who are mourning the loss of their children," said a woman who for two weeks had received no news of her two brothers who departed on a raft.

At the end of the day, when it was time to say goodbye to the miraculous Virgin of Regla, the multitude raised their hands and waved them as they sang the Ave María. In the hands of the believers were the brightly clothed black dolls representing Yemayá and Ochún, who in the Afro-Cuban pantheon represent the Virgins of Regla and la Caridad, respectively.

The great exodus of Cuban raft people was about to end. It had lasted a little less than forty days, from August 7 to September 14 of 1994. In that short period of time, an estimated 32,300 people left Cuba for the United States in the most primitive, rudimentary, and, on occasion, exotic vessels.

Thor Heyerdal and his raft *Kon-Tiki,* the Viking and Phoenician ships, and the *piraguas* of the Caribbean Antilles were not so extraordinary in the annals of world navigation when compared to the epic of the Cuban raft people. Of so many hopes, dreams, sufferings, agonies, dramas, and tragedies, there remained the bitter taste of the bad memories and thousands of anecdotes told by the survivors on being picked up at sea by the U.S. Coast Guard. Looking at one of those roughly constructed rafts, floating alone at sea, that bunch of rotten ropes joining a couple of old boards with holes in them for inserting pieces of plastic, anyone in his right mind would bet that the raft would sink as soon as it was put in the water. But nevertheless, alone or in families, raft people dared to cross the one hundred and forty kilometers between the western coast of Cuba and the Florida Peninsula.

The raft people generally lashed inner tubes together and then tied them to a board or piece of plastic that would float on the turbulence of the waves. During the first days of the wave of refugees, the rafts were usually wrapped in jute to protect the rubber from the pernicious effects of long exposure to the sun and the salt. In the eyes of those who saw them arrive, their bodies toasted by the sun, dehydrated and hungry, the appearance of the rafts indicated that their flight, however crazy it might appear, had been prepared carefully in advance. But later, a few days after the great exodus began, the floating objects identified from the air by Brothers to the Rescue pilots included a truck tire floating adrift, a strip of wood with nothing attached, or, in the best-case scenario, a "luxury launch," constructed of two barrels or a pair of large metal cans tied to a board.

One survivor swore he had seen a man set out swimming north from Tarará Beach, with the dream—or perhaps the firm conviction—that swimming in a straight line without stopping, after passing the three-mile limit of Cuba's territorial waters, he would find his golden dream: a U.S. Coast Guard ship. The swimmer did not take any kind of raft or even a life preserver. A Brothers to the Rescue pilot stated that on Tuesday, August 23, he saw a sugarcane cart floating at sea. Its occupants had ingeniously tied several tractor tires under it. The enormous tires turned slowly, appearing over the waves, leaving behind them a frothy furrow in the depths of the Gulf Stream.

Even after the mass exodus of raft people ended, many solitary rafts were found floating in the waters of the Florida Straits. The National Association of Boat Owners began to warn its members of the accidents the abandoned rafts could cause. To others, however, the expanse of sea separating the United States from Cuba is so large, and the rafts so small, that the danger seemed a real exaggeration. That was not the opinion held by one of the employees of the tugboat service, who was surprised that there had not been more accidents, such as one he witnessed in the middle of Biscayne Bay. A rubber tire became caught in the propeller of an outboard motor, destroying its steering system.

Bill Hicks, owner of the South Dade Dockside towing service based in Homestead Bayfront Park, declared to the Miami press: "We have found some rafts constructed around fifty-five-gallon steel tanks; any vessel hitting one of these will sink . . ." According to Hicks, approximately every fifteen minutes his company's radio received reports of sightings of empty rafts. In all, twenty-four accidents due to abandoned rafts had been reported.

For Cubans desperate to escape across the sea, any object is capable of being turned into something useful to make the precarious journey safer. Towels, pieces of plastic, blankets, and box-spring mattresses are not usually considered standard materials for boat construction. Nevertheless, they were essential for raft people. In the opinion of Arturo Rodríguez, president of the Casa del Balsero in Miami, some of the rafts found at sea could win a prize for ingenuity; one raft was built of bamboo stalks, like the Vietnamese sampans that travel the Mekong River. The base of the bamboo raft consisted of four tires, covered with red and green blankets to absorb shark attacks. On top of the blankets was a metal sheet welded to several lead pipes, which served as handrails for the passengers on the endless journey. Then, nine pipes tied tightly with a rope covered the metal sheet. In front, on the prow, there was another collection of welded pipes, which together formed the ship's mast. Shreds of white and yellow cloth still hung from the mast. The bamboo raft was picked up well northeast of the Florida peninsula, in the residential area of West Palm Beach.

Another revelation of the nautical engineering of the raft people is the craft nicknamed "Bebé Rebozo's Yacht." (Bebé Rebozo, a well-known political figure in the Cuban exile community, was a close friend of the late President Nixon.) The raft bearing his name measures nineteen feet by six feet. It is made of wood and weighs about fifteen hundred pounds. "It's so heavy it ruined my trailer," said Ricardo Medina, who found it and brought it home. "Bebé Rebozo's Yacht" was found floating near Bay Side Park in perfect condition and bearing a mark indicating its occupants had been rescued by the Coast Guard.

During the first weekend in September 1994, Bill Hicks, also noticed something strange floating in the sea. Curious, he approached the unknown object aboard his commercial craft. What he saw left him astonished, unable to believe his eyes. Next to his boat floated a box-spring mattress, three feet wide by six feet long, welded on all four sides to metal tubes. "The ingenuity of these people is incredible," declared Hicks. "When my friend tried to lift the raft onto our boat, he almost sank it." Hicks is not easily surprised, as he has seen countless abandoned rafts floating at sea. Their peculiar manufacture ranges from tubes roped to twenty-five-gallon steel tanks to bus roofs turned upside down to float, to soft, modern, comfortable polyfoam cushion mattresses that will glide across the impetuous Gulf Stream.

Another polyfoam craft, also of interesting manufacture, consisted of twenty attached sheets covered with asphalt, on a wooden frame. Hicks said that, of all the rafts found, close to forty percent had one-cylinder motors that originally belonged to motorcycles, tractors, or lawn mowers. "They've done whatever was necessary to adapt the motors for the rafts; they've welded pipes, invented axles and propellers, everything," exclaimed the amazed Hicks. He stated that he had picked up from ten to twelve rafts per day and that the sea near the beaches of Biscayne National Park and the Homestead area was then still full of abandoned rafts. "We will continue to pick them up until there are none out there," added Hicks.

The residential area of South Beach in Miami is one of the most snobbish and cosmopolitan areas of the city. Its modern avenues such as Ocean Drive and boulevards such as Lincoln Road compete for the tourists' favor with other equally popular and populous areas such as Coconut Grove. One morning, an extraordinary object appeared in the middle of a South Beach fountain: a gigantic raft! The unusual artifact had a triangular shape and was made of heavy fence posts, canvas-covered inner tubes, and a heavy reed mast. The raft was immediately given the nickname of *Tio-B*. It measured ten feet in length. It was found empty and abandoned on September 2 in the Elliot-Key area. It is very probable that its owners and occupants never dreamed it would end up as an *objet d'art* on public exhibition in the busy South Miami Beach area. The raft was found during a yachting excursion to Elliot-Key by two Lincoln Road businessmen. Tim O'Walker, a gallery owner, and Steve Rhodes, owner of the World Resources restaurant, were the people who happened to encounter the remarkable artifact.

The last two rafts that arrived during the massive exodus were held at North Beach Park while the authorities tried to find them a place of honor. "They are a part of recent history which must be preserved," said Commissioner Nancy Liebman, one of the people looking for a place for the rafts. In the preceding two months, Dade County work crews had recovered more than fifty rafts between Government Cut and the Broward County line. Jim Hoover, supervisor of those jobs, said that nearly ninety-five percent of the rafts bore the customary Coast Guard initials, indicating that those aboard had been rescued. The rafts were immediately transferred to warehouses from which they could be easily removed using trucks. As time passed, very few were claimed, and many of them had to be destroyed due to the lack of available space. Hoover remembers, among other maritime curiosities he saw, a raft formed of two fifty-five-gallon barrels tied end to end and driven by a one-cylinder Soviet motor such as those used by Cuban lawn mowers. Hoover also remembers a raft whose top was a Soviet bus roof, turned upside down so it would float, equipped with three wooden benches and a plastic windshield and driven by a BMW motorcycle engine.

How far could a raft go when pushed capriciously along by the impetuous Gulf Stream?

That was a question asked frequently by all who had closely followed the exodus—pilots, sailors, journalists, relatives of raft people—every time a raft appeared. Nevertheless, perhaps very few dared to consider the possibility that one of these homemade rafts could be found floating in the middle of the Gulf of Mexico, fifty miles from

Louisiana's Terrebonne Bay. Upon the solitary wooden frame lay the dead body of a Cuban. The crew of a navy supply boat found the raft and towed it to Morgan City in southwestern Louisiana. When found, the raft was exactly 745 nautical miles from Cuba.

The forensic doctor who examined the body reported that the victim was 1.67 meters tall and weighed between fifty-seven and sixty-eight kilograms; his hair was black and he had a beard and moustache. "You see these things on TV all the time. But one day, a body appears in front of you on a raft, and it's then that these things make you react," said Dr. F. H. Metz, working doggedly alongside a forensic anthropologist to construct a model of the victim's head in order to try to identify him. The raft, made of foam rubber, metal, and wood, had six oars, their wood worn from cutting through the waves.

Who was the owner of the craft found in the middle of the Gulf of Mexico? Neither the doctor nor the anthropologist nor INS officials familiar with the case could answer the question, in spite of the fact that they quickly contacted the Miami offices charged with identifying disappeared Cubans. The question did not fall on deaf ears. Mercy Basas, a Cuban hairdresser who had lived for many years in Morgan City, devoted herself completely to the task of locating the victim's relatives, if he had any. After countless inquiries, she found out that the man was Omar Granda Rosales, age twenty-five, who had left Cuba with his friend Gilberto Samuel, also presumed to have died in the crossing. One month after the discovery of the cadaver of the solitary raft person, his mother, Doña Felicia Rosales of Nueva Gerona, Cuba, arrived in Miami with the permission of the Cuban and U.S. governments to attend her son's funeral. It was then that the rest of the story of this mysterious discovery was clarified.

Her son's attempted clandestine departure from Cuba was not his first. In 1991, Granda had been arrested in Santa Cruz del Norte while attempting to leave. The following year he was sentenced to a year in prison. He was released in 1993. One year later he was again on a raft with a friend who had encouraged him to leave. Although Mrs. Rosales was unaware of her son's plans, she knew of his desire to leave Cuba and come to the United States, since on more than one occasion he had said to her, half-joking, that he "preferred to be eaten by an American shark," because in Cuba there was one that was eating him slowly . . .

Winnie Gilbert, a primary school teacher, never thought that during her vacation she would be caught up in the whirlpool caused by the maritime exodus of Cubans for the United States. Winnie Gilbert was participating in a fishing derby in international waters. About thirty miles east of Key Largo, Winnie saw an object floating. It was a raft, adrift at sea. When she boarded it, she felt a chill run up and down her back. She wished it had never occurred to her to climb aboard. In a corner of the raft was a little pile of clothing. Closer to her were some crackers soaked by the salty water, a plastic bottle of water, and a teddy bear whose discovery plunged Winnie into a sea of anguish. And finally, the most revealing discovery of all: Inside a plastic envelope placed under the pile of clothing, Winnie found thirty photographs of various members of a family. There was everything: baptisms, weddings, birthday parties, parties with friends . . . Winnie clutched the plastic envelope full of pictures to her chest and turned to look around. Nothing. No one. Only the immense sea, and the rhythmic movement of the waves. Was she in the midst of an endless nightmare? Was what was happening real, or was it a figment of her imagination? Was she hallucinating? What was she doing standing on a solitary raft floating aimlessly in the Florida Straits?

Winnie shook her head and clutched the photos more tightly against her chest. What had happened to those people? Who were they? Where were they? Why had they left their most basic and beloved possessions hidden in that little corner of the raft? Had a storm come up suddenly, surprising them? Had they been attacked? Had they been devoured by sharks? Winnie began to cry as she looked at the teddy bear, thinking that a little boy or girl might have clung to it during the last seconds of life. And the blood, where was it? And the signs of violence, where were they?

When she reached shore, Winnie immediately contacted her brother Alfred Gilbert, vice president of a detective agency. Her brother, offered to cooperate in the task of locating the people. By then they had been identified as Cubans, thanks to what they had written on the backs of the photos, indicating the place, date, and names of those appearing in each one. Alfred Gilbert showed the photos on a television program that, miraculously, was seen by Tomás Cabrera, a resident of New Jersey, as he was eating scrambled eggs and bacon before leaving for work.

Alone in his solitary apartment on the outskirts of New York, Tomás Cabrera screamed like a caged gorilla. As soon as he saw the photos, he recognized his daughter, sister, nieces, and nephews. For thirteen consecutive days, Cabrera had been calling the INS trying to find out the fate of twenty-one raft people. Each day, Cabrera logged on to a computerized system that displayed the names of Cubans rescued by the Coast Guard. Each day, his attempts had been fruitless. Nevertheless, when he saw the photos on the television screen, Cabrera knew his luck had changed because there, within his reach, was his family!

That same day he purchased a ticket at La Guardia Airport and took the first flight to Miami. Along with the Gilberts, he began the task of locating the lost raft people. Hours, days, and then a week of inquiries passed without a word of them. Through questions directed to the Gilberts, Cabrera began piecing together the fragments of the story. He saw the raft. He confirmed that it was a raft that one of his nephews, Nelson, had constructed for his family. He had added a four-cylinder engine, a roof made of a pair of sheets, and a light bulb powered by the energy from the engine—a light that might be spotted by the U.S. Coast Guard. And, in fact, Tomás Cabrera discovered the letters "USCG" written in red ink on the cover of the motor. It was customary for the Guard to leave those initials each time they found a raft, whether empty or occupied. "Then," said Cabrera, about to explode, "where are my people?"

At last, in the middle of the second week of his constant search through all possible agencies that had anything to do with the rescue and sheltering of Cuban raft people, he received a phone call from Guantánamo Naval Base on the island of Cuba. An anonymous voice confirmed, "Yes, Mr. Cabrera, they're here; they're alive, safe, and sound, all the relatives who appeared in the photos shown on television."

Before leaving Cuba, Máximo García Sánchez had selected thirty-three of his favorite family photos: those of his wedding, the baptism of his first son, the birthday of the second . . . Every time he looked at one of the pictures, knowing that within a few hours they would set sail, Máximo would start crying. Máximo placed the photos inside an old manila envelope. He put the envelope inside a plastic case, and enclosed the entire contents in seven bags he had acquired at a super-market for tourists and foreigners in Havana. The bags bore these words: CARACOL ALL YOUR SHOPPING IN CUBA. He gave the package of photos to Amelia, his ex-wife and the mother of his son, so she could carry it on board the raft. But in the rush to leave from the cove of Brisas del Mar on August 31, amidst the crying of the children, the last-minute checking of supplies, and the need to inflate the raft in the darkest night, soon after departing no one remembered at sea if the photos had been taken or not.

Máximo García Sánchez never imagined that it would be those photos that would compel an American woman, a stranger to him and his family, to undertake a search filled with curiosity and faith. Winnie Gilbert's search began by saving the raft found adrift at sea and with it, the belongings of the unknown Cuban family. The search would end when she finally, one afternoon in Miami, embraced Máximo and his family. They had been permitted to leave the Guantánamo tent camp to visit their relatives in the United States and the person who did so much, altruistically, to find them.

According to Máximo, amid tears and expressions of amazement, they had left Cuba on a twenty-six-foot raft christened *Faith, Hope, and Charity*. It was a meticulously constructed vessel, with a canvas roof, a barrel hull, ten wooden planks tied at both sides, and an enormous tank of gasoline that they could use to drench their bodies if, by chance, they fell into the sea and found themselves surrounded by sharks. The group of refugees, which included four children and one pregnant woman, could still make out the coast of Cuba in the distance at the moment they were intercepted by a U.S. Coast Guard patrol.

The raft would be left adrift on the waves, the photos and other belongings still on board, until, providentially, it was found by Winnie Gilbert. From there began the intense search for the disappeared refugees by Winnie, her brother, and Tomás Cabrera. The determined search would end the night when, under a kerosene lamp that hung from the door of the canvas tent in which they were sheltered, Máximo García Sánchez read in *El Nuevo Herald* that they were being desperately sought throughout the United States by their relatives. "Finally, they found us!" shouted the shocked Máximo, awakening everyone in the tent. Some days later, Máximo and his family were embracing Tomás Cabrera and the incomparable Winnie Gilbert who, trembling with emotion as she embraced the strangers who were so familiar and beloved, could not stop repeating the name of the solitary raft: "*Faith, Hope, and Charity!* I always thought that must mean something great, in the midst of the sea of lost rafts!"

Chapter VII

Guantanamera

WHEN SOME OF THE CUBAN RAFT PEOPLE detained on Guantánamo heard that the United States was constructing in Panama a camp of tents with cement floors, electric light, cafeterias, and telephones, they immediately considered the possibility of moving. Emilio Moreno Torres was brought by the Guantánamo authorities to inform the rest of the refugees of the advantages of the Panama camps. Armed with color photographs of the Panamanian base, the forty-year-old economist said that he, his wife, son, and mother-in-law had moved. In spite of his best efforts, most of the raft people detained in the Guantánamo tents did not believe the U.S. authorities about the positive attributes of other installations established in the Caribbean area.

To them, the U.S. military authorities' keeping them in deplorable living conditions had no purpose other than to pressure them to return to Cuba. "The camps that many raft people initially saw as the waiting room to freedom have become concentration camps," stated a volunteer of one refugee agency. Alberto Grau Sierra, a former political prisoner imprisoned for more than two decades in Cuba who now works with the International Rescue Committee, was emphatic: "Human rights are being violated." At no time, explained Grau, were humanitarian organizations permitted to enter the camps and have direct contact with the refugees.

Two weeks after the first detainees were taken to Guantánamo, an uncontainable stream of problems broke out in the camps. Among the most shocking testimony was that of Elsa González, a former political prisoner, who was detained on the base for protesting lack of medical attention for a baby and for insulting a guard. According to a note that World Relief volunteer Moisés González was able to bring out of Guantánamo, Elsa González and Enrique Valdés were mistreated by military personnel. "We were taken to the most severe prison, which is called 'Hell.' We were mistreated, beaten, and humiliated with obscene words," Elsa González wrote. "We were thrown on the ground and they held sticks, threatening us and saying many bad words close to our ears, like they were trying to drive us crazy," she declared.

Reports from the visit carried out by World Relief volunteers indicated that there were raft people still wearing the same clothing in which they had left Cuba almost two months before. Most of the refugees had no shoes, and some were nearly naked. There were women covering themselves with sheets and towels to complement the few items of clothing they had. Others wore the swimming suits in which they had been rescued. The report said that thousands of raft people were living amidst dust, rocks, and the stench of latrines and showers. Many of them suffered from a variety of ailments, such as conjunctivitis, kidney problems, and asthma. Medical attention was not what it should have been, according to World Relief volunteers. There were reported cases of people denied access to medical treatment. Others, the volunteers explained, went to the infirmary only to be told that the personnel there did not have the medicines needed to treat them.

Twenty-two-year-old refugee Alcides Suárez died of a heart attack after U.S. military personnel told him four times that he could not see the doctor until 8 A.M. "They told him to go to bed . . . and in the morning he was dead," said World Relief volunteer Moisés González. A two-month-old baby girl was bleeding from her rectum, but the soldiers guarding the camp where her family was held did not grant them permission to take her to the doctor. "This is unacceptable," said Alberto Grau Sierra.

Receipt of letters and correspondence in general was another nagging problem affecting the raft people detained at Guantánamo. Thousands of letters sent by relatives in Miami had not been delivered to them, it was reported. And the same occurred with packages containing clothing. First, the authorities alleged that the postal service did not permit the delivery of letters without stamps. Later they added that the process was being made more difficult by the number of refugees and the confusion of correctly locating them in the different tents they occupied.

Grau Sierra and González, both of whom spent the first days of their visits to Guantánamo with the refugees, speculated that the poor treatment of the raft people was intentional on behalf of the U.S. authorities, that in this way they sought to force them to return to Cuba. "They don't want to give them anything; they're doing this so they'll leave," said Grau Sierra. "With what they're doing to the raft people on Guantánamo, they are trampling on the U.S. Constitution and slapping the Statue of Liberty," stated Moisés González.

Brothers to the Rescue pilot Humberto Sánchez could not find words to express the irritation he felt at seeing his compatriots detained at the distant Guantánamo Naval Base. Perhaps that is why Sánchez took advantage of a short visit by Bill Clinton to Miami to express his feelings in an unusual way. Motorists traveling calmly around the Blue Lagoon area on Monday morning, October 17, 1994, saw a raft floating on the calm sea. It was similar to those that arrived on the coast on a daily basis. Looking more carefully, they were able to make out a sad-looking solitary man sitting in the middle of the raft. In place of a mast or sail, the solitary raft person showed a poster that said in large black letters: AUSCHWITZ TREBLINKA GUANTANAMO.

Humberto Sánchez never imagined that the symbolic protest he carried out on the calm waters of Blue Lagoon would gain him, a few days later, heated protest from some representatives of the Jewish community of Miami. One of the first to respond directly to Sánchez was Bob Kunst, president of Shalom International, who said he was deeply offended by the parallel the poster established between the Cuban refugees at Guantánamo and the Nazi concentration camps. "I understand his motives, but you can't do that. You cannot compare mass industrial-level murders with thirty thousand Cubans detained on Guantánamo who receive three meals a day. That is to trivialize the Holocaust. Brothers to the Rescue should apologize to the Jewish community and to Holocaust survivors," explained Bob Kunst. Immediately, Shalom International, an organization whose main objectives include extraditing and processing Nazi war criminals, held a protest against the protest, on the corner of Dade Boulevard and Convention Center Drive in Miami Beach, a block from the Holocaust Monument.

In response, José Basulto, president of Brothers to the Rescue, felt obligated to explain that it had not been his organization's intention to trivialize the magnitude of the Jewish Holocaust, but rather to get a dramatic message to President Clinton. "What the sign says," stated Basulto, "is that these are three concentration camps, and it is not intended to offend the Jewish community. Having Cubans detained without the opportunity to apply for political asylum, and in living conditions that leave much to be desired, makes Guantánamo a concentration camp." Finally, Basulto added that several Brothers to the Rescue pilots were Jewish, and none of them were bothered by the poster or took it personally. "Of course, we feel a great respect for the Jewish community. Kunst took it wrong," Basulto concluded.

Since no one knew how much longer the Cubans might remain detained at Guantánamo, the raft people began to create entertainment and amusement out of their daily reality. A thirty-eight-year-old civil engineer turned a piece of cardboard from the containers of dehydrated food they were given into a game related to his many misfortunes as a raft person. His name: Martín Barquín. The game, called "Raft People 94" ("Balseros 94"), was similar to Monopoly. Early every morning a group of refugees lined up in front of Barquín's tent to wait their turn and sit down at the Balseros 94 board for a game. Instead of kings, queens, bishops, knights, rooks, and pawns, the players used spoons, forks, and knives cut into different shapes to substitute for the usual game pieces. The most important object of the game: not to stray off course with a bad play and thus arrive safe and sound in the Promised Land, the city of Miami. All along the way, the players had to overcome numerous obstacles that could cost them their lives: storms lying in wait, sudden wind shifts, torpedoes from Cuban Navy warships, and the U.S. Coast Guard, which, though their savior, would take them farther from their destination.

Near the place where the refugees waited patiently in the morning sun for their turn to play Balseros 94, Mrs. Leyvis Ruiz, nine months pregnant, squeezed into an old red T-shirt that made her protruding stomach seem even larger, complained that she had no alternative than to enter one of the foul-smelling latrines. She did not know why the soldiers insisted on calling them "portable bathrooms," as dirty and small as they were.

For Luis Rodríguez, the greatest distress of camp life came from the fear that one day he might miss his necessary insulin injections. If that happened, he could go blind, or die, during one of his customary morning walks around the camp. Knowing that without two injections per day, one in the morning and the other in the evening, his disease would worsen disproportionately, Luis had brought his insulin injections along on his raft. In front of his traveling companions, amidst raging waves or in hot sun and maddening calm, he had religiously given himself his injections every morning and evening during his three days at sea. But when he arrived at Guantánamo, the insulin remaining became useless due to lack of refrigeration. He reported his case to the authorities, and now he, like other diabetics, had to be taken to the military clinic for their daily injections. "But the transportation never arrives on time. We line up at 7 A.M., and sometimes it's 2 P.M. and no one has come to pick us up. How long can this go on before we begin to go blind and die?" asked the anguished Rodríguez.

U.S. Army officers in charge of the refugees' health care admitted that there were problems in providing appropriate medical care to the more than thirty-one thousand Cubans held on a base that was originally equipped to handle five thousand Navy employees and their healthy families. But, at the same time that they recognized shortcomings, they pointed out that the problem was not as critical or widespread as the refugees described in many of their statements. And they suggested that some were feigning illness to be able to leave the camps. On the other hand, however, they conceded that there existed problems of lice, various skin diseases, and severe conjunctivitis.

On the other side of the fence surrounding Guantánamo, in Cuban territory, General Carlos Manuel Pérez, base commander in the zone known as Melones, told international journalists that he and his U.S. counterparts were very concerned about those who escaped from the base across the mine fields. In the opinion of international political

analysts, some type of direct communication—telex or telephone—
was necessary between the commanders of the Cuban and U.S. bases
in case of increased tension among the refugees, which could result in
a riot that might send thousands of them out into the double mine field,
considered by military experts to be the largest in the world. The mine
fields are a reminder that in spite of the destruction of the Berlin Wall
and the collapse of the Eastern European Communist bloc, the Cold
War era—at least in the Caribbean—has not ended.

In Washington, federal officials had still not determined what procedures would be used for the voluntary departure from Guantánamo
for Cubans who wished to return to their country. The State Department stated in a report in late September 1994, that up to that time fifty
Cubans had requested voluntary return, and their names had been sent
to the Cuban authorities. In a report issued by the Cuban Interior Ministry, the statistic offered by U.S. authorities was confirmed; that report
stated that fifty-nine Cuban refugees had left the Guantánamo camps
and returned to Cuba, some of them swimming.

The possibility of riots on the base led U.S. military authorities to
reinforce internal security measures. On Monday, October 17, at midnight, soldiers conducted a search and confiscated a large quantity of
weapons, including stakes, posts, sticks, metal bars, and pieces of aluminum that had been torn from the bases of the cots and sharpened. All
that and much more was found hidden under the cots, or buried near
the tents of the Noviembre I and Noviembre II camps, where those raft
people who wished to return to Cuba were held. U.S. officials suspected that many of those detained in those areas had criminal records.
That same night, during the search, one of the raft people, elected as
their leader by more than six hundred refugees in the Noviembre II
Camp, declared emphatically that they were running out of patience.
"We are warning that Cubans are known for our bravery, and if we've
had the courage to cross the ocean on rafts, we have enough courage
to face the marines," announced camp leader Dante Roche.

In another area of the base, a poster hanging at the entrance to one
of the Lima Camp tents expressed clearly the desire of its residents:
"TO CUBA."

"We all want to go back; the situation we have here is very bad. The misinformation, the deceit, the uncertainty . . ." said Víctor Luis Guerra.

"We live more freely in Cuba than we do here. Here they treat us like murderers. We aren't used to being locked up. With each passing day we're becoming more like animals," said thirty-year-old Jorge Luis Flores Medina.

The Cuban and U.S. governments discussed the possibility of the voluntary return of raft people during negotiations held in early September in New York. But there was delay in working out the details. "We are anxious to find a mechanism by which that can happen," said Brigadier General Mike Williams, base commander. The military was processing the applications of those refugees who wished to return, who were taken to a separate camp so that they would not be harassed by the others. "We want to avoid others saying to them 'You want to go back to Cuba; you must be Communists,'" said Williams.

In early October, a total of forty-eight raft people had found ways to return to the Cuban side, by their own initiative. Some of them had risked crossing the mine field. Others had jumped into the sea, swimming steadily until they reached Cuban shores.

The first formal repatriation occurred on October 7, 1994, when seventeen Cubans were flown from Guantánamo to Havana. On Monday, October 10, another twenty-five followed. These came from a list that the State Department had previously presented to the Cuban government for its approval. The official stated that the Cuban government had the names of all the detainees at Guantánamo who wanted to return to Cuba. Ten days earlier the U.S. government had sent a list of one-hundred forty names; the list of the rest, more than eight hundred, was sent to Cuba with the twenty-five repatriated refugees.

How did things go back in Cuba for those who chose to return? Did they regret their decision? Did they change their minds soon? Did they stand firm? And what did their friends and relatives think of their return? And how did the Cuban authorities treat them?

Several foreign journalists accredited in Cuba followed the steps of the refugees who returned between October 1994 and February 1995. Twenty-six-year-old Orlando Rodríguez's despair was evident as he spoke of his return to Cuba and the opportunity he left buried behind the barbed-wire fence at Guantánamo. "This is never going to change. You can die of old age here in Cuba, and you'll never be anything. My advice to those who stayed behind on the other side of the fence is to wait; they are already under the American flag, and sooner or later they must accept them into the United States."

After many efforts, the four Mujica brothers had managed to leave Cuba on a raft that was intercepted at sea by a U.S. Coast Guard ship, which immediately transferred them to Guantánamo. Up to that point, their story is very similar to those of thousands of other raft people, were it not that it involved four brothers, and that their father, a few days before his death, had made them swear that they would leave Cuba. One of the Mujica brothers, thirty-two-year-old Rolando, had a case pending against him for attempting to leave the country illegally. Fidel, the youngest of the four at nineteen, was a deserter from the general military service and was sought by the authorities. The four brothers, then, were forced to move up their departure date for fear of being discovered. Once at Guantánamo, the four brothers offered to be voluntarily transferred to the Panama camps, because they believed that it would be easier to enter the United States, or a third country, from there. According to one brother, there in Panama they enjoyed better living conditions, including movies and recreational activities. As the months passed, Mujica missed his people more and more. When he returned to Guantánamo, he lost patience and jumped the fence. But his three brothers, watching him move away across the mine field, thought of their mother, whom they hoped to help someday, and decided to remain on the base. "They say they already jumped the puddle, so why should they come back here," stated Mujica, as his mother, next to him, caressing his hair, told a reporter, "Since he couldn't stand to wait anymore, maybe the others will wait . . ."

※ ※ ※

At the same time that the first repatriations of raft people to Cuba were occurring, the Cuban and U.S. governments began a new round of negotiations. The Cuban government was seeking to expand the negotiations to other topics besides immigration, as it felt that the exodus of raft people was directly related to the U.S. economic embargo against Cuba in effect since 1962. The Clinton administration publicly continued firm in its demands that the Cuban government adopt democratic reforms before negotiating an end to the embargo. The Cuban delegation would be led by Ricardo Alarcón—president of the Popular Power Assembly and former Cuban ambassador to the United Nations—while the United States would be represented by Dennis Hays, coordinator of the State Department for Cuban Affairs.

Near the end of this new round of negotiations, news involving the migratory limbo of the Cubans on Guantánamo changed the course of the agenda. A lawsuit was filed against the U.S. government on Monday, October 24, 1994—the same day the new round of U.S.-Cuba talks began—by a group of Cuban-American lawyers in Miami. The filing halted the takeoff, in mid-runway, of a plane in which twenty-three raft people who had asked to return to their country were going to be repatriated. When news of the lawsuit broke, Justice Department spokesman Carl Stern stated: "Some Cubans reacted with tears at the news that they will not be able to return to Havana until they receive legal advice . . ."

A sixty-three-page document signed by the lawyers alleged that the policy of detaining raft people indefinitely was illegal. The suit sought direct access to the refugees at Guantánamo and in Panama to explain to them their options and rights. It included a demand that the Cubans be permitted to apply for entry into the United States without having to return to Havana. The case was filed in Miami, where Judge C. Clyde Atkins ordered that a call be made to stop the departure of the plane, just minutes before its scheduled takeoff. Judge Atkins' decision was the first victory for the group of plaintiffs.

Harold Hongju Koh, professor of law at Yale University and part of the team that sued the government, explained that the legal challenge consisted of four points:

(a) it was illegal to pressure the Cubans;
(b) living conditions in the camps must be sufficiently adequate as to not cause the detainees' return;

(c) Cubans on Guantánamo must have the chance to apply for political asylum;
(d) Guantánamo was U.S. territory, like Puerto Rico or the Virgin Islands.

Koh, who had been one of the defenders of the Haitian boat people since the first days of their clandestine arrivals in the United States, stated: "U.S. policy has taken a one hundred and eighty-degree turn, but the law has not changed. Until the other day, Cubans were being welcomed with open arms. This is not consistent with the law . . ."

The matter of the Cuban refugees on Guantánamo caused a great deal of tension among the Cubans and Cuban-Americans in Miami. Each day, news of the exodus introduced new elements into the discussion. Afro-Cuban singer Celia Cruz, world-renowned for her popular performances of Cuban *guarachas* and *salsa* music, hastened to put a sweet tone of "*¡Azuuuucccaarrr!* (Suuuugggaar!)" into the soured relations between Cubans and non-Cubans when she was invited to the White House on October 14 to receive the National Medal of the Arts—the highest national honor for an artist—from President Clinton.

That same day, as Celia Cruz filled the White House gardens with a Latin flavor, the Washington government was announcing that it would release up to five hundred raft people, including the chronically ill, unaccompanied minors, and those over age seventy.

The day after, President Clinton arrived in Miami for a whirlwind political visit. Thousands of Cubans took to the streets and stopped traffic in downtown Miami and in the aristocratic Coral Gables neighborhood. About five thousand people shouted at the president, demanding the freedom of their parents, siblings, spouses, children, grandchildren, friends, and all the detainees held at Krome and Guantánamo since September. As the president's motorcade passed, Martín Pérez Baster held his sign as high as he could: "President Clinton, your daughter is in the White House, mine is on Guantánamo. Please, have compassion!"

In such comments one could feel the tension over the refugee situation. The announcement that about five hundred Cubans detained on Guantánamo would soon be released evidently satisfied some Cubans and merely infuriated others. To others, the recent presidential decision was nothing more than a political maneuver. "He did it, yes. But it was nothing more than political maneuvering. He just wants to ingratiate himself with the Cuban exile community," said a Mr. Vidal. "That's why he released five hundred out of more than thirty thousand. That's why he gave a little culture medal, or whatever, to Celia Cruz. Quite a coincidence, isn't it?"

Jorge Mas Canosa of the Cuban-American National Foundation considered it appropriate to go on record once again to state his position. "I'm going to talk with President Clinton on Saturday. I'm not going to argue or insult the President of the United States. First, I'm going to speak in favor of freedom for Cuba, then for freedom for the Cubans on Guantánamo," said Mas Canosa. During President Clinton's visit to Miami, Mas Canosa had been in a controversy that included a defamation suit against Lázaro Barredo and Reinaldo Taladrid, authors of the book *I Am the Chairman* (*El chairman soy yo*), in which they attempted to implicate Mas Canosa in espionage and terrorism activities from the time of his exile to the United States in 1960.

According to Barredo and Taladrid, during Mas Canosa's first months in the United States he had been recruited for the Central Intelligence Agency by a youthful George Bush. At that time, according to the authors, Mas Canosa worked as a milkman, a job that was nothing more than a CIA cover so that he could take food to secret agents who were hidden in "work houses" and thus be better able to spy on them. Mas Canosa called the book "a desperate attempt by the Cuban government and by Fidel Castro, who wrote part of the book, to discredit the Cuban democratic opposition."

On Friday, October 28, 1994, the day after Judge C. Clyde Atkins ordered the suspension of the repatriation flight from Guantánamo, the Justice Department began a rapid counteroffensive. Attorney Allen W. Hausman argued that the lawsuit on behalf of the raft people was outside the jurisdiction of Atkins, because the detainees were not protected by U.S. law. "They have no rights as long as they do not reach our shores," said Hausman in a hearing that lasted about three hours. Hausman argued that under two cases that dealt with the treatment of Haitian refugees, all the Cuban raft people could be repatriated.

The legal and international juridical philosophy argument caused Ricardo Alarcón, president of the Cuban National Assembly and Cuba's representative in the immigration negotiations, to remark: "I share the opinion of the U.S. officials regarding the suspension of repatriations and agree that the judge's decision endangers the immigration accord . . ." As the good Florentine diplomats used to do during the glory days of the Médicis, Ricardo Alarcón commented obliquely, "It's a dangerous idea that a group of people who want to voluntarily return to their homes can be prevented from doing so."

Roberto Martínez, a former federal district attorney in Miami and one of the lead attorneys defending the Cubans, felt obligated in turn to execute his own corresponding pirouette. "It does not surprise me that this time the two governments have similar viewpoints. They had previously reached an agreement against the detainees," stated Martínez.

The day following the tense debate triggered by Judge Atkins' decision, twenty-one of the twenty-three raft people on the suspended repatriation flight wrote an unexpected letter to Judge Atkins indicating that they indeed wished to return to Cuba. The letter swore that its signatories did not desire "any type of political status," nor did they wish to travel to the United States. "We do not want visas. I would not be interested in going to Miami even on a boat full of money," said Manuel Iglesias.

The contents of the letter, of course, caused deep shock and concern among the Cuban-American lawyers defending the "raft people's cause." The surprising message punched an enormous hole in their future arguments. "There is no way the same refugees could have written this letter," said the perplexed Roberto Martínez, and added that, in his opinion, the letter contained evidence that government officials had been conversing with the detainees. Meanwhile, another attorney from the group, trying to turn the setback into future victory, insisted that the letter did not weaken the case, as the case involved not twenty-three but thirty-two thousand people.

The main questions about the letter concerned the source of the detainees' information and how they got the letter to the Miami judge. The letter was received by fax in Judge Atkins' office. Guarioné Díaz, who since early September had served as civilian liaison between the authorities and the refugees in the camps, partially answered these questions in an affidavit presented to the court by attorneys for the government. In the affidavit, Díaz stated that in his zeal to save the Cubans who were desperate to return to their homes, he had provided them with pencils, paper, and a copy of an article published in *El Nuevo Herald,* in which the events were explained. "When I returned, they had already written the letter," said Díaz in his affidavit. "I took the letter; I did not talk to anyone except my assistant about my intentions. From my office on Guantánamo I faxed copies of the letter to my office in Miami and to a friend of mine, also in Miami, who is a lawyer." According to Díaz, the letter expressed the exact thoughts and feelings of the twenty-three Cubans who were going to be repatriated. Nevertheless, only twenty-one of them signed it. Díaz's affidavit did not explain why two signatures were missing. The absence of those two signatures pushed the plaintiffs' lawyers to continue with the case.

"In reality, this is more evidence than ever before that those people need access to lawyers before they give up the rest of their lives," stated the attorneys vehemently.

On Monday, October 31, 1994, three days after the plane was stopped on the runway, Judge Atkins reiterated that the raft people detained on Guantánamo had rights under the U.S. Constitution, including that of legal counsel. "The United States has complete jurisdiction and control over the base at Guantánamo. Therefore, the First Amendment is applicable there." Atkins also ruled that the Cubans could not be repatriated until they had access to independent legal counsel.

Two days later, Judge Atkins, in surely one of the most spectacular weeks of his judicial career, issued a new order blocking the deportation of fourteen Haitian refugees from Guantánamo. The order was issued by Atkins in response to a motion by the Haitian Refugee Center in Miami, which asked to join the suit brought in favor of the Cubans detained on Guantánamo and in Panama. Atkins allowed the Haitian Refugee Center to join while he studied the matter in depth.

On November 3, 1994, however, a federal appeals court in Atlanta authorized the return of one thousand Cubans from Guantánamo, and rejected the portion of the lower court order that prohibited the repatriation of the refugees. The Eleventh Circuit Court of Appeals in Atlanta made its decision late Thursday afternoon, after the federal government presented an emergency appeal in which it stressed the serious threat of violence among the frustrated refugees. "We are concerned that without this order . . . the risk of loss of life will continue," said a three-judge panel of the appeals court in its short decision. The panel also blamed Judge Atkins' decision for the disappearance of nine Cubans who had attempted to swim back to Cuba. "It appears that loss of life may have occurred as a result of the reaction to the district court's decision prohibiting repatriation," the decision said.

The attorneys for the raft people were extremely restrained in their response to reporters' questions about the decision issued in Atlanta. "Evidently, the court reacted to what it considered an emergency, as described by the federal government. We will wait until oral arguments are presented to the court . . ." said Roberto Martínez. Nevertheless, the reactions and opinions expressed by many of the one thousand refugees who wished to return to Cuba made things more difficult for the Miami attorneys. In several interviews granted to reporters visiting Guantánamo during the first week of November, the raft people expressed themselves violently with regard to the attorneys who were battling bravely to achieve significant changes in the detainees' status. One of the raft people even urged publicly ". . . that the lawyers be thrown to the sharks . . ."

The forty-page appeal filed by the U.S. government in the federal appeals court in Atlanta warned of the increase of violence in the camp where a thousand Cubans were being held separately from other refugees on the base. The report stated that more escape attempts and fights had occurred in the Noviembre camps since Judge Atkins' decision. According to the document, the repatriation flights provided a necessary escape valve at a critical moment to alleviate the tensions in the community. But the district court's decision had closed off that escape valve, and the immigrants had reacted with riots and violence directed against military personnel. To assure that all returns were completely voluntary, the U.S. government promised in its appeal that it would allow United Nations workers to interview those who wished to go back to Cuba.

Not giving an inch, Miami lawyers said they were investigating the possibility that the U.S. Army was using military personnel specializing in psychological manipulation to persuade thousands of refugees to return to Cuba. The attorneys were in the process of requesting permission from Judge Atkins to interview two Radio Martí employees and one member of the military regarding the use of Psy-Ops. Those they hoped to interview included Radio Martí's director Ricardo Bonachea, his assistant David Rivera, and Major Barry Keith, director of the Communications Unit on Guantánamo. According to a document presented in court on Monday, October 31, the attorneys believed that specialized troops had as their objective the psychological manipulation of the raft people so that they would ask to be returned to Cuba.

Major Rick Thomas, base spokesman, said on Tuesday, November 1, that it was true that the Psy-Ops troops were on Guantánamo. But, he added, their mission was not the traditional one. "They are only disseminating information. They are publishing the newspapers and operating the radio stations." The mission of the Psy-Ops troops during the recent marine invasion of Haiti against the dictatorial regime of Raoul Cedras was to operate local radio stations to keep citizens informed of the latest events. Previously, these troops had been among those who forced former Panamanian military leader General Manuel Antonio de Noriega to surrender, partly through the use of deafening music broadcast constantly at maximum volume. Bonachea and his assistant Rivera refused to comment to *El Nuevo Herald* on the presence of the highly specialized troops on Guantánamo. Nor did Major Barry Keith answer the newspaper's calls. As a result, the presence of the Psy-Ops troops and their mission remained shrouded in mystery. The press had to be satisfied with the information previously supplied by Major Rick Thomas, who said that the Psy-Ops troops read press cables, reported on camp activities, and retransmitted Radio Martí programs.

"They take the pages they don't want us to read out of the newspapers," said twenty-four-year-old Angel Jesús Yáñez Martínez. Yáñez explained that groups of men and women who spoke Spanish had visited the camps on five or six occasions. "There is no doubt they're from the government," said Yáñez. "They talk to us with the psychological factor, trying to convince us." His companion in resistance, thirty-three-year-old Cenén Delgado Vilar, added that these people worked "very intelligently and indirectly. In normal conversation, they show us that we have no alternative."

For Cubans, a *ball* can just as well belong to the world of billiards as to baseball, basketball, or universal geography—whether it's a ball or a globe representing the world—but the same word is also used in Spanish to refer to gossip or slanderous comments. For Cubans, to get a "ball" rolling is to allow gossip to go beyond certain permissible limits. To "listen to balls" often means to let yourself be tricked or deceived by confirming as true comments that are nothing more than pure inventions. The U.S. Naval Base at Guantánamo, occupied by more than thirty thousand Cubans, could not be the exception to the rule of popular Cuban psychology. In spite of the U.S. military's attempts to ensure that the refugees received only information previously filtered through the command, rumors flew with the dust from one camp to another, lifting the canopies and entering the tents. According to one of the most common rumors, in mid-November the Cuban-American attorneys from Miami would come to the base to provide legal counsel to the refugees. It was also rumored that the women living in the tents were being raped at night, that the detainees at the Loco Camp were being tortured, that the sick children would soon be able to travel to the United States, and so on.

In truth, on Thursday, November 3, federal authorities announced that mail would be delivered to the detainees for the first time. Also, telephones were installed from which collect calls could be made. And it was announced that big-screen televisions would soon be installed. Even so, between realities and unfulfilled promises, the intensity of the rumors or "balls" did not stop. Among the most-believed stories was one that specified the date when the Miami attorneys would arrive; the rumor also said that the attorneys were authorized by the government to grant visas to enter the United States. Much of the raw material for these rumors came from a group of refugees who had portable radios at their disposal, tuned to Radio Martí in Florida, Radio Rebelde in Havana, Haitian stations broadcasting in Creole, or Dominican stations dedicated exclusively to playing *merengue* music.

The tension in the Guantánamo tent fortress at times was nearly unbearable, and events unfolded with astonishing speed. On Sunday, November 6, the detainees were shaken by the news that thirty-nine refugees had escaped. They had headed toward Cuban territory after knocking down two fences, jumping from the edge of a forty-foot cliff, and swimming a mile. A group of eighty-five managed to get out of the camp; forty-six were detained by military personnel and placed in confinement. Major Thomas, spokesman for the camp military command, said the group had escaped by piling up cots and boards to knock down two six-foot-high bars. Then they jumped from a nearby cliff onto the beach forty feet below. Without so much as catching their breath, they swam a mile to get beyond the mines in Cuban territory and, finally, went ashore on another beach.

The fate awaiting those apprehended during the November 6 escape attempt would surely be similar to that of another group of fourteen captured attempting to escape the previous week and penalized with one hundred and twenty days in prison. Scott Willie, head of the Preventive Detention Center of Operation Safe Refuge, said that another thirty-two Cubans who participated in a fight on October 31 would have a hearing on Wednesday, November 2. As of the first week of November, a total of eighty-six raft people, including five women, were imprisoned for various infractions. Scott Willie stated that punishment for detainees who violated camp rules included: cutting the grass, picking up stones around the camp, and other "voluntary jobs," which caused one of those punished to exclaim: "Here on Guantánamo, I feel as free as I did in Cuba . . ."

The situation of conflict between the detainees and the military personnel charged with their indefinite custody resulted in a strange political game of "give and take." One example of the unusual dialectic was in the release of a group of thirty-two Cubans, including six children, women, elderly people and their companions, who were transferred from Guantánamo to Homestead Base outside Miami. Flown there on a Boeing 727, they became the first group of freed raft people.

Their relatives in Miami did not recognize many of the new arrivals. The refugees stated that on Guantánamo "there is no food, medicine, or milk for the children, nothing . . ."

"I thought we would all die there," said thirty-eight-year-old Nancy Rodríguez. "Don't let them fool you; it's a true hell. If the rest of the people aren't released from there soon, they'll all die."

Just a week before the first group of liberated raft people was sent to Miami, military and civilian authorities were discussing the adoption of reforms and new measures intended to improve the conditions of the refugees. A telephone survey of a representative sample of 467 raft people, carried out by the Finlay Medical Society, an organization of medical professionals, had as its objective to determine whether the detainees, lacking enough fresh vegetables and some meats in their daily diet, could be vulnerable to colds, viruses, and other infectious diseases. The physicians also wanted to establish whether the diet, abundant in carbohydrates, could affect people who suffered from diabetes or were predisposed to diabetes and others who suffered from gastric upsets. "If we compare it to what they had in Cuba, the diet they receive on Guantánamo is magnificent. But if we compare it with a well-balanced diet, it is not the best; it has deficiencies," reported Dr. Antonio Gordon, president of the Finlay Medical Society.

In direct response to the medical survey, First Lieutenant Peter Mitchell stated that in the preceding two weeks, the diet had improved. In addition to the breakfast, cold lunch, and hot supper the detainees received, the camps had begun to provide fresh fruit and milk for the children. For his part, Guarioné Díaz, civilian liaison between the U.S. military and the Cuban detainees, stated that they were studying how to improve the diet, although limitations would always exist. For example, to provide vitamin C, they would have to have tens of thousands of oranges shipped to the base daily, and that would require logistics that did not as yet exist in the camps. "We're going to improve the diet, not in the nutritional sense, but rather so that it will be more pleasant and varied," said Díaz.

The dialectic of "give and take" appeared again on Wednesday, November 9. It was announced in Washington that the government would improve its policy toward the raft people. The Clinton administration considered it opportune to expand its policy to allow nearly three hundred children to come to the United States within the next week. The original policy permitted giving asylum only to the elderly, the gravely ill, and to orphans under age thirteen. The redefined program included unaccompanied minors under age seventeen. The administration's decision was announced one day after the election of Florida Governor Lawton Chiles, who, in response to the Mariel exodus in 1980, had coordinated the work of Operation Distant Coast in case a new migratory exodus was forced by Castro. Chiles had won by a narrow margin, in part due to his strict attitude toward immigration, which barely left margins open to Cubans who wished to escape from the island, whether for political or economic reasons or both. On several occasions, White House officials had promised that they would not soften their stance toward the refugees until the election was over, out of fear that the decision would affect Chiles' chances.

While the first groups of Cuban refugees—children, the elderly, and the severely ill—were en route to Miami, many of those left behind on Guantánamo were becoming ever more desperate, with no hope on the horizon of an opportunity to make new lives for themselves in the United States. However emotional, irrational, and desperate it may seem, the only way out the detainees could see was to return to Cuba, the country they had left two months earlier. It seemed to them that things were no different for them on Guantánamo, since there was no end in sight to their confinement. Statements made by some of the refugees to visiting reporters indicated that often the clandestine departures were not planned in advance but came up suddenly in the midst of conversations. The air, then, according to the vivid descriptions provided by refugees and reporters, became filled with a strange mix of confusion, euphoria, and fear.

News spread like wildfire through the Noviembre camps. Seven detainees had just jumped into the ocean. A crowd of refugees ran toward the barbed-wire fence. Alarmed, the military personnel mobilized quickly; five of those who had jumped in were caught almost immediately; the other two managed to reach Cuban territory. It was the fourth time during the first ten days of November that an incident like this had occurred. "It's becoming a daily event," said Major Rick Thomas, military spokesman for the base. With each passing day, emotions became more explosive in the Noviembre camps, where about 650 Cubans awaiting repatriation were being held. According to statements of the detainees themselves, the Noviembre camps were "a time bomb." At dawn on one early November day, thirty-one-year-old Rafael Salgado Silva tried to escape for the third time. From the top of a thirty-foot cliff, he jumped into the sea in a fantastic dive worthy of Olympic competition. A short time later, he was picked up by a U.S. military patrol and taken under arrest to the base prison. Salgado told the troops that arrested him that he would try it as many times as necessary if in January—two months later—he was still on the base. "I don't want to hear anything about Miami anymore. My whole family is in Cuba. I want to go back to Cuba," declared Salgado, who had left his wife and six-year-old son in the town of San José de las Lajas.

The "give and take" between the U.S. authorities and the Cuban refugees also included the cases of raft people who set aside the inner tubes they brought from Cuba and became swimmers to return to their point of departure. Concerned for the lives of the Cubans who had indicated their desire to swim back to Cuba, the camp commander was considering the idea of making the trip safer for those who somehow managed to jump the barbed-wire fence, elude the armed guards, descend across coral reefs, and swim nearly two miles against strong currents to Cuban territory. The other escape route was across the mine field that surrounded the base. The camp commander figured that if he could somehow move the potential fugitives closer to the Cuban border, the risk that someone would drown would be greatly reduced. The U.S. troops themselves told reporters that they had seen Cuban vessels pick up some of the escapees. But, they added, this was only on a very few occasions, and therefore the fate of such escapees was generally uncertain and unknown.

Anything can happen when creativity and resourcefulness are focused to achieve an objective. This had already been demonstrated when, using any material that would float, Cubans had risked crossing the Florida Straits in great numbers. But surely what occurred on Tuesday, November 1, 1994, was among the strangest episodes in the entire history of navigation. The base commander could not believe what one of his officers was telling him: At least fifteen Cuban detainees had just set sail on an unknown course using as aquatic vehicles more than a dozen portable latrines! When the military personnel reached the beach, they saw the group of floating toilets, and very close behind them, the guards in charge of their custody. "It doesn't surprise me that they use latrines to escape; they float," said Major Rick Thomas.

※ ※ ※

In the 1940s, Joseíto Fernández, traditional Cuban folk-music singer, made a fabulous innovation. He took advantage of the opportunity provided him by a radio show, in which the bloody events chronicled by the newspapers were dramatized, to debut and popularize his sensational song, "Guantanamera." The voice of Joseíto Fernández lyrically singing "Guantanamera, guajira guantanamera . . ." served as a sharp contrast and musical counterpoint as the announcer and actors narrated and dramatized the episodes of blood, pain, misery, suffering, and death transmitted daily over the radio waves. In time, "Guantanamera" became the melodic-dramatic symbol of the Cuban people. In the 1960s, it became known worldwide when American singer Pete Seeger adapted a unique version, further popularized by a folk trio called the Sandpipers, that traveled all around the globe. "Guantanameeeraaa!" chorused thousands of young Americans in the folk-music festivals of the 1960s, unaware that they were repeating the musical refrain made popular in a tiny radio studio by Cuban troubadour Joseíto Fernández twenty years earlier.

During the same time that more than a dozen Cubans formed the first flotilla of floating latrines in nautical history, another great Cuban artist, movie director Tomás Gutiérrez Alea, was visiting the area around the town of Guantánamo, with its arid landscape, looking for an appropriate location for the filming of what would be his last movie, *Guantanamera.*

The story Gutiérrez Alea intended to tell had to do with death, as had his movie *Death of a Bureaucrat,* shown in 1966. The story of the film *Guantanamera* pays tribute to Joseíto Fernández. It tells the story of a singer who dies in Guantánamo and, as her last wish, asks to be buried in Havana. This is practically impossible, due to the enormous number of bureaucratic rules that would have to be broken in order to transport her body through the fourteen new provinces into which the island of Cuba has been divided, at the very moment when the new Socialist Constitution has just been approved.

Gutiérrez Alea ("Titón" to his friends) died on Tuesday, April 16, 1996, not long after the opening of his film *Guantanamera* and just as the author of this book was finishing up recording the sufferings of thousands of Cubans on Guantánamo. And still the suffering of the Cuban people continues.

Chapter VIII

Panameña, Panameña

THE MORNING OF THURSDAY, SEPTEMBER 15, 1994, Panamanian Congressman Alberto Cigarrustia of the opposition Authentic Liberal Party (PAL—Partido Liberal Auténtico), left later than usual for the general session called by Parliament. Standing on the corner of one of the main streets in Panama City, the congressman was nervous. He extended his long right arm as far as he could when he saw an old taxi jerkily winding through the heavy traffic like a fly with clipped wings. Cigarrustia took out the card that identified him as a member of Parliament, and prepared to wave it at the taxi driver. Upon doing so, he could not help but remember the amusing comment of his parliamentary colleague Rubén Blades who, half-joking, had said that he did not need the card to get a taxi on a busy street; all he had to do was discreetly groom his magnificent Pancho Villa-style moustache or sing one of his favorite melodies, to stop even speeding taxis. Coincidentally, when Cigarrustia opened the door of the taxi, the driver's cassette player threw in his face the melodious voice of Blades.

Cigarrustia longed for the return of the good old days of Latin-American liberalism, as opposed to the decadent populism of the postmodern Panamanian era. He wished that instead of old songs, there would be a return to the glory days of the knights of industry and free enterprise who now sat waiting for death in rocking chairs, their hands gripping pearl-handled canes.

"Get in back, Congressman," said the taxi driver, and Cigarrustia could not help but smile. *I am as well-known as Rubén Blades,* he thought. His satisfied smile turned immediately to a look of astonish-

139

ment when he saw two young women seated in the back seat of the taxi, wearing white T-shirts and tight blue-jean shorts with suspenders. Their outfits revealed their arms and shoulders completely, and highlighted to perfection their large breasts. Once in the taxi, and having gotten over the initial annoyance of the long wait, Cigarrustia, still blinded by the morning sun, had the opportunity to return the welcoming smile that the two young women gave him. He noticed, even if for a few brief seconds, that one of them had extremely light skin, with tiny freckles marking the top of the curvature of her shoulders, while in the soft shadows of the intimacy of the car, the intensity of the dark skin and long curly hair of the other stood out.

"They are Cuban refugees who just arrived, Congressman," commented the taxi driver, looking toward the back seat through the rearview mirror.

As they traveled through the city on the way to Parliament, the young women told the congressman how those evil American Army boys had put them behind bars and barbed-wire fences in a concentration camp. Yes, Congressman, this had happened to them, innocent people who had never done anything wrong and wanted only the freedom that Castro denied them. "You know him, don't you, Congressman? You know who I'm talking about, the one that doesn't take off his boots or uniform even to *go to bed?*" Listening to the girls' vehement words, the taxi driver turned and looked at the congressman's distressed face through the rearview mirror: "What do you think, Congressman, should we send them back to Cuba?" The melodious voice of Rubén Blades sang out again from the taxi's tape player, this time his version of "Material Girl / La chica plástica." The young women raved about how beautiful the song was, while the congressman tried to come up with a wise answer to their question. After meditating for a while, and observing how the girls crossed and uncrossed their beautiful legs, the congressman ordered the driver to make a quick U-turn in front of the imposing Parliament building and rush back to the camp where he was to deliver the fugitive raft girls safe and sound.

The congressman's unusual experience, made public that same day by the Panamanian press, unleashed a wave of public comment and official refutations. No one knew or wanted to know of the presence of

Cuban refugee camps in Panamanian territory. In a press conference the following day, a spokesman for the U.S. Army's Southern Command headquartered near the Canal, responsible for the Cuban refugee operation, denied the veracity of the story and stated that custody of the refugees on the military bases was rigorous.

Cigarrustia defended the truth of his story to reporters. He added that the two young Cubans, probably eighteen or twenty years old, seemed extremely nervous and upset at having arrived, by pure coincidence and in the company of a congressman, at the door of the Panamanian Parliament.

In a downtown Miami hotel room, people came and went quietly at all hours of the day and night. A quick look inside revealed lots of first-aid equipment on the beds and furniture. There were also, throughout the room, colored lights, especially blue flashlights, and in the center of the room, next to the bathroom door, an unlikely stack of fourteen metal briefcases nearly reaching the ceiling.

"What's the mystery inside the metal briefcases?" a visitor to the room asked naively.

"If we told you, it wouldn't be a mystery. That's why this is called the Secret Service," responded Roger Blakenship, a support technician.

If protecting a president and his wife is a challenge under any circumstances, protecting thirty-four presidents and their wives for several days is exponentially more complicated and risky.

Jack Kippenberger, officer in charge of the Secret Service Office in Miami, called the Summit of the Americas the most complex security operation in the history of south Florida and possibly of the United States. For the moment, prior to the beginning of the summit, all the elements of the protection system that would be employed originated in the mysterious room with the fourteen metal briefcases on the second floor of the Sheraton Hotel on Brickell Avenue. Dozens of Secret Service agents coordinated a veritable army of agents, including sharpshooters stationed on the roofs of the main buildings in downtown Miami, dogs for detecting hidden bombs and explosives, and divers and frogmen with sufficient training to blow up submarines.

Jack Kippenberger was proud to say that the number of special agents involved included more than eleven hundred agents and thousands more belonging to other organizations, such as the FBI, the State Department Security Service, the U.S. Marshal's Office, the Florida State Police, the Miami City Police, and even the U.S. Army, which could be supported by the Air Force Reserve and National Guard if necessary.

Apart from the complexity of the summit and the risky situations that could arise, the Secret Service's mission was constant, according to Kippenberger. "We try to foresee the worst possible situation and prepare for it, and then hope that our efforts cause the best possible situation to occur."

"This is where we follow the movements of those who must be protected," said Daniel Curran, a special agent from Miami. "We will be with those we are charged with protecting twenty-four hours a day, as long as they are in this country."

In late October 1994, the news that the U.S. government had again stated that Cubans detained in third countries would have to return to Cuba to apply for immigrant visas created an immediate sense of uncertainty in the Cuban refugee camps in the Panama Canal Zone. Not even the better living conditions enjoyed in the Panama camps— much superior to those of their Guantánamo counterparts—were any comfort. The generally accepted opinion in the Panama camps was that not one of the six thousand Cuban refugees being held there would accept the offer. "The only way I would return to Cuba is dead," declared twenty-eight-year-old Ana Rosa Rodríguez Madrigal, who had left the island with her husband and children, ages three and eight. "After putting my children's lives in danger at sea, I will not change my mind," Mrs. Rodríguez insisted. The family had been detained for more than a month in Camp #1.

Foreseeing future conflicts or misinterpretations of the agreement, U.S. officials Rob Malleany, of the National Security Council, and Brad Hittle, consul general of the U.S. in Panama, arrived at the camps that afternoon and asked to meet with Cuban representatives from the tent section. The news, according to later press accounts, hit the camps like a nightmare, especially since the Cubans had spent most of the day waiting for an announcement they hoped would give them a positive message. "The procedures were explained to them, and how this was going to work," said Mike González, a member of the civilian-military operations headquarters of the Southern Command, who acted as interpreter for the meeting. "They feel extremely frustrated; it's another obstacle they have to overcome."

≈≈ ≈≈ ≈≈

Although moved by the drama of the raft people detained in the Guantánamo and Panama camps, even the newspapers, which closely followed the vicissitudes of the mass exodus of Cubans, gave less space in their pages to the Cayman Islands and the Bahamas. The total number of Cuban raft people confined on the white sands of the Cayman Islands was almost fifteen hundred and rising. The magnitude of the number was cause for alarm for the authorities of the small Cayman territory, which had always been a British trust. The alarm was so great that, with or without an agreement between the United States and Cuba, the island governments were seriously considering the possibility of starting to repatriate the Cubans. Aware of the difficult situation of the Cubans on Grand Cayman Island, U.S. Congressman Lincoln Díaz-Balart of Florida asked Michael Gore, governor of the islands, not to repatriate the Cubans. Governor Gore responded that the U.S. government had not permitted the raft people detained there to go to the camps established for them in Guantánamo or Panama. "The only alternative you may wish to propose to the U.S. authorities," Gore told Díaz-Balart, "is to reconsider their refusal to accept these immigrants at any of their camps."

Yet after Governor Gore's statement, the number of raft people on Grand Cayman Island tripled. Given the worsening of the situation, Díaz-Balart sent another letter to Governor Gore, again asking that the raft people not be repatriated. The letter also stated that organizations of Cuban exiles were willing to send supplies and specialized personnel to help his government with the Cubans "now in grave danger of being deported." The British Ministry of Foreign Relations announced that it was considering the possibility of sending police to the Cayman Islands at the request of the local authorities who could not handle the continuous arrival of Cuban refugees.

The situation of the Cuban raft people on the Bahamas did not differ much from that of their compatriots detained in southern Cuba. Anchored on the sunny sands of the Bahamas, they continued as adrift as when they were picked up at sea in tiny rafts about to capsize. Surrounded by two high fences and barbed wire, 286 raft people, including thirty children, slept on the ground and ate only one meal a day, which consisted of a little rice and beans. They had insufficient water for bathing, and their weakened bodies suffered from skin rashes and lice. In addition, the Cuban raft people were now intermingled with a true "international refugee community," made up of two hundred Haitians, Indians, Peruvians, Dominicans, and two Croats who had escaped from the ethnic conflict in the former Yugoslavia. At the back of the camp was a pit that overflowed each time it rained and much more so with the strong tropical downpours that often occur in the Bahamas. When that happened, the field around the camp turned into a swamp of human excrement. When the burning tropical sun dried it, the field was flooded with worms, which crawled and teemed everywhere.

The awful description provided by the refugees was immediately contradicted by the Bahamanian authorities, who characterized the refugees' statements as exaggerated. According to Tofwell Coakley, the Cubans received at least three balanced meals per day, and he was aware of no infections in the camp. The Nassau detention camp was composed of three long shelters arranged in a U-shape. The Bahamanian patrols were accompanied by German shepherd dogs, but the relationship with the guards was not bad, according to some of the detainees. At each corner, beyond the fences, soldiers in watch towers were armed with long rifles, and the detainees were counted three times each day.

⚓ ⚓ ⚓

Anticipating the importance of the agreements that might be reached during the Summit of the Americas, various Miami organizations, anxious to make a good impression on the distinguished visitors, prepared welcome gifts. Each of the thirty-four heads of state from Latin America and the Caribbean would take home nine watches, an Art Deco-style porcelain box, a silver paperweight, an engraved crystal sphere, a gift of crystal from the president, and a leather-bound journal, as well as a silver pen for each wive.

Leading the organizational welcome for the distinguished guests of the continent was Dade County. The presidents would honor four local governmental entities with their presence during the course of the official events. In terms of welcome gifts, that meant a present for each of the distinguished guests from the City of Miami, the City of Coral Gables, the City of Miami Beach, and Metro-Dade. And, of course, there was also a gift from the host country. Whatever the gift, it was most likely to be from Tiffany. "I believe that people think of Tiffany when they think of gifts for a world leader," said Paula Musto, spokesperson for the Metro-Dade municipality. How about a silver paperweight in the size and shape of a calling card, courtesy of Metro-Dade? These gifts, created by Tiffany, were engraved "Summit of the Americas, December, 1994, Metropolitan Dade County." The cost: one hundred and fifty dollars each. For each of the first ladies, Metro-Dade would have a hand-painted ceramic vase, approximately a foot in height. Some one hundred ministers and other high-level representatives would receive *Over Miami,* a book of photographs with the cover laminated in gold, courtesy of the Burdines department stores. The vases cost forty-two dollars each, and the books were donated.

There would be no doubt as to which city gave the four-inch round porcelain Tiffany boxes with shiny buildings painted in the best Art Deco style and lighted by the golden rays of the sun. A gift like that could come only from Miami Beach. "This is a good opportunity to continue promoting our city," said the Miami Beach tourism coordinator. "Every time one of the recipients sees the box on his desk, he will remember Miami Beach." Miami Beach ordered a hundred of the boxes, at a price of forty dollars each, made specially for the city. Thirty-four would be used for the summit; the rest were for future high-level visitors.

The City of Coral Gables opted for something truly useful: a navy blue leather-bound journal—from Tiffany, of course—engraved in gold: "Summit of the Americas." The cost: fifty-five dollars. The first ladies would receive elegant Tiffany silver pens each valued at forty dollars. Two other high-ranking delegates from each country would receive gold pens valued at twenty-eight dollars each, engraved with the emblem of Coral Gables. The City of Miami, breaking the Tiffany mold, went to Miami Beach artist Jeffrey Glick for its purchase. The gift: the world. The five-inch-high spheres created by Glick weighed more than five pounds each. Looking into these crystal balls, one saw the silhouette of the Miami skyline, with the shape of the continents visible behind it. Each sphere had its own special presentation case measuring eight inches in height, made of Brazilian wood and bound in blue velvet. The price about four hundred dollars was definitely beyond the reach of many inhabitants of this world when compared with the other local gifts.

For its part, the White House also chose crystal. The official White House gift was a three-faceted crystal column designed by Peter Yenawine, former Steuben head of design. Each face was engraved: one had North America and South America; the second had the U.S. Capitol and the Washington Monument; and the third had a forest, symbolizing growth and renewal of resources, family, and community. It was mounted on a mahogany base bearing the presidential seal. In addition to the governmental gifts, each world leader would also receive a set of nine brilliantly colored watches with the emblem of the 1996 Olympics. Swatch, which created the watches, was a sponsor of the Olympics; Mayor's Jewelry and the local Star Art Foundation assisted in the preparation of the gift.

Southern Command officials were concerned that, even though living conditions were better in the Panama camps than on Guantánamo, the detainees would resent that there was no end in sight to their stay. Therefore, the authorities disseminated comments that poisonous snakes, iguanas, and a multitude of wild animals abounded in the dense Panamanian jungle surrounding the canal, and that these animals were capable of devouring a human being in a matter of seconds. The result of the attempt to psychologically dissuade future escapees backfired, judging from some detainees' statements. "If we weren't afraid of the sea, we aren't going to be afraid of a snake or a panther in that jungle,"

stated Wilfredo Alfonso, who had arrived at Camp #4 just a week earlier. "There are a lot of people here who are desperate, and they can't find any solution other than jumping the fence," added Alfonso, alluding to a group of twenty-one raft people who had escaped from Camp #3 and fled into the jungle.

The escapees were found through a cooperative operation between the Panamanian police and the U.S. military, according to a spokesman for Operation Safe Refuge. The goal of the escapes, hunger strikes, and other threats was to pressure the United States and make clear that the Cubans were not willing to remain detained in the camps and that what they wanted were visas to enter the United States, where many had immediate family members. The raft people stated, however, that they were treated well in the camps, where they had sports facilities, music, and daily meals. But even so, they were desperate, because they were not free.

The Cubans in Panama stated that the best Christmas gift they could receive would be to leave the camps where they were confined and be reunited with their relatives in Miami and other U.S. cities. "If we don't get out of here by the end of the year, this is going to get ugly," opined Wilfredo Alfonso. "We aren't here for the food or the music; what we want is to be free, anywhere," stated twenty-eight-year-old J.C. Jiménez.

The terrible fear that they might be deported at any moment overcame the patience of a group of Cuban raft people detained on Grand Cayman Island. They decided not to wait for the result of the trilateral negotiations initiated between Lincoln Díaz-Balart (as spokesman for exiled Cubans), Governor Gore of the Cayman Islands, and the U.S. government. Ten raft people declared that they were going on a hunger strike. Prior to lying down on their thin mats, the detainees, saving their energy for the long fast that awaited them, explained the principles that led to their act of rebellion: "We want to be free. We are not in agreement with the soft policy Bill Clinton has toward Cuba." The striking Cubans stated that their prolonged fast would be peaceful, since they did not wish to cause problems for the government of the Cayman Islands, which had been so "good" to them. Ramón Olazábal de la Torre, age fifty-two, one of the leaders of the hunger strike, said "The U.S. government is playing with us. Our only crime is being anti-Communists."

Pushing baby carriages and chorusing "Freedom! Freedom!" some three hundred women and children paraded down the beaches of palm trees of the tourist paradise of the Cayman Islands, a few days before the beginning of the Summit of the Americas, demanding U.S. visas in order to escape the dusty refugee camp where they were being held. "We want humanitarian visas!" shouted Omar Agüero, a Cuban refugee who spoke to the demonstrators as they converged peacefully on the doors to the governmental seat of the British colony. "How can they speak of development and human rights at the Summit of the Americas while 296 children, nine elderly, and thirteen chronically ill people are living in a camp in the middle of an island on the American continent?"

Although many Cubans were grateful to the inhabitants of the Cayman Islands for giving them food, tents, and showers, their frustration was increasing. The previous week, a hundred and fifty refugees had fled through a hole in a barbed-wire fence. Most of them returned later that same day—distressed, sad, and tense. Nine of them opted to return voluntarily to Cuba; another eighteen were thinking about doing the same. Others, incredibly, proceeded to the beach where they picked up their tiny rafts and set out to sea again, this time hoping to reach Costa Rica, Honduras, or whatever place destiny might provide.

At the last minute, with the fireworks opening the Summit of the Americas only hours away, Dade County authorities were still searching to find enough photographers to cover the various activities of the Latin-American presidents in Miami. This time, suitable technical personnel were dug up in a most unusual place: the city morgue.

The morgue photographers were used to photographing cadavers, but never presidents or heads of state. Todd Reeves, supervisor of photographers for the Legal Medicine Department of the county, could not help but smile at the recruitment of his employees. The walls of his office were literally covered—Reeves insists on calling them decorations—with a sort of horror map of dead bodies. The photos also showed bullet trajectories photographed with ultrasensitive lenses, dismembered human bodies, wounds caused by vicious dogs and wild beasts, and the main attraction of his exposition: a living man with a pencil protruding from his head.

When interviewed by Dade County authorities, Reeves stated, "Of course we are willing to photograph this type of event . . ." Another morgue photographer, thirty-one-year-old Ruben Marichal, appeared equally enthused at the possibility of photographing presidents at an event of the magnitude of the approaching Summit. "We'll meet more people than we can meet here [at the morgue] . . ."

Once an agreement was reached, Dade County authorities provided the morgue photographers with a program of activities, including the opening of the trade show; the Children's Summit sponsored by First Lady Hillary Clinton; a presentation by Secretary of State Warren Christopher; and at least one event with their boss, Art Teele, president of the County Commission. "Yes, we already know all the jokes they'll be telling about us," Reeves said to reporters, referring to the fact that they would now have to photograph people who moved, not those in absolute repose.

On Thursday, December 8, 1994, Miami was abuzz with activity; President Clinton would be arriving that day followed by some forty jets carrying the various presidential delegations from Latin America and the Caribbean. The pressure was enough to make the Miami International Airport air traffic controllers' hair stand on end. Since very early that day, the thousands of Secret Service agents controlled by Officer Kippenberger had been mobilized; specially trained dogs were sniffing every downtown Miami corner for bombs; frogmen were submerged in the rough waters of the port and the gray waters of the Miami River; Mr. Reeves' "photographers of death" turned photographers of the international jet set were ready; the Miami Beach Tourism Commission was prepared with a pile of tourist maps and visitors' guides to important places; and Paula Musto was ready with her silver paperweights, notebooks with gold-edged pages, and beautiful pens to give to the first ladies.

When President Clinton arrived in Miami, he was welcomed by Senator Bob Graham, and by Governor Lawton Chiles, a key player in the presidential decision to interdict the raft people and send them to Guantánamo. It was likely that some member of the president's entourage, while the president dispensed smiles, greetings, and hand-shakes to those in attendance, whispered in his ear the news that had just come in on the wires: about two hundred U.S. soldiers and three Cuban refugees had been wounded in a violent riot in the Panama camps.

As the hours passed and the activities of the Summit of the Americas continued, a less glamorous panorama of the events in Panama was unfolding. The disturbances began the morning of Wednesday, December 7, 1994, in Camp #1, called "Willie Chirino," where about 2,238 raft people were sheltered. Some one hundred of them began to throw stones at military installations and vehicles, wounding more than sixty soldiers. By that evening, the situation was under control. But the disturbances broke out again the following morning. About two hundred refugees from Camp #2 had violent confrontations near the U.S. installations, according to a spokesman for the U.S. command. But the worst occurred some hours later, when a furious mob of about a thousand raft people attacked fences and soldiers with sticks and stones and managed to escape from the camp.

The approximately one thousand refugees knocked down the barbed-wire fences surrounding the camp and fled into the jungle, ignoring the soldiers' shouts promising they could return without fear of reprisals for their actions. It was not until late that night that the refugees returned to the camps. Although a full evaluation of the damages was not complete, it was clear that about ten military vehicles were seriously damaged. "I want to clarify that the Cubans' attacks were not directed at the U.S. soldiers, but rather at the installations. If there are wounded soldiers, it is because they were near the vehicles," stated spokesman Levy-Dutram, analyzing the riots. He added that, in his opinion, the cause of the riot was the slowness of the departure process for the Cubans authorized to travel to the United States or third countries. "This has been their way of expressing themselves, because they're desperate. There are very decent people here, who are peacefully awaiting a solution. The rioters are a small percentage of the total," reported Levy-Dutram.

As the days passed, more details of the violent riot were made public. The disturbances lasted two days; the wounded included 221 soldiers and twenty-eight Cuban detainees. The rioters also damaged twenty-three military vehicles, and burned several tents and latrines and the installations containing a small school and library. Most of the wounded soldiers suffered cuts and bruises, and some of their injuries were serious, according to U.S. authorities. Shortly after the incident, twenty-five U.S. soldiers and nineteen Cubans were hospitalized with fractures and contusions. Accounts by Cubans who participated in the riot indicate that the soldiers used primarily tear gas against them.

On Saturday, December 10, U.S. Southern Command officials confirmed that Panamanian authorities discovered the bodies of two Cubans who had drowned in international waters in the Panama Canal. Vigilance around the four refugee camps was reinforced with two thousand U.S. soldiers. On Saturday, approximately thirty-one fugitive raft people were still wandering in the Panamanian jungle. The Southern Command chiefs showed the local and international press a video in which Cuban raft people appeared with handkerchiefs covering their faces, in the style of the Zapatista rebels in the mountains of Chiapas, Mexico. The Cubans were armed with sticks and were throwing stones at the U.S. military police. The officer in charge of presenting the video to reporters added that the rioters had also used razor blades, wooden clubs, and metal bars to attack the U.S. authorities. Of the more than eighty-five hundred raft people held in Panama, for the moment only eighty-six had been accepted in accordance with the requirements of a federal program permitting temporary entry into the United States of orphans under age thirteen, elderly over seventy, and the chronically ill.

It was logical that one of the first to be questioned regarding the events that had occurred in Panama was that country's president, Ernesto Pérez Balladares. Pérez Balladares, along with the rest of the

Latin-American and Caribbean heads of state, was in Miami participating in the Summit of the Americas. "I dare to propose that the U.S.
have a more open policy toward the Cuban raft people. Tell them if
they can immigrate to the U.S. or not, but do not hold them there indefinitely, telling them absolutely nothing," recommended Pérez Balladares, who until that moment had stayed out of the controversy. In an
interview with the press, U.S. Vice President Al Gore, also attending
the Summit, stated: "The riots will not have repercussions in U.S.
immigration policy. We are taking steps to find a country that will
accept them. We are diligently examining the humanitarian cases, and
we have improved living conditions in the centers."

Many of the U.S. troops stationed on Empire Range (Panama)
regretted that the friendship that they believed had been established in
their daily relationships with the detainees had been broken by the
riots. According to the soldiers, the detainees received three meals a
day, had a small theater, had fields in which to play sports, were given
packages of clothing and cigarettes, and permitted to call their relatives
in the United States. In addition, they received frequent visits from
well-known Cuban performers from Miami: Willie Chirino, Celia
Cruz, and Jon Secada. "It is something [the soldiers] were not expecting; the violence of the Cubans took them by surprise," said one of the
U.S. military spokesmen.

The Legislative Assembly of Panama warned that it would demand
the immediate departure from the country, before the stipulated six
months, of 840 raft people from the U.S. military bases in the Canal
Zone if further riots occurred. The statement was made on December
13 to a local radio station by the president of the Foreign Relations
Commission of Parliament, Legislator Oyden Ortega of the governmental Democratic Revolutionary Party (PRD). At the same time,
word was received that the U.S. Southern Command had stated that, as
a result of the riots, it had detained some six hundred raft people, 490
of whom were accused of provoking the incidents. These latter
detainees would be subjected to a summary process in which the possibility of their being sanctioned with return to Cuba was not out of the
question.

Among the Cuban refugees interviewed after the riot, there existed a gamut of opinions. Alcides Barrera, one of the raft people, stated that he feared what might occur. Agitators were trying to provoke problems in the camps just a few days after the bloody uprising. In spite of various warnings from the Panamanian government and the U.S. military, the situation in the camps remained tense, and if the graffiti on the walls of the latrines was to be believed, it was only hours before the next uprising would occur.

Most of the 8,480 raft people held in the camps seemed to be against the violence, but their desperation was growing by the hour and many were pressuring from inside the tents for a new outbreak of rioting. In preparation for possible further violence, U.S. anti-riot forces patrolled the four camps night and day, carrying shotguns and nightsticks, while armored assault vehicles remained stationed on the outskirts.

Detainee Alcides Barrera was of the opinion that Fidel Castro had sent some infiltrators as *agents provocateurs* among the more than thirty-four thousand Cubans who fled the island during the summer. The infiltrators' main objective would be to create problems at the camps. "People are afraid they'll think we're all the same and treat us as agitators, reducing any hope of our going to the United States," said Barrera.

The week following the disturbances there was an early-morning raid in which troops removed approximately six hundred presumed agitators and placed them in a separate, strictly guarded camp. There, each case was reviewed, using witnesses and videotapes to determine the extent of each person's participation. The Cubans who took part in the riot could be detained indefinitely in the provisional camp, which did not have television, recreation facilities, or any amenities.

Other stories circulating among the refugees indicated that the treatment they received from the U.S. military following the riots in Camps #1 and #2 had been extremely unpleasant. A group of soldiers, suddenly sent to carry out a search, arrived at the camp before dawn and awakened the detainees by hitting them with nightsticks. This occurred at 4 A.M., and the soldiers were constantly shouting "Get up! Get up!" as they struck the prisoners. The raft people complained that since the riots, they were required to keep their tents open all day.

"There is no privacy, and the heat is bad for our health. The children are afraid of the armed soldiers," said one woman.

A more accurate account of the December riots in the Panama camps was obtained from Guillermo Rodríguez, who finally managed to reach Miami on December 21. His new-found freedom would be dramatically tested when he attended the funeral of his brother Rolando, who had drowned two weeks earlier in the Panama Canal. Guillermo and Rolando Rodríguez had escaped from Cuba that August, being detained first in the Guantánamo camps and finally in Panama, where both had participated in the riots. "My brother Rolando was left behind. I am very sorry, but it is better to risk one's life than to die a slave in Cuba," Guillermo stated at a press conference in a Miami hotel a few hours after being released from the camps out of humanitarian considerations.

After two weeks of intense negotiations, Guillermo Rodríguez landed at Homestead Air Force Base, with a visa to live in the United States, obtained through intense pressure by Congresswoman Ileana Ros-Lehtinen and Arturo Rodríguez, director of the Casa del Balsero in Miami. "It is lamentable that in order to come to this free country, Guillermo had to lose his brother. It is a tragedy that burying his brother is one of the first things this man must do," said Ros-Lehtinen. Guillermo, a thirty-three-year-old father of two children who remain in Cuba, stated that in spite of having lost his brother, leaving Cuba had been worth the risk. His parents and an older brother have lived in Miami for two years. Guillermo and Rolando escaped from Camp #2 during the riots. Rolando drowned in the Canal, and Guillermo was detained by the Panamanian police, who turned him over to U.S. authorities. "After I escaped, they took me back to the camp. The soldiers beat me. As they handcuffed me, they kicked me while I was on the ground. I don't like violence, but if they try to return the refugees who are in Panama to Guantánamo, there will be more incidents." Guillermo saw the waters of the Canal swallowing his brother, but was unable to save him. Nor could he rescue another refugee, Lázaro Jirones, who also lost his life in the always-dark waters of the Panama Canal.

According to statements by Guillermo to reporters at his brother's funeral, word had reached the Panama camps on December 7 that the detainees would be sent back to Guantánamo. The Cubans asked to see representatives of the U.S. Embassy to obtain an explanation of the situation. That same day, the first incidents occurred, when a food truck was trapped in the camps. "That day some U.S. officials arrived at the camps, but this did not calm the detainees," he indicated. "We got the impression that they were not diplomats, and we were not able to converse much with them because they didn't speak Spanish." The most serious incidents took place during the morning of December 8. "The situation exploded when we realized they had reinforced the fences surrounding the camps and that they had anti-riot teams." Guillermo and his brother were among those who battled the U.S. soldiers until they managed to escape from the camp through a hole in the fence. Their first instinct was to run toward the jungle, but they soon encountered eighteen others. "We decided that we had to go to Panama City to present ourselves at the U.S. Embassy and ask what they were going to do with us." Pursued through the air by artillery helicopters and on land by special forces made up of U.S. troops and Panamanian police, the rebel band of twenty Cubans managed to travel some three kilometers through the jungle before reaching the shore of the Panama Canal. "We had no choice but to throw ourselves into the water, because they were chasing us." They all jumped into the canal. Guillermo, a mechanic by trade and a strong man, reached the other shore in ten minutes. "I saw that my friend Lázaro Jirones was drowning; I tried to get him out, but I couldn't. He sank away from me. I returned to the shore and turned to look for my brother, but I couldn't see him either. I kept looking, and they shouted that he had drowned. I couldn't believe it, because he was such a good swimmer. Maybe by the time we started swimming he was already exhausted from being chased." Right there on the banks of the Canal, Guillermo was detained by the Panamanian Police and turned over to U.S. soldiers. "They took me back to the camp and locked me up in what they call the 'five-and-a-half unit'. It's a place full of filthy mud; you have to stay there for days, dressed only in your underwear," said Guillermo Rodríguez. He was punished in this manner for several days, along with four hundred other raft people. He began to think he would never reach the United States.

Nevertheless, amazingly, when he believed all was lost, as in Balzac's novels, on December 16, 1994, he was told that he had a U.S. resident visa. It would initially permit him to attend his brother's funeral in Miami. Early that same morning, a military truck took him from the camp to the Panama military airport. "The people who are in those camps are good people, most of them professionals, who have sacrificed everything for freedom. I don't understand why they aren't admitted into this country. I can't accept that the dead arrive here before the living," Guillermo told reporters upon his arrival.

Christmas week brought an unwelcome surprise to many of the detainees in the Panama camps suffering the consequences of a forced relocation. The U.S. military began transferring families and single women from Camp #1 to other camps, as Camp #1 had been the scene of violent riots and escape attempts just two weeks earlier. Now only men would live in Camp #1. The measure, of course, was disapproved of by many of the relocated refugees, who said that now their compatriots in Camp #1 were without the presence of women and children. In addition, the phones had been damaged, and as a result, the detainees could not communicate with the outside world. Nor were the men in Camp #1 permitted to watch television, which drastically limited their receipt of information. According to U.S. authorities, the transfer of some seven hundred raft people, including families and single women, was carried out in order that those people might be more comfortable in the camps. Captain John Thomas, Operation Safe Refuge spokesman, said that no additional changes would be made. The relocation was carried out without incident during the early morning of Friday, December 23.

One of the relocated refugees said that the soldiers stationed at the entrance to Camp #1 cried as they said goodbye to the women and children they had come to know. "Not all the men left in Camp #1 are bad. There are professionals and decent people who liked to watch the children play and conversed very respectfully with us," said one woman. The raft people requested that reporters not mention their names, for fear of reprisals by the soldiers. "Locked behind barbed wire, with no contact with the outside world, and without seeing women and children, those men will die of sadness," said one detainee in reference to the more than fifteen hundred single men sheltered in Camp #1.

Amidst sighs of sadness, lost hope, relocated and postponed dreams, Christmas came to the Panama camps. At the entrance to Camp #2, on a large Christmas tree, was a sign proclaiming "Happy 1995." The detainees were aware that that night they would eat pork, black beans, and cassava . . . but without the seasoning of the Christmas spirit. Some pointed out that the children would receive toys donated in Miami; nevertheless, no one was sure when they would be distributed. The refugees' lives were becoming a darker gray with each passing day. "Christmas is a minor thing here," said thirty-two-year-old José Jiménez González. "We are waiting for something else: to get out of here."

Near the close of the Summit of the Americas, the U.S. government announced that nine hundred Cubans who had fled to the Cayman Islands would be sent to Guantánamo. The announcement came after several months of negotiations with U.S. officials, and the day after more than three hundred Cuban women and children marched peacefully through the streets of the tourist area on Grand Cayman Island, asking for permission to enter the United States. When they received news of the accord, many Cubans expressed satisfaction mixed with concern, since the Guantánamo Naval Base is so close to the country from which they had fled. In addition, they were not looking forward to the idea of being held in camps with other refugees whom they did not know.

Coinciding with the end of 1994, which for international organizations was "the year of tolerance" and for Cubans could well be called "the year of the raft people," a group of more than three hundred *santeros* and *babalaos* met, as was their custom, to elaborate the prophesies and recommendations that, by divine mandate, the Orishas had in store for 1995. The Cuban *santeros* predicted the presence of diverse illnesses, coups, betrayals, religious wars, marriages broken due to infidelity, and the deaths of well-known personalities. If anyone had hope, or repeated the refrain that "things could only get better," certainly after the *babalaos* cast the shells and studied their positions, there was no doubt that worse disasters could still occur.

The *santeros* belonging to the IFÁ IRAN LOWO association made public the document that included their predictions and advice for the year. When they presented their forecast, the *santeros* stated that it had a broad horizon and a framework of "universality" that concerned not only Cuba but the entire world. An increase in violence and criminality, a decline in parental authority, religious wars and struggles for hegemony, cattle epidemics, astronomical phenomena, housing deterioration, broken marriages due to adultery, and an elevation in sea level were among their gloomy predictions for 1995.

For the raft people detained indefinitely in the Panama camps, the new year of 1995 began with the bad omen revealed by the colorful shells tossed by the *santeros*. The Orishas of the Afro-Cuban pantheon of gods had reached an agreement with the officials of the U.S. Southern Command on January 1 when they informed them that very soon they would be relocated again, this time back to the tent fortress—the great circus of the U.S. Navy—at Guantánamo. For refugee Martín González, that was tantamount to death. González, a Cuban soldier, had deserted from his guard post in August 1994 when he saw a solitary raft floating near shore. In his rush to leave, he did not take off his uniform, and he took with him his regulation rifle. A lieutenant in the Interior Ministry, González assumed that if caught in Cuba, he would likely end up in front of a firing squad. "Imagine, I'm a deserter, a traitor to my country," said the thirty-one-year-old former soldier.

Many of the Cuban refugees in the Panama camps stated that they had no desire to be relocated to Guantánamo, which they called a "nest of absurd contradictions." The U.S. government was permitting the entry of only a small group of the more than thirty thousand Cubans who had left the island in the massive exodus of rafts in August 1994, exhorting the remaining Cubans to return to their country and apply for entry visas to the United States, thus making use of the twenty thousand immigrant visas that the U.S. government had agreed to grant each year.

Most of the refugees laughed at this option, and morale in the camps was declining rapidly, according to some of the leaders in the

Panama camps. "There are people here who want to commit suicide," said González, the leader of a group of eighteen tents in the "Willie Chirino" Camp. According to U.S. Southern Command spokesman Col. James Fetig, several suicide attempts had already occurred. "One individual swallowed a piece of metal, and another stabbed himself in the abdomen with barbed wire. Part of the violence in the camps, self-inflicted or not, is designed to attract attention, and does not result from severe desperation. We have had several faked epilepsy attacks."

After the December riots, soldiers brandishing clubs patrolled the camps and frequently conducted searches for rudimentary weapons and contraband liquor. On occasion they used "bomb-hunting" dogs and metal detectors in their raids. U.S. Army Captain John Legget reported "picking up knives and other instruments which can be used for beatings . . ." Legget described the agitators as a minority, and said that the U.S. military was well prepared to effect the transfer. The imminent departure for Guantánamo was beginning to wreak havoc on the refugees' psyches. Vladimir Rojas, age thirty-four, who had been an announcer at a Havana radio station, meditated doubtfully about the possible transfer, balancing positive and negative aspects. "Perhaps someday people will resign themselves to the idea that they have to leave. Really, there is no alternative. Either we go back voluntarily, or they'll force us to go back. If I say I won't go, they'll hit me with a stick, tie me up, and take me back anyway . . ."

At the end of the interview, Rojas, leader of the detainees in the "Celia Cruz" Camp, indicated that he knew that some refugees were making new plans to jump the fence or riot, to stop the relocation plans. Some leaders of other camps were seated next to Rojas; they appeared furious at the presence of a visiting reporter—according to the description of the encounter in the *Nuevo Herald*—but, at the same time, anxious to obtain information about things that could affect them. One of them, forty-eight-year-old singer Juan Sánchez, spoke up: "We're in a zoo here, where a series of celebrities come to visit us, including many reporters like you . . . And you never publish anything that helps us."

The year 1995 had a fateful beginning for a group of Cuban raft people held at the Nassau Detention Center in the Bahamas. At 2 P.M. on January 5, two armored police cars arrived at the center, and behind them some two hundred riot police. They ordered the Cubans to get into the cars and drove them to the Fox Hill Jail, in the capital. "The problems started on Sunday, December 31. The guards were drunk, and four Cubans and one Dominican escaped. After that, the repression started," said Pedraza Polanco. On Wednesday, January 3, some thirty Cubans had escaped, and an operation began that managed to recapture twenty of them. One of the fugitives was Yamelis Pérez, only sixteen years old. When they were bringing her back to the camp, the police hit her on the legs, said Pedraza. When the refugees began to protest the beating, the police hit Yamelis Pérez in the head with a nightstick. "That was when Troy burned . . ." said Pedraza. The Cuban refugees began to throw stones at the police, and the uniformed guards responded with gunshots. A short time later, they forced their way into the camp and began to beat the prisoners indiscriminately. Seventy-year-old Alcides Valbuena was kicked as he was sleeping in his bed. The tension between the police and the refugees continued throughout the following day. Finally, on Thursday, the armored cars arrived, and the men were taken to Fox Hill. "Now we're desperate. The guards still have their long weapons, and they stick them in our faces for any reason," reported Pedraza. He added that two armored cars and fifty police were still guarding the camp.

In Miami, Ileana Ros-Lehtinen asked the government of the Bahamas for an immediate investigation into the alleged mistreatment of the Cuban refugees. A press release from the congresswoman's office indicated that, according to groups of religious workers and volunteers who maintained contact with the refugees, the Bahamian guards had beaten several of the detainees. Ros-Lehtinen stated that her office was trying to obtain more information about what had happened. "Of course, the officials have to control the situation. The first priority is the safety of the people." The congresswoman called "worrisome" the versions of events that she had heard so far. Ros-Lehtinen denounced the inclusion of an eight-month pregnant woman among the detainees. "I am completely opposed to Cuban refugees being sent to prison, especially the woman who is eight months pregnant. To mistreat refugees who are only seeking freedom is a violation of human rights," she concluded.

The government of the Bahamas defended its jailing of dozens of Cubans, alleging that the measure was necessary to keep order. The Bahamian authorities stated that the Cubans had not been beaten or mistreated. "We categorically deny that. It is incorrect and false. In accordance with the proceedings of the United Nations High Commissioner for Refugees (UNHCR), the government of the Bahamas has taken the measures it considers necessary to assure the security of its installations and the safety of the detainees," added the communique issued by the government.

Meanwhile, in the Panama camps, located between the jungle and the canal, the U.S. soldiers in charge of more than eight thousand refugees were preparing for any contingencies that could result from the Clinton administration's plan to send most of the refugees back to Guantánamo. A substantial number of the detainees swore they would resist. "It is not going to be a peaceful thing, because no one wants to go back to Guantánamo," said Jorge Luis Alvarez, a twenty-eight-year-old refugee. One official warned that the United States would deploy a massive show of force in relocating the refugees. "We're going to prepare for the worst," stated a U.S. Army officer. Col. Jim Greenwood, commander of one of the four tent camps, was much more emphatic in his statements. He reflected the general climate when he said: "What am I going to do with people who tie themselves to the tent poles because they don't want to go? Panamanian government officials fear that will happen."

However, on Friday, January 13, 1995, ninety-one Cubans detained on the Cayman Islands calmly boarded a U.S. military transport plane that would take them to the Guantánamo Naval Base. "We were so miserable on Grand Cayman, that for many of us it's better to accept the transfer to Guantánamo. There was no hope," explained Juan Rodríguez, a thirty-five-year-old Cuban doctor. Recently, the prime minister of the Caymans had argued that the island had a population of twenty-eight thousand people and that it was therefore impossible to integrate the more than a thousand raft people. "For us, more than a thousand Cubans is the same as if ten million people arrived in the U.S. at one time," stated a Cayman Island government spokesman.

The Cayman authorities offered another option to those Cubans who wished to emigrate to places other than Guantánamo. If, by chance, any of the Cuban refugees on Grand Cayman Island raised their hands and asked to set sail again, destination unknown, the Cayman authorities immediately provided them with everything necessary for repair of their rafts: wood, paint, gas, and oil. When the Cubans were ready to set out, the Cayman authorities added six days' worth of food and water. "We don't want them to be at sea without provisions for the voyage. We try to give them humanitarian aid," said Grand Cayman government spokesman Pat Ebanks.

With the iron will demonstrated by the Cubans, and the help supplied by the Cayman authorities, during the preceding two weeks three groups of raft people had reached the coasts of Central America. One group of twenty arrived in Belize, and two groups of fifteen each reached Costa Rica. The arrivals posed a problem for Costa Rica, which was experiencing economic difficulties. President José María Figueres was forced to assume emergency measures, and warned that Costa Rica was in no condition to grant political asylum to Cubans. "This is a problem that, for a country like ours, is beyond our possibilities," said Figueres.

It is very probable that upon hearing or reading the Costa Rican president's words, the Cuban refugees looked at each other and, unanimously and without a word, picked up their oars, willing to set out to sea again. Had they not already traveled nearly the entire Caribbean? From the coasts of Cuba to the Florida Peninsula; from Florida to Guantánamo; from Guantánamo to Panama; from Cuba to the Bahamas; from the Bahamas to the Cayman Islands; from the Cayman Islands to Belize; from Belize to Costa Rica? And now, in what direction should they steer their rafts?

꒖ꜝ ꒖ꜝ ꒖ꜝ

In the Panama camps, the situation was growing worse. A wave of frustration, defeat, and desperation, higher than those they had to battle during their odysseys on rafts in the Florida Straits, was threatening to bury the raft people forever. The U.S. military made public the decision to transfer them back to Guantánamo. The news was truly alarming. Brigadier General James Wilson, commander of Operation Safe Refuge, confirmed that some twenty raft people, desperate, had attempted suicide in recent weeks, because they did not wish to be returned to Guantánamo. On Thursday, January 12, the State Department announced that the eight thousand detainees from the four Panama camps would be returned to Guantánamo in six weeks, after the temporary stay granted by Panama expired on March 6. The news was communicated to the refugees through the camp chiefs, while U.S. soldiers warned the detainees not to resort to violence, because that would affect their chances that the United States or a Latin-American country would grant them visas in the future.

The military command ordered as a precaution that dozens of tanks and assault vehicles be stationed around the camps, while security by soldiers with anti-riot gear increased. On Thursday, January 12, as the bad news of the transfer to Guantánamo was being announced, several artillery helicopters were patrolling the area. The most calm and sensible refugees afterwards stated that tension in the tents was so great that many detainees manifested severe psychological symptoms. Some tried to hang themselves with the ropes that held up the canvas tents. Others overdosed on pills or tried to slash their wrists with sharp pieces of metal they pulled off the cots. Had it not been for the quick intervention of the calmer detainees, a group suicide might have occurred. A few hours after the fact, the story of the wave of suicide attempts was confirmed by military sources. "It's criminal what they've done with us. We don't deserve this kind of treatment," María Dumenio said tearfully. "They'll have to take me to Guantánamo dead," shouted another detainee.

Other groups of refugees, even more furious at the thought of the imminent transfer, threatened to burn the tents or attack the soldiers with stones, as they had in December. Groups of up to five soldiers carrying clubs patrolled Camp #4, while several armored assault vehicles, ready to put down any riot, waited on the other side of the barbed-wire fence. General Wilson stated that security forces made up of more than two thousand troops in combat gear would act immediately against any violence during the transfer of the raft people. "Their human rights will be respected," added the general.

In a press conference in Panama City, Colombian writer Gabriel García Márquez said that he was deeply concerned at the uncertain situation in which the Cuban detainees lived and that he "wholeheartedly" hoped for a solution. García Márquez was in Panama visiting President Ernesto Pérez Balladares. "I am extremely concerned about the situation of people who believed they were leaving to seek happiness, and I believe they have found something substantially less than happiness. It is unfair that this is occurring," declared García Márquez.

"Gabo," as he is known to his friends, had not visited Panama since the death of General Omar Torrijos in 1981. "I had sworn I would not come until there was a president like the one you have today, of whom I have been an old friend since back then," concluded the Nobel laureate. García Márquez stated that he and President Pérez Balladares had had a "long conversation of memories, just memories."

This last statement caused reporters covering the press conference to smile cynically. They did not believe that García Márquez had suddenly lost his memory; and that now, in conversations with his friends, he would be like Proust, embarked on a demented search for the lost days through conversations in which the only permissible topic is memories. Current political topics must, in fact, have ranked high on the agenda of the conversation between Pérez Balladares and García Márquez. But that was news these journalists would not find out.

Did García Márquez bear a last-minute message from Fidel Castro? Perhaps a recommendation from Bill Clinton?

The struggle continued . . . and, meanwhile, Gabo remained silent.

Chapter IX

Undertow

MELCHIOR, CASPAR, AND BALTHAZAR, the Three Wise Men of Christian tradition, arrived punctually at Guantánamo Naval Base in the early morning of Friday, January 6, 1995. But, this time, there were a few changes in the ritual. Instead of camels, they used an old twin-engine plane from the glory days of World War II. Melchior, Caspar, and Balthazar were really Juanito, Tacho, and Manuel, three Cuban residents of Louisiana who, wearing brightly colored, rented robes, and artificial beards, landed on the airstrip of the U.S. base.

It was the first time in their lives that most of the Cuban children had had contact with the Christian holiday tradition of the Wise Men. On the other side of the barbed-wire fence, in Cuba, the Marxist-Leninist instruction received by children does not leave much room for epiphany. In the best scenario, the Three Wise Men might be treated as just one more myth. Or, if the teacher involved is an imaginative pedagogue, he may well substitute for the bearded Kings the equally bearded Comandantes Fidel, Che, and Raúl.

For Maggy Schuss, wife of one of the founders of Brothers to the Rescue, which helped collect and distribute approximately five thousand new toys to Haitian and Cuban children detained in Guantánamo, Panama, the Bahamas, and the Cayman Islands, the mission of distributing toys to children is "almost comparable to the satisfaction of saving a life . . ."

A week earlier, in the last days of 1994, when the *santeros* and *babalaos* on the island were preparing to toss their colored shells onto the Ifá board to inquire and foretell the future, some important changes were taking place on the Guantánamo Naval Base. Guarioné Díaz, who since September had held the position of civilian liaison between the U.S. military and the detainees, was relieved of his duties and not replaced. When interviewed, Guarioné Díaz informed the press that he was returning to his position as president of the Cuban-American National Council, since his commitment in Guantánamo, according to what he was told at the outset, was not to exceed three months, and that time was up.

Guarioné Díaz's work in the camps was evaluated as positive. Among his greatest achievements were cooperation in the collection of approximately one hundred thousand pounds of donations for the refugees; the obtaining of approval for weekly visits from the Miami medical team; and the facilitating of communication and flow of information between the detainees and the outside. At his departure, Guarioné Díaz felt satisfied at leaving behind Cuban children who were receiving milk every day, refugees preparing to live in small wooden houses instead of canvas tents and using regular toilets instead of the portable latrines previously provided. Many of the Cuban refugees on Guantánamo felt that Guarioné Díaz could continue looking out for their interests from the high executive position he occupied in the Council offices in Miami; others felt that his departure gave way to a period of uncertainty as they knew nothing about his replacement. "Who knows what will happen now?" wondered a discouraged Joaquín Menéndez.

Also near the end of 1994, prior to the visit of the Wise Men to Guantánamo, the U.S. Department of Defense announced that it would begin to carry out important works that would cost tens of millions of dollars, with the purpose of detaining approximately thirty thousand raft people for an indefinite period. The announced plans for the base prompted complaints from the Cuban government, which opposed the United States employing the base as a detention center for thousands of Cuban and Haitian refugees. According to statements by Ricardo Alarcón, president of the National Assembly and chief of the Cuban delegation in the conversations about migratory matters between the U.S. and Cuba: "Filling the Guantánamo Base with refugees is a criminal act . . ." In the opinion of Dennis Hays, director of the Office of Cuban Affairs of the State Department and head of the U.S. delegation in the negotiations with Cuban officials: "The Cuban authorities hold an interpretation of the base transfer agreement that we do not accept . . ."

The Cuban government alleged that Article 3 of the 1934 treaty between the United States and Cuba contemplated only two possible uses of the territorial concession in Guantánamo. One was that of using the base as a deposit for coal or fuel; the second was using it as a naval base. The Cuban government also insisted on pointing out that the accord signed between the two countries on July 2, 1903—a year after the establishment of the Republic of Cuba—indicates: "The U.S. agrees that it will not permit individuals, societies or companies to be established or make commercial, industrial or any other type of use . . ." In the opinion of Cuban jurist Rolando Amador, a resident of Miami and specialist on the base transfer agreements, the Cuban government's interpretation was incorrect. "There was always a civilian population on the base, and now there are nearly thirty thousand people," he said.

From the moment the old plane carrying the Three Wise Men landed at Guantánamo, the landing strip became the most popular place for the detainees. Who are they? Why did they come? Who was leaving? What were the reasons? These were the questions that came up in the detainees' conversations each time a group of passengers boarded or deplaned. Fifty-four Haitians, of a total of four thousand, were forcibly repatriated by U.S. authorities. The refugees were returned to Haiti where Red Cross workers welcomed them and gave them a couple of cold sandwiches and twelve dollars with which to begin the process of reintegration into Haitian society now that the dictatorship of Raoul Cedras had ended. The Cubans on Guantánamo commented: "Ten more days and there won't be a single Haitian left here!"

Several days after the return of the Haitian refugees to their country of origin began, two planes passed each other on the landing strip at Guantánamo, framed by the magnificent peaks of the Sierra Maestra and the blue depths of the Caribbean. A white jet took off carrying a hundred and seventy excited Cubans authorized to reside in the United States, while a green Hercules C-141 military transport plane landed with one hundred sad Cubans aboard. Guantánamo is too close to Cuban soil not to arouse the most varied feelings—from nostalgia and the desire to return, to the most profound hatred toward the political power of Fidel Castro and the Communist system of government. Near the airstrip, an enormous poster next to the U.S. flag caught the attention of the new arrivals; in Spanish, it proclaimed "WELCOME BACK."

When they got out of the plane, the detainees returning from Panama complained of the suffocating tropical heat of Guantánamo as they received glasses of orange Kool-Aid. The refreshing drink prompted embittered comments by some of the new arrivals when they remembered that around a thousand people had been poisoned in Guyana by drinking Kool-Aid in innocent little plastic cups. The incident occurred during the Carter administration, when the Reverend Jim Jones had attempted to found an empire in the midst of the jungle. Going through customs at the airport, the refugees were reminded that those guarding them were not responsible for the policy that kept them imprisoned. The group was processed with astonishing speed: The soldiers, dressed in bright, shiny khaki uniforms, took only eight and a half minutes to verify and distribute documents. At the end of the line, a U.S. soldier handed each of the new arrivals a piece of paper with an enigmatic message printed in black letters: "BE PATIENT. STAY ALIVE." From customs, the group proceeded to a school bus and from there to the deck of a ferry that carried them across the bay. It was the second day without delays in the air bridge established between the Panama Canal and the Guantánamo Naval Base. By the end of the afternoon, approximately five hundred refugees had been settled in the new camp, christened "Echo Village." It consisted of a group of tents with strong frames mounted on wooden platforms instead of on the ground as before. But even so, the refugees resented the harmful effects of the orange-colored dust cloud that weighed upon them eternally, like a curse. "A beautiful seafront property," Major Rick Thomas said, welcoming them.

Several of the recently settled refugees looked carefully around, and did not wait long before taking advantage of the optimal location of the camp: the shortest route to return to Cuba. One of the raft people read aloud the message written in black letters that they were given when they went through customs: "BE PATIENT. STAY ALIVE." Within hours of the arrival of the first five hundred new inhabitants of Echo Village Camp, eight raft people left their tents at midnight and entered the largest mine field in the world. The following day at 6 P.M., as several detainees contemplated, or pretended to contemplate, a beautiful tropical sunset, four of their companions took the same route. The U.S. military did not pursue them or even seem to notice. An hour earlier, nearby, three Cubans from the other side of the fence had been begging the U.S. sentry to take pity on them and give them asylum inside the base.

In mid-January 1995, two weeks before the arrival of the first groups from Panama, two U.S. Marines had been seriously wounded when a mine exploded outside the U.S. area of the base. One of the marines, age twenty-four, had his left leg amputated at the knee, while the other, age nineteen, suffered severe shrapnel wounds to several parts of his body. The explosion of the mine occurred as the two were on a routine patrol on the perimeter of the base; for reasons that are still not clear, they crossed the border and entered the zone mined by the Cuban Armed Forces (FAR). According to a subsequent Pentagon report, the U.S. mines are perfectly mapped; detailed records are kept of the positions they occupy, and old or defective mines are replaced periodically for safety reasons. The same report stated that U.S. military personnel stationed at Guantánamo confirm that the mine fields in Cuban territory are not adequately mapped, nor have they been properly maintained.

A week after the mine explosion, history repeated itself, this time with different victims and an even more tragic toll. Two raft people were blown to bits by the explosion of a mine as they and five others who wanted to return to Cuba attempted to cross the area categorized as mortally dangerous. According to the report from the U.S. side, an explosion was heard on the Cuban side at 12:30 A.M. on Friday, January 19. "Two of them must be dead. We haven't seen them move at all," said Major Rick Thomas. The following afternoon, Cuban soldiers on the other side of the fence were still attempting to retrieve the bodies and assist five others who appeared unharmed.

Desperation drove detainees not only to risk their lives in a type of gigantic Russian roulette trying blindly to cross the biggest mine field in the world, but there were also other more sure ways of reaching death quickly, incited by despair and hopelessness. Every morning and evening the horizon surprised them with radiant dawns and golden sunsets, but the sun's rays, emerging or dying in the sea, did nothing to provide the necessary ray of hope to brighten their lives in detention. That quick, cruel way to death is suicide. On Monday, January 23, 1995, at 3:30 P.M., twenty-three-year-old Emilio García Reyes became the fortieth raft person to attempt suicide in the tent fortress of Guantánamo. García Reyes' family in Miami received a telephone call from the base only moments after the young man was taken to the military hospital. "It is something terrible. I spoke with him this morning. I could tell he was very depressed, but I never thought he would slash his wrists," said his friend Arnadis Valdés Pérez.

According to reports of the incident circulating in the camp, García Reyes had a discussion with his friends in Camp McCalla regarding the possibilities of leaving the camp legally. But the young man had no chronic illness, nor did he have relatives among the refugees through whom he could obtain a humanitarian visa. "He was desperate. He saw how people were able to get a visa because they had asthma, or were elderly, or had a child accompanying them. And he had nothing to help him get a visa, no one," said García Reyes' friend Arnadis Valdés Pérez in a telephone interview from the base. "Suddenly, they told me that there was blood in the room, and I saw that they were taking Emilio to the hospital in an ambulance."

Most of the suicide attempts in the camps employed the most unlikely objects to cause self-harm. Those intent on taking their own lives used razor blades from disposable razors to slash their wrists; they used the tent ropes to hang themselves, and chemical products to burn their skin. According to Valdés Pérez, "Emilio took apart the disposable razor, took out the blade, and made a deep cut in one of his hands. When they were taking him away, I heard one of the guards saying 'He's a homosexual.' I asked them to let me go with him, telling them that I was his partner, but they didn't let me."

A few days later, another young man in Camp McCalla #3 attempted suicide by slashing the veins in his arms and neck. A couple of weeks later, during his recovery, he managed to be processed to receive a humanitarian visa. A seventeen-year-old by the last name of Baquero injected petroleum into his left leg, which caused several wounds and an uncontrollable infection. "I wanted to die; it didn't make sense to keep trying. By luck, I don't know if good or bad, I am now recovering from the operation, and I don't know what they're planning to do with me," said Baquero. The operation on Baquero's leg was done in the camp hospital, lasted several hours, and included skin grafts.

One case was discussed with particular horror by the male detainees. A refugee injected tabasco sauce into his penis and testicles, and doctors were forced to amputate part of his penis. There were still other cases in which human ingenuity turned into an effective means of self-destruction and physical mutilation. This occurred in the cases of detainees who, in the early morning, took cold showers and then drank large quantities of water mixed with detergent, for the purpose of pro-voking severe asthma attacks. Others placed knotted towels into their anuses to cause sudden inflammation of hemorrhoids. Detainee Virgilio López stated that the wounds on his right leg, which accompanied him as an unpleasant memory of Cuba, did not help him at all in applying for medical parole. "The soldiers think I caused the wounds myself, but I didn't. I've lost almost all feeling in the leg, and can barely walk."

Another particularly extraordinary case of a self-destructive nature was that of a transvestite nicknamed Rachel, who had attempt-ed suicide several months before. But instead of one cut he made sev-eral deep gashes the length of each arm. Sixto Lozano, age twenty, known to his friends as Rachel, obtained a visa for medical reasons and was awaiting transfer to Miami. "At night, you lose your mind. I cut myself several times so they wouldn't be able to save me. I truly wanted to die, but as you can see, thanks to my friends, I'm alive."

The epidemic of self-mutilation among the raft people diminished shortly thereafter, as they realized that there was nothing to gain by committing those actions, not even medical parole. "There was a case of a detainee who swallowed two "C" batteries," Captain Grey of the Public Relations Office of the base reported to the press. There have also been many cases of women who became pregnant as another means of obtaining the coveted medical visa. As of Thursday, April 6, sixty children had been born at the base hospital. But, in accordance with current immigration laws, the children born in that hospital were not U.S. citizens.

For their part, the U.S. military stated that most of the suicides occurred among men between the ages of sixteen and thirty who had no relatives in the United States. According to medical reports, there had been forty-one suicide incidents among the approximately thirty thousand Cuban refugees at Guantánamo. Since authorities began to investigate these incidents in late 1994, twelve cases had been classified as suicide attempts. "These individuals truly wanted to die," stated the report. Twenty-nine other attempts were really suicide "gestures," described by doctors as "intentionally harmful" self-inflicted actions carried out in circumstances in which it was likely that the person would be saved. Doctors estimated that most of the refugees did not really wish to die. They only wanted to reach the United States any way they could, even by becoming so ill that they had to be hospitalized.

Physicians were concerned at the emotional deterioration resulting from the indefinite detention of people already scarred by an extremely difficult life in Cuba and an even more difficult journey at sea. "We're talking about people who have already done dramatic things to fight for their lives. They have thrown themselves into the sea, and believe me, I know what I'm talking about. I spent ten hours in a storm. Our raft was constantly dragged to the heights of the waves, and below we could see the abyss. And now, I live in a camp; I'm a prisoner like them," said Carlos González, a psychologist who assisted the U.S. medical team.

Ironically, the suicide attempt that gave people the idea of doing the same to obtain release on their own recognizance had very little to do with their detention. It began with a love triangle in the camps. "A Cuban *Romeo and Juliet*," said Col. Celso Bolet, chief of the Army Mental Health team. The man was upset because his wife left him for another man that she met in the camp. When she moved to her lover's tent, her husband tried to hang himself. He was taken to the camp hospital, taken care of, and told he would be taken to the United States. He wanted his wife to go with him, and when she was not allowed to, he begged them to leave him in detention with her.

The love triangle and suicide attempt occurred in late 1994, and after the story began to spread, the number of refugees who ingested bleach, swallowed entire bottles of pills, slashed their wrists, or tried to hang themselves quickly increased. It was then that the military command decided to rush a team of bilingual psychiatrists, psychologists, social workers, behavior experts, therapists, and psychiatric nurses from Eisenhower Medical Center in Fort Gordon, Georgia, to Guantánamo. They were part of an independent team formed several years earlier to travel to combat zones and conduct psychological evaluations of soldiers overwhelmed by stress. The U.S. mental health group estimated that the indefinite nature of the detention was causing most detainees enormous anxiety and depression. "They don't know when they'll be able to leave, if at all. If we could tell them they could leave in six months, their anxiety would be alleviated. They see flights and people being transferred and they wonder, 'When will my turn come?'" stated one of the physicians.

Along with periodic visits from physicians, what also reached the camps was news from the outside world about their former companions. The raft people were tremendously attracted by the possibility of finding out details about life across the sea in Miami, the Mecca of their golden dreams of future settlement. Therefore, under the protective canvas of the tents, the raft people milled around anyone who managed to somehow get hold of a *Nuevo Herald*. The paper often contained reports of families being reunited, and, of course, future hopes and dreams. One example was an article on extraordinary and daring raft person Aníbal Rodríguez.

Every morning Rodríguez enters a cage full of ferocious alligators. He spends some time with them, playing with the animals until he manages to infuriate them. Only then does he choose his opponent. "The alligator that is most aggressive and anxious to fight, that's the one I choose," Rodríguez explained. Rodríguez works in Native Village on the Seminole Reservation in Florida. "I grab them, open their mouths by holding their jaws . . . and try to neutralize them . . ." stated Rodríguez, who, despite more than ten years' experience working with heavyweight crocodiles and alligators, is conscious of the enormous danger he faces. "These creatures are not trained, and at any moment they could strike me with their head, tail, or even their sharp teeth," said Rodríguez, explaining his daily activities. Aníbal Rodríguez has huge scars everywhere on his body, as well as a dislocated shoulder, but the danger he faces every day not only attracts but thrills him. At times he feels fear, but the risk in being among dangerous animals gives him such great satisfaction that it truly excites him. His first contact with crocodiles and alligators was in Cuba, where he worked as a diver doing oceanographic research. "I was given some crocodiles to care for. Immediately, I began to get to know them and play with them. Later, I raised a few. Some even lived in my house, along with some snakes." Without another word—according to the report—Aníbal entered a metal cage full of alligators and crocodiles. The most striking was a magnificent specimen named Long Jaws, a male American alligator measuring eleven feet in length and weighing 340 pounds. "The alligator has every right to bite me. I mustn't forget that I am the one intruding on his territory," warned Aníbal from inside the cage, as if bidding the reporter farewell.

After reading the article, one of the refugees addressed his companions: "A free ticket to Miami for the first five people who volunteer to work with Aníbal!" Not a word, not a hand went up among the group. "Read something else, come on, my friend," said one detainee finally. "Let's see, let's see," the reader looked the newspaper's pages over carefully, "what do you think of this article?" He began to read a story about the Palma de Mallorca Restaurant, whose owners specialized in keeping Cuban raft people afloat. "What do they mean by that?" chorused several voices from within the group. The detainee-turned-reader informed his companions that four raft people worked at the Palma de Mallorca: William Rodríguez, a chef's helper, who was picked up at sea on August 13, 1994; Raquel Leal, who works in the cafeteria along with her son; the chef of the house, José Hernández, who worked as a chef at the Mexican Embassy before travelling to Miami with a visitor's visa eight months earlier and deciding to stay; and Raúl Reyes, who spent a week at sea and was rescued on April 21, 1994, currently employed as a waiter's assistant.

The group of raft people employed at the Palma de Mallorca Restaurant got together to celebrate their common employment, and decided to prepare a special dish that would become part of the restaurant's menu. That is how the Tostón Balsero ("Rafter Tostón") was born. A fried plantain in the shape of a boat, filled with shrimp, lobster, and seasoned crab and served with two side dishes, the Tostón Balsero is offered to customers at a price of $8.45. Raft people on the menu; raft people working in the restaurant kitchen; raft people serving coffee in the dining room; raft people everywhere. "That's great, my friend. Look in the paper and read us another story like that one about the raft people at the Palma de Mallorca," requested the detainees gathered under the tent.

With the increase in arrivals and departures of planes at Guantánamo came an increase in the number of journalists, physicians, attorneys, politicians, and representatives of international humanitarian institutions interested in finding out more about the fate of the raft people since their confinement in the great U.S. Navy tent circus began in late August 1994. Hidden among the sea of canvas tents spread across the arid surface of the military base, incredible stories awaited the reporters, tales of people who set sail seeking the freedom and well-being that the paradise of the United States could offer them, and on the way found only death and despair. Finally, they were pushed by the undertow to that tiny fortified territory surrounded by barbed-wire and mine fields. By strange coincidence, that territory was as much a part of the hell from which they wanted to escape as of the paradise they yearned to reach. And, as the last straw of their misfortune, they were continuously watched by two armed powers as if their arrival might signal the beginning of World War III.

The camp was full of incredible stories, like that of the group of young swimmers made up of Jaime Ruano, Israel Lara, Javier Castaneda, Reynaldo Martínez, Ernesto and Urbano Olivares, Angel Martínez and Arnaldo Muñoz, who, in separate incidents, jumped into the sea at different points along the southeastern coast of Cuba—where the water is as much as three thousand meters deep—and swam to Guantánamo. Jaime Ruano, a refrigeration technician, had been previously sentenced to eighteen months in prison for attempting to leave Cuba. Then he tried again, and was arrested again. He stated that on this second occasion the police beat him brutally. Wearing a swimsuit and with two bottles of water tied to his belt, Jaime Ruano tried his luck for the third time, and swam for a couple of hours. But the waters of the bay were very rough, and he decided to take a break on the beach. When night fell, he realized that the seas were calmer, and he set out again. Swimming slowly, guided by the distant reflection of the waves crashing onto on the coral reefs and trying not to lose sight of the shore, he swam all night. "From time to time I hung from a tree trunk to rest. When I became too exhausted and hungry, I returned to the beach." To calm his hunger, Ruano ate snails he pulled off the rocks.

Another of the young swimmers, Urbano Olivares Batista, preferred to crack open crabs and suck them. "I just drank the juice of the crabs," he explained. "It gave me the strength to keep going." The third to join the group was Ernesto Olivares, Urbano's brother, who stated that he had served six months in two Cuban jails, accused of being a liaison of the Cuban-American National Foundation. "Somebody turned me in. All I did was put up posters and recruit people." A few kilometers before reaching the base, the Olivares brothers were forced to stop. "We didn't have the strength to go on," said Urbano. "We came out of the water in front of a Cuban guard post, and the sentry told us that we could turn back, that it wasn't too late, and that the area ahead of us was mined. We told him we weren't interested in turning back, and that we preferred to die on the other side." While the Olivares brothers carefully crossed the field mined by the Cuban army and were sighted by the U.S. guards on the base, near them, in the water, a line of eight young swimmers continued their steady maritime march toward the base.

At the head of the group of tireless swimmers was Israel Lara, better known to his courageous companions as "The Fat Guy on the Tree Trunk." Astride a thick bamboo trunk, Lara propelled himself forward by paddling steadily with his arms. Behind him swam twenty-five-year-old Reynaldo Martínez, wearing flippers. Panting, in last place in the string of surprising swimmers, stroking hard to stay afloat, was Georbis Fuentes Blanco, a university student from Santiago de Cuba who, unfortunately, felt the first twinges of an appendicitis attack as he swam. When he felt he could not go on, his companions encouraged him. "The last thing I would have done was to go back," said Fuentes, who was admitted to the base hospital with peritonitis and spent eight days there before being sent to Panama.

The group took four days and nights to complete the maritime journey to Guantánamo. In the early morning of the last day, when their legs and arms no longer responded, one of them saw a light in the distance and exclaimed excitedly: "That's the base, friends!" Some of the swimmers did not believe him until two hours later when they saw the U.S. flag flying above a sentry box, from which a U.S. Marine guard showed them the way.

There were stark stories, such as that of Alexander, an eleven-year-old boy who was selling peanuts in paper cones on the Havana waterfront and decided to escape, alone, on a raft. When he reached Guantánamo, he was in the company of a woman who, during her voyage, had lost her husband, her two children, her sister and sister's children, and her brother-in-law.

And there were bizarre stories like that of eighteen-year-old Russian Sergei Vladimirovich Chernosov, a tale that borders on legend and myth. Sergei used his life savings to take a four-day cruise from Moscow to Havana. His secret desire was to obtain a U.S. visa and travel from Cuba to the United States. But his plan failed when he was denied a U.S. visa in Cuba, just as he had been in Moscow. It was then that Sergei decided to board one of the many rafts on which thousands of Cubans were attempting to cross the Florida Straits. It was August 1994, and Sergei, like more than thirty thousand Cubans who made the same trip, was captured by the U.S. Coast Guard and taken to Guantánamo, where, after preliminary questioning, he joined the thousands of Cubans in their migratory and legal limbo. The fact that Sergei was the only Russian inhabitant of the refugee camp made him the object of constant jokes and ridicule. "I am alone in the world. No one cares about me. What can I do?" he said in a telephone interview with the Jacksonville, Florida *Times-Union*.

Officials from the Russian Embassy in the United States said that Sergei could return to his country of origin whenever he wished, but Sergei would not accept their offer, according to State Department spokesperson Hazel Reitz.

Russell Bloom, refugee director for Lutheran Social Services in Jacksonville, met with Sergei in late 1994 while doing volunteer work at Guantánamo for World Relief. "He's determined. The effort he has made is impressive. He's young and healthy and wants to work." Sergei told World Relief volunteers that the Cubans at Guantánamo had ostracized him; they laugh at him, throw stones at him, steal his clothing. "They think I'm a Soviet, a Communist. I try to explain to them, but they laugh at me," said Sergei of his contradictory situation. Bloom said that it would be difficult for Sergei to obtain permission to enter the United States, as he had no relatives here and had not been persecuted in his home country. "We could help him, and get him a job, but getting him *here* is the problem," stated Bloom, whose organization has assisted other Russian refugees in resettling in northwestern Florida. The young Russian raft person regretted greatly that the only photographs of his mother and from his childhood, which he brought with him as treasured memories, had been ruined by the seawater.

There were also harrowing stories, like that of Jorge Hernández Avila, one of the thirty-one survivors of the sinking of the *13 de Marzo* tugboat in mid-July, 1994. When Hernández Avila arrived in Miami from Guantánamo, he stated that the most terrible moment for him was seeing the children on the old tugboat crying for help and drowning. He related in detail how at 4 A.M., the one-hour pursuit of the old wooden tug and its seventy-two passengers ceased. At that moment, a government ship, the *Polargo 5,* rammed and split the stern of the fugitive boat. Hernández Avila dove into the water in an attempt to save himself. "I didn't want the suction of the sinking ship to swallow me up," stated Hernández. Hernández had no doubt that the main responsibility for the sinking lay with the skipper of the *Polargo 5,* a Party militant known as Jesusito. He added that the escape was organized by fifty-two-year-old Fidencio Ramón Prieto, a State Security Department official in charge of periodic review of an entire section of the port. Fidencio Ramón Prieto was another of the victims in the sinking of the old *13 de Marzo* tugboat. "He was the official operative of the Maritime Services pier the night of our escape," said Hernández.

About nine miles from the Havana coast, in a place known to sailors as La Poceta, the *Polargo 2* tugboat cut off the *13 de marzo* while the *Polargo 5* rammed it, cracking its stern. The prow of the *13 de marzo* was lifted out of the water by the blow, and the deck began to flood. "After that, everything happened so fast . . ." said Hernández, who estimated that it took fifteen seconds for the *13 de marzo* to sink. "The last thing I remember were the screams of the people who were trapped in the hold and the sound of the engine when the water snubbed it. As they drowned, almost all of the children were screaming one word: Mamá!" said Hernández, clearly shaken.

The scene of bodies disappearing under the water could be seen clearly, because the *Polargos* had withdrawn to a distance of about fifty meters away and were illuminating the scene with their reflectors. "It was about forty minutes before we received any help," said Hernández. In his opinion, at the moment it sank, there were about twelve people in the hold of the *13 de marzo*. Of a total of seventy-two, only thirty-one survived. According to this last estimate, at least forty-one people drowned while the authorities stood by and watched, emotionless. Remaining calm, according to Hernández, was what saved his life, as he managed to remain afloat and grab two small life preservers thrown from the *Polargos* a half hour later. The most moving moment he remembers was when Mayda Tacoronte swam over to him begging for help, holding her small daughter, whom she believed already dead. "My little girl! My little girl!" Mayda was shouting. "But I saw the little girl's face and realized that she was still alive, so we immediately put her on top of the life preservers," Hernández related. The report was made by Jorge Hernández Avila in late February 1994 in Miami, at the same time the *13 de marzo* case was being presented before the Human Rights Commission in Geneva.

Despite their harsh living conditions, daily life with its routines, hopes, and frustrations began to germinate under the hot canvas of the great tent circus at Guantánamo. In early March 1995, a group of thirteen Cuban-American and three Haitian-American teachers arrived at Guantánamo on flights chartered by the U.S. government for the purpose of implementing an educational program for the children detained on the base. In addition to educational activities, another development on the base was active commerce, not organized by the U.S. military and almost completely out of its control. Just like in Cuba, cigarettes had become a monetary unit. The refugees on the base had found a way to convert the three cigarettes they received each day into objects of exchange. "It's one more way to survive," explained nineteen-year-old Ariagna Tabares, who was pregnant and just two weeks from giving birth. "My pregnancy makes me very hungry. This morning I traded five cigarettes for an MRE," Ariagna told a reporter. In base jargon, "MRE" refers to the famous "Meals Ready to Eat," packaged in brown plastic bags that the refugees call "the little caramels." The clandestine commerce of cigarettes took care of many small necessities as, for example, when they wished to have a snack between their breakfast of oatmeal, lunch of MRE, and dinner of rice with corned beef.

At times, the trades became complicated. One visiting journalist relates that, as he was interviewing a detainee, a pair of new athletic shorts flew like an arrow above the sheets that served as the interior walls of the tents. The shorts turned out to be a gift for twenty-year-old Justo García Muñoz, elected tent director by his fellow refugees. And, although they were too big for him, he insisted that he was not going to return them. "I'll trade them for another pair, or for cigarettes!" said García Muñoz.

The barbed-wire fences separating the various camps did not restrict commerce at all. The refugees would shout their asking price to someone in a neighboring camp, and then throw the merchandise over the fence. The usual price of a cigarette was three small bars of soap, each one enough for one shower. "Sometimes when an inveterate smoker is dying for a cigarette, he'll trade as many as twelve bars of soap," reported García.

*   *   *

Another manifestation of the creative civilian life beginning to appear in the Guantánamo tent camps was art, practiced in numerous forms. Every morning Luis Rolando Vázquez would melt plastic food trays with a cigarette lighter. One by one he would put them together, forming a black base on which to begin to carve his small sculptures. "We survive thanks to imagination," said the sculptor.

The camps could not be without music. The trio Los Balseros was the most outstanding of the various groups and soloists; their concerts were held in Alpha Camp. Their repertoire consisted of traditional Latin American and Cuban music, but they also took requests and played by ear. In Alpha Camp, in addition to musicians, painters, and sculptors, there had to be an actor. On holidays or whenever visitors arrived, Juan Bautista Sosa, by popular request, would do his best imitation. Can you guess? Yes, of course, it was Fidel Castro. "I do several imitations, but what everyone requests is Fidel Castro," said Sosa, dressed in the olive-green uniform that characterizes Castro, a long artificial beard, a hat, and even the commander-in-chief's stripes.

The physicians from the Miami Medical Team Foundation who visited Guantánamo on a regular basis to take care of the growing medical and health needs of the refugees, besides seeing a face of Cuba they never knew, made another sensational discovery. They encountered a group of Cuban painters, creating genuine raft-person art, which enchanted and dazzled all of them. The doctors applied for financial and logistical support from the Miami-Dade Public Library System; in this way they were able to rescue the Cuban art made in Guantánamo even as the various artists arrived in the United States. The work of those artists who spent such miserable times at Guantánamo reflects all the tragedies they experienced: rafts, the sea, loneliness, terror, sharks, death, and the hope of protection and help represented by the U.S. flag. That hope and despair is also evident in their works, as explained in the introductory words to the exhibit catalog, written by Nunzio Mainieri.

Juan A. Amaro was born in Havana and studied art at the San Alejandro Art Academy and the Instituto Superior de Arte. His works have been exhibited in private collections in the United States, Puerto Rico, and the Dominican Republic. He considers *La niña del violín (Girl with Violin)* to be one of his best works. It is based on the anecdote of a Cuban girl who went around the refugee camps with the violin she had brought on her raft, playing the U.S. National Anthem, which she had learned by heart from the marines. Amaro conceived the girl as an evocation springing from nature amidst a landscape that includes distant mountains and a dark blue sky with white clouds. The girl's golden hair and her sad, ghostly appearance lend a note of magical realism to the painting, reminiscent of some of the fantastic and surrealistic creations of Marc Chagall and Giorgio de Chirico.

Carlos Aulet was born in Havana in 1962 and studied art at the San Alejandro Art Academy. He made his painting debut in the Guantánamo exposition. His unique vision of the overcrowding of camp life, circumscribed within the fenced environs of the tent camp, is displayed in his painting *The Last Train*. Through an expressionistic conception of camp life, Aulet allows us to feel the overwhelming sensation of claustrophobia and hopeless waiting, represented by five men waiting patiently in their tents for the humanitarian parole that will allow them to reach the paradise of the United States. The five men are presented as marble busts, fixed, motionless, implacable in their prolonged wait, plunged into the dense and suffocating interior of the tent, as if they had been there for centuries. The contrasts of gray and brown, and the pictorial technique of separating the figures and their surroundings into several planes, recall the brushes of Picasso, Braque, and Gris.

Conrado Basulto Romero, born in 1967, began to paint at the age of eighteen while serving in the Cuban military. Because of his natural artistic talent, he was assigned the task of painting portraits of several members of the Political Bureau of the Cuban Communist Party. From his terrible experience at Guantánamo, Basulto drew the material necessary to paint *Hablando duro (Talking tough)*, an unusual painting with mystical overtones. This composition presents a perspective of the infinite that goes beyond the clouds and allows one to see God shedding tears of pain amidst a circle of dark clouds. In the lower strata of the painting the author shows us bodies of newborn children floating, suspended in a sort of timeless limbo, a symbolic allusion to the lack of definition of nationality to which children born in the Guantánamo and Panama camps are subjected, as no government agreed to give them citizenship. The final circle of this Dantesque representation is occupied by the tranquil landscape of the mountains and the Caribbean, which, like an enormous calm lake, provides a sharp contrast to the rest of the infernal vision of children moving in space with their umbilical cords floating adrift.

Bernardo D. Caballero (Lele) was born in 1968 and studied at the School of Art Education in Havana. His work *Genesis* has the bright colors of pop painting. Lele uses this to give us his unique vision of the U.S. flag, presented as a hood covering something like a voluminous shapeless body painted red, on whose extremities there appear rolls of thick barbed wire. In its left hand, the body holds the Torch of Freedom, whose flames permit the viewer to see, in the background, a wall of shadows, painted in strong expressionistic tones ranging from yellow to mustard, from gray to magenta.

Omar Esquivel, born in 1963, founded the Hard Times Gallery at Guantánamo. His painting *Hard Times* uses one of the best-known symbols of the United States, the bald eagle, to offer his testimony of the refugees' experience at Guantánamo. Esquivel's eagle is huge; its open wings shelter a heterogenous humanity: tents, fences, watchtowers, armed soldiers, couples embracing in secret . . . At the height of the eagle's white neck feathers, a plane flies toward a distant city. Its skyscrapers and suspension bridges blend perfectly into a vast sea where rafts float adrift. Helicopters move above the waters, searching for those lost at sea. The late afternoon sky warns of an imminent storm. Esquivel's bright metallic colors, and the sharp, hyperrealistic vision of the eagle, make this painting one of the most powerful in the Guantánamo exposition.

Finally, Armando Mejías, born in 1961, graduated from the San Alejandro Art Academy. He left Cuba with his wife and daughter in 1994, arriving in the United States on March 8, 1995, after spending several months at Guantánamo. Mejías' painting, titled *Price of Freedom,* is a strongly autobiographical piece. In it, a solitary man and woman, dressed in rags, face a tempestuous sea. They are on a raft, and are trying to pull the unconscious body of another traveler aboard. The sea and sky are painted in strong dark green tones, while in the distance the sun shines its last rays on the water, creating a thick layering of colors, a mixture of red, orange, green, and black, in a multi-colored totality that translates desperation and death and would make Munch's famous expressionistic painting *The Scream* green with envy.

᧙ ᧙ ᧙

This account of civilian life on the arid plains of the Guantánamo camps would not be complete without reference to religion. In the refugee camps there was a Catholic church and a Protestant church. But many detainees also had their small syncretic altar on which the Catholic deities met the unique vision of *santería*. A remarkable altar, containing no crosses or images of Christ, but never without the figure of Saint Lazarus, with his ulcerated skin and his crutch under his arm, or the dark image of the Virgin of la Caridad del Cobre, or the popular Virgin of Regla. In addition to all these deities, many refugees believed that the best protection they could possess was Elegguá, the god that paves or clears the way. For shows and festivals, the detainees selected a group of dancers to play the role of the African goddesses. "The camp transvestites, a group of gays, have helped us with costumes and choreography for the show," said one of the festival organizers. Luis Martínez, who identified himself as La Colorá, played Obatalá. "She's my goddess," said Martínez, who assisted in making the costumes. "We've all been able to work on this, thanks to the help of the U.S. military women, who have given us material, makeup, and everything we've needed." In the camp the transvestites are known as the "Brown Sugar Girls," and they live in a separate cabin near the beach. Benito Martínez, nicknamed La Rumbera, stated that although initially they experienced discrimination, they had finally gained the understanding of the heterosexuals in the camp. "But we always prayed to the gods, and now the others have realized that we are useful, and they treat us like the women of the camp," stated Martínez (La Colorá), his face made up and his fingernails painted red. In the cabin full of women's clothing, a sewing machine, and the rest of the costumes for the show, there stood an Elegguá behind the door. "We have to be protected," declared La Colorá.

Although many detainees were able to bring their Elegguá, others were not able to get their holy protectors onto their rafts. During U.S. Navy rescue operations to try to save the more than thirty thousand Cubans who left the island on rafts in August, most of the refugees lost their saints. But Omar Madruga, the only *babalao* in Alpha Camp, managed to load all his saints on his raft and escape the island, where he was rescued at sea by an enormous U.S. Navy destroyer. Once again, he found a way to get his precious load of Afro-Cuban saints aboard. "I left Cuba with all my warriors aboard," Madruga told reporters. "I brought Orula, Odduá, Elegguá. I know I was really lucky, because many *santeros* were forced to throw their saints overboard." In his cabin, Madruga carefully showed reporters the stands where his Afro-Cuban saints were kept. But his religion would not allow them to be photographed. "The saints cannot be photographed," insisted Madruga, wearing a necklace of yellow beads and a small white beret.

Meanwhile, in Miami, Rigoberto Zamora, director of International Yoruba Rights, an organization dedicated to protecting the rights of *santería* and Afro-Cuban religions, said that he was willing to send religious aid to the *santeros* at Guantánamo. "We can send them the oracle. An *ecuele,* so they can consult," stated Zamora. In the jargon of *santeros* and *babalaos,* an *ecuele* is a chain strung with small coconuts, used to read the oracle. "The *ecuele* is a great help for the *santeros* because it's the only thing that can make the future clear for you," explained Zamora. With or without the assistance of the *ecuele,* a rumor was spreading through the tents in late April 1995. More than a rumor, a premonition that something important was about to happen surfaced amidst solitary prayers, invocations to Elegguá, and divination with multicolored shells tossed into the divining circle.

What could it be?

The news ricocheted from ear to ear among the thousands of Cubans in the Guantánamo camps, and it is very probable that its echo crossed the sea to the tent fortresses of the Panama, Grand Cayman, and Bahamas camps. In an unexpected turnabout—as radical as the policy change implemented in mid-August 1994—the U.S. government announced on Tuesday, May 2, 1995, that it would take in most of the Guantánamo detainees and would thenceforth immediately deport to Cuba those interdicted in the future.

The joint agreement between Washington and Havana, announced by Attorney General Janet Reno, provoked an angry reaction in Miami and obvious disagreement from top officials in charge of Cuban matters at the State Department, who requested transfers to other areas. "Cubans must understand that the only way to enter the United States is by applying for entry from Cuba," said Reno during a press conference in Washington. Reno said that by virtue of the accord, the Cuban government would accept back any raft people who wanted to return, as well as those ineligible to enter the United States for health reasons or due to a criminal record. And any Cubans arriving illegally at Guantánamo after Tuesday, May 2, would be deported.

The joint agreement had been secretly negotiated in New York and Toronto by Peter Tarnoff, assistant political affairs secretary at the State Department, and Ricardo Alarcón, president of the Cuban National Assembly. The secret negotiations were begun during the fourth round of immigration conversations between Cuba and the United States in mid-April. Dennis Hays, coordinator of Cuban Affairs at the State Department, who headed the U.S. delegation at the immigration talks, was not informed of the other negotiations. When news of the accord was made public on May 2, Hays and Nancy Mason, assistant coordinator of the Cuban Affairs Office, requested transfers to other positions within the State Department.

According to State Department political adviser Richard Nuccio, "The agreement involves an unprecedented level of cooperation. This is a recognition that, in order to resolve some problems, it is necessary to negotiate with the Cuban government." For his part, Ricardo Alarcón, head of the Cuban delegation, indicated, "As in all good agreements, both sides win."

Gabriel García Márquez also expressed his opinion regarding the problematic accord: "The agreement evidences a true change in the U.S. government's attitude toward Cuba. Cuban raft people are no longer going to be considered heroes. The accord puts an end to the calamitous situation of indignity of the Cubans detained at Guantánamo. The raft people crisis occurred because the United States did not keep its old commitment to issue twenty thousand visas per year to Cubans who wish to leave the island."

On the other side, the opinion of Miami city administrator and *ad hoc* group member César Odio stood out among those who did not agree with the new measures. "We are against any agreement with the Cuban government," he stated. Congressman Lincoln Díaz-Balart felt obligated to issue this reminder: "Never has there been an agreement with a Communist dictatorship for the systematic return of refugees. The Berlin Wall has fallen, but now there is a wall in the White House."

Ileana Ros-Lehtinen said that the agreement was a huge setback in efforts to bring democracy to Cuba. "It's incredible and lamentable. It undoes thirty-five years of recognition that Cubans should be granted certain rights."

José Basulto, president of Brothers to the Rescue, used harsh words in referring to the accord: "It is repugnant and tragic. We will not be aerial informants for the Coast Guard. We will not turn refugees over to the Cuban government."

What interests had mobilized to cause things to change, practically overnight? In the talks between Cuba and the United States on immigration matters, it seemed that anything could be achieved except a satisfactory agreement. What could have caused those talks to change course suddenly and both nations to sign a pact after whirlwind secret conversations? According to some analysts, the coinciding of interests among influential sectors of the White House and the Pentagon made the radical policy change possible. According to the same source, Morton Halperin and Tony Lake, members of the National Security Council, who along with State Department political adviser Peter Tarnoff favored a normalization of relations with Cuba, had found support for their positions among high Pentagon officials. These Pentagon officials, "powerful and cautious," sought to avoid U.S. military involvement in Cuba at all costs. They felt that such involvement could be provoked by two causes: (1) a mass exodus; or (2) a civil conflict, both possible consequences of the deepening political and economic crisis on the island. According to analysts, the White House found a strong ally in these judgments by important Defense Department officials.

As had happened so many other times during the "raft people crisis," an unexpected event again complicated the situation further. On Thursday, May 4, 1995, thirteen Cubans traveling in two small motorboats were rescued forty-five miles south of Little Cayman Island by the cruise ship *Majesty of the Seas,* said Coast Guard spokesman Dan Waldschmidt. The raft people had left Camagüey several days earlier, and when they were rescued, they asked the ship's captain for political asylum. The ship, flying the Norwegian flag, was owned by Royal

Caribbean Cruise Lines of Miami. According to reporters, the raft people would be transferred from the cruise ship to a U.S. Coast Guard
cutter, which would turn them back over to Cuban authorities.

Miriam Malpica, mother of one of the raft people, said on Friday,
May 5, in Miami that she would not permit the Coast Guard to detain
her son. Her twenty-nine-year-old son held an advanced degree and
had been trying to leave Cuba for years. "I lost my daughter ten years
ago in Cuba, because the Cuban government would not give her permission to travel to Miami, even though she was very sick," said
Malpica. Mrs. Malpica, age fifty-two, employed in a Miami factory,
stated that her son would not be a public charge. Hours after talking to
the *Nuevo Herald,* she collapsed and was taken to Panamerican Hospital in Miami.

Shortly after the interdiction of a boat carrying several Cuban
refugees, four Brothers to the Rescue planes set out again on Saturday,
May 6, in search of more raft people in the ever-tumultuous waters of
the Florida Straits. The pilots not only wanted to find survivors; they
also scanned the horizon in search of U.S. government officials. Part of
their new role: to witness the U.S. Coast Guard's surrender of raft people to Cuban patrol boats or to Havana authorities. "From now on, we
will be the eyes of the community. Even if we have to enter Cuban air
space," declared José Basulto. In a meeting with his pilots, Basulto
proposed the idea of entering Cuban air space to detect detentions of
raft people. It was optional, but if they agreed to do it, they would bring
back proof of violations.

Hearing that, despite the protests, the U.S. government would return
their relatives detained at sea May 4, Miami residents made strong statements against the new deportation measures. "They sent them back right
away, because they knew we would not be silent, that we would scream,
and, if possible, go get them," declared Miriam Malpica, mother of the
recently repatriated Camilo David Rodríguez. "What this government
has done is inhuman and will be punished by God."

News of the first group of repatriates' return to Cuba was not long
in coming. The returnees were taken to the island aboard the U.S.
Coast Guard cutter *Durable,* which docked at the port of Cabañas, west
of Havana, escorted by a Cuban Navy patrol boat. Six of the thirteen

raft people deported to Cuba stated soon afterward that they and their relatives had been harassed by Cuban State Security since they returned to their homes. "They've stationed an Interior Ministry officer in front of our house," said Ulises Cabalé, one of the repatriated raft people, in an interview with the *Nuevo Herald.*

Jorge Acevedo, age seventeen, was one of the raft people repatriated on Friday, May 12. One month later, in an interview with a foreign journalist, Acevedo reported that he feared for his life if he remained in Cuba. He hoped the U.S. government would grant him a humanitarian visa. "My life is a shambles. They watch me on every corner; they pursue me. I am constantly fleeing." The State Department was studying Acevedo's case, and the possibility of granting him a humanitarian visa. "A final decision has not yet been made," said a State Department spokesman who asked to remain anonymous. A week earlier, Acevedo had left his home in Caibarién and begun hiding in a nearby wood. Friends and relatives were taking him food. Acevedo explained that he decided it was necessary to go into hiding when two State Security agents attempted to detain him as he was going to a nearby store to buy cigarettes. "If they caught me, they were going to give it to me harder than the other time," said Acevedo. "Before I left Cuba, they were harassing me, saying that I was leaving the country because my father stole a boat. But since I returned, it's worse."

Five days after being deported, young Acevedo was detained by Officer José Antonio (Tony) Martínez, chief of the Caibarién sector of the National Revolutionary Police. According to Acevedo, the police beat him, kicked him, and sprayed mace into his face. In May, Officer Martínez confirmed that Acevedo was beaten, and stated that the young man was transferred to the police station because there was an outstanding warrant for his arrest from the provincial tribunal. On that occasion, Martínez said that no superior officer had told them the repatriates could not be mistreated.

The news that, as of May 2, 1995, Cuban raft people captured at sea by the U.S. Coast Guard would be immediately returned to Cuba, was taken seriously by the main political commentators in the Cuban exile community. Analysts Carlos Alberto Montaner and Agustín Tamargo published editorials on the subject in the *Nuevo Herald* in the days following.

Commentator Carlos Alberto Montaner, in his article "Cuba and USA: The Conflict Continues the Same," stated:

> The Comandante, like everyone else, read in the papers that Clinton's modest objective regarding Cuba was "to not have problems with Castro." And as a good tactic, the old dictator deduced that if he wanted to modify Washington's policy toward Havana, all he had to do was create those new problems for the occupant of the White House, and then eliminate them in exchange for the concessions he wished to obtain. What were those concessions? In the first place, something that turned out to be indispensable after the disappearance of the USSR: a lifting of the economic embargo and the normalization of relations with the U.S. government without having to make political changes and without negotiating the transition to democracy with the internal or external opposition. Castro's sending the raft people to Florida in the summer of 1994 is part of this general vision, but Castro's calculations turned out to be partially incorrect. As Castro had supposed, Clinton did not resort to force or military reprisals to stop the exodus but, surprisingly, he did not sit down at the negotiating table to discuss global matters either. His response was limited to detaining the raft people at Guantánamo in the hope that they would return to Cuba voluntarily. Clinton was also convinced that this measure would serve to discourage other Cubans from leaving the island on rafts. Naturally, Clinton's two presumptions were wrong: Ninety-five percent of the detainees preferred to remain at Guantánamo indefinitely rather than return to Cuba, and many others were willing to suffer the same fate of detention at Guantánamo in order to leave Castro's "paradise." So a strange tie had occurred: Neither Havana nor Washington achieved its goals, but Castro was in a better playing position. He could throw his migratory bomb again at any time, since Clinton, a stubbornly fainthearted man, planned only to expand the Guantánamo camps in response to that hostile act. He had already planned for another 30,000 people, but no one in his administration had the slightest idea what they would do with raft person number 60,001.

With these cards in its hand for two months, the Cuban government began to threaten and give indications that it could again resort to sending huge numbers of refugees if its requests for a comprehensive, direct dialogue received no response. Washington took careful note of the blackmail, but the presidential advisers immediately divided themselves between those who prescribed a hard line and those who proposed conciliation and appeasement. The latter, nearer Clinton's heart, were those who negotiated the announced agreement. Where are we now? Apparently, both sides got what they wanted. At least that's what they're saying. Castro began a sort of dialogue with Washington, which he is now attempting to deepen using an elementary syllogism articulated as follows: if the White House does not want riots and a flood of Cuban exiles, it will have to alleviate the economic situation on the island and reduce tensions; ergo, the reasonable thing to do is to lift unconditionally the embargo, normalize relations, and abandon the adversarial posture now held by both countries. . . .

Cubans don't rebel because they can't, not because they have other, better options. Throughout history, with the exception of the present, Cubans have chosen to rebel rather than flee. And that change is due not to a sudden decrease in their bravery but rather to the scrupulousness, cruelty, and extraordinary efficiency of the repressive apparatus.

In synthesis, we are still on approximately the same page in the penultimate chapter, with nothing substantial having changed.

Commentator Agustín Tamargo stated his position on the matter in an article titled "Parable of Infamy":

The U.S. Coast Guard is turning over not people but principles. And in the forefront, the most important one of all: resistance to tyranny. The international moral doctrine of the United States was at its lowest point that day. There in Cabañas, in that dark hour, with the harsh reality of the situation, President Clinton was telling Cubans: "Don't count on us anymore. Get used to the tyranny however you can, because to us it is no longer tyranny. Whitewash the blood on the execution walls, paint the bars of the political prison, bury your dead, and swallow your cries of pain. Everything we have said and done to the contrary for the last thirty-six years has passed into oblivion. On this side of the Florida Straits the sun continues to shine as if nothing happened . . ." Clinton's decision to return forcibly to tyranny those who flee it ends one chapter and begins another, as Ricardo Alarcón, who should know better than anyone, declared in Havana. It ends the era of confrontation and begins the era of collaboration. If there were a traditional government in Cuba, this would not matter much. Washington has almost always supported traditional Cuban governments, and even those that weren't. But today this is something else; this is a tyranny, still militarily powerful, attempting to force itself on eleven million frightened beings who detest it . . . Does the book end here? No. One act ends, but others are still to come. Who will play the leading role in those coming acts? Who will it be? Obviously, not Clinton or Morton Halperin, nor Chiles, nor Tarnoff, but the Cuban people. Abandoned once again, the Cuban people will have to redouble their efforts now to prevent their freedom from being taken from them again . . .

The climax of the raft people crisis was represented by the statistic of some 31,500 people who fled the island for the United States in a period of only five weeks—between August 7 and September 14, 1994. This number is almost ten times the total number (3,656) who departed on rafts in all of 1993. To have an idea of the progressive increase in clandestine departures that at one point becomes exorbitant, it is necessary to take note of the qualitative changes produced as the month of August 1994 approached: 1989: 319 raft people; 1990: 457; 1991: 2,203; 1992: 2,557; 1993: 3,656; 1994: 37,145.

This is the greatest concentrated exodus that has occurred in Cuba since 1959, when an armed revolution, directed by Fidel Castro, overthrew the mediocre dictatorship of Fulgencio Batista and established a single-party Marxist-Leninist regime supported—back then—by the Soviet Union.

In statistical terms, the most significant years of previous migratory exodi were: 1959: 449 people; 1960-62: 196,111; 1963-64: 24,992; 1965-72: 352,806; 1973-79: 21,178; 1980: 141,742; 1981-89: 84,147.

Approximately one million Cubans abandoned their country over thirty-six years, employing the most diverse means of transportation, from ultramodern jets to the most insignificant rafts constructed of inner tubes and propelled by sails made of tattered sheets and underwear.

~~ ~~ ~~

What remained of the Guantánamo camps after May 1995, when unpredictable fate decided the destiny and order of priorities for the refugees' departure?

On Saturday, January 6, 1996, the *Nuevo Herald* reported that as of January 31, the Guantánamo camps, which once housed more than thirty-two thousand people, would be closed. The last raft person was leaving for Miami, approximately 525 days after the Clinton government had announced that they would never reach the United States.

At the moment the announcement was made, there were fewer than two thousand refugees on the base; another two thousand had returned to Cuba. The remaining twenty-eight thousand raft people had traveled silently to U.S. territory on weekly flights to an air base outside of Miami. The cost of detaining the thousands of raft people at Guantánamo for a year and a half was estimated at a million dollars a day. The total expense for the delay, then, came to more than five hundred million dollars from U.S. taxpayers.

The Guantánamo base again became the subject of scandal when the news broke that about twenty-six refugees who had arrived at the base after the signing of the May 2 accords were in grave danger of being returned to Cuba against their will.

The level of desperation was so great that one of the refugees ran out into the biggest mine field in the world, and threatened to blow himself to bits if the authorities did not grant him political asylum. Several U.S. soldiers convinced the man to return to the camp unharmed, but to avoid future problems, he was placed in protective custody. Some refugees misunderstood this status, believing it to be the equivalent of political asylum. As a result, they threatened drastic action in order to obtain release from the camps. "I am terrified of what might happen," said a military spokesman familiar with the situation. "I was horrified by what I saw there."

The refugees who reached the base after May 2 were finally deported. "It makes me sick. I am extremely disappointed," said New Jersey Representative Robert Torricelli, who had fought hard against deportations. His hope had been that a dramatic letter he sent to INS Commissioner Doris Meissner might forestall the deportations.

The closing of the Guantánamo camps also affected high-ranking State Department officials. Richard Nuccio was Clinton's adviser during the brief period of time when there seemed to exist a diplomatic rapprochement between Cuba and the United States. In mid-April 1996, Nuccio, surrendering to the evidence of the comments circulating in the carpeted State Department hallways indicating that he would very soon be replaced, submitted his resignation. When questioned by reporters, Nuccio stated that it was a purely personal decision, based on a commitment he had made to himself after a visit to Cuba in 1994. At that time, seeing the living conditions of the Cuban people, he decided he would not encourage the imposition of more economic sanctions against the Castro government if it was not possible to offer greater support to the population. "It was no longer possible to maintain a balance between sanctions against the Castro regime and support for the Cuban population," declared Nuccio. In conclusion, he added that the saddest aspect of the Cuban situation was that, in order to wound the government, it was necessary to hurt the eleven million Cubans Castro was holding hostage.

For his part, State Department official Dennis Hays, who had directed the second round of immigration negotiations with Cuba and publicly defended the right of the Cubans at Guantánamo to enter the United States, received an international press prize for the position he assumed during the conflict. Currently, Hays is quite far removed from secret political meetings in Washington, holding a diplomatic position in Surinam.

Will the Cuban refugees ever be able to forget what they suffered at Guantánamo?

Gerardo Alfonzo Piquera was detained at Guantánamo for fifteen months. Minutes before boarding the plane that would take him to Miami, his last act as a refugee at the camp was to leave a permanent record of his stay at the Officers' Club, so the memories would not be erased too soon. He chose an area of the wall by the dance floor in Rick's Lounge in the Bayview Club. The painting shows a raft, a torso with wings nailed to a post, and a barbed-wire fence. With this design, he won the contest in which seven artists competed to represent symbolically the odyssey experienced by thousands of raft people over the previous two years. Taking his leave, Cuban artist and raft person Alfonzo Piquera had the great idea, in addition to hanging the symbol of the raft people on one of the walls of the Officers' Club, of writing a slogan to accompany the recently created emblem of the refugees: "The price of freedom is the fair value of life."

When the waves tire of beating and biting the coral reef that resists their advance toward the coast, this produces undertow, which is nothing more than the slow, deliberate retreat of the waves following their frenzied beating of the steep, rocky shore. Among the waves float jellyfish, seaweed, sand stirred up from the ocean bottom, pieces of coral, tiny bits of the reef, fish crushed by the violent whirlpool of foamy water, squashed crabs. And above all this shapeless mass reigns the wind, which, with its continuous gusts, tosses the wave back onto the calm sand of the beach, causing an endless rolling, continuous advances and retreats, a world of infinite undertows.

The southeastern coast of Cuba at Guantánamo is no exception to the universal movement of the tides. There, the Caribbean, like the Mediterranean Sea, or the Red Sea, or the Baltic Sea, causes any human being, faced with its immense grandeur, to recite nostalgically, with French poet Paul Valéry:

La mer, la mer, toujours recommencee . . .

The sea, the sea, forever starting and re-starting . . .

Could there be a more appropriate metaphor than the undertow to explain events at Guantánamo in 1995 and their worldwide repercussions?

Chapter X
Cessna 337 is not Responding

FEBRUARY 24, 1895, IS ONE OF the most significant dates in the history of the Cuban nation and people. That is the day the second Cuban war of independence began. Paradoxically, this new war was not led, like the prior one, by large landowners like Carlos Manuel de Céspedes, Ignacio Agramonte, or Francisco Vicente Aguilera. Rather, it was conducted by intellectual leaders from the small, semi-ruined *bourgeoisie,* like young Havanan José Martí—then in exile in the United States— and mulatto Juan Gualberto Gómez. They were supported in this formidable task by two old military leaders with dozens of battles under their belts, and hundreds of scars spread like infinite puzzles over the entire geography of their bodies: Dominican General Máximo Gómez and Cuban mulatto General Antonio Maceo.

The first war of independence, Cuba against Spain, had lasted ten years, from 1868 to 1878. It left the island almost depopulated, deep in a ruin of fright, and with independence still not achieved. The second, begun on February 24, 1895, would end three years later, in July of 1898, with the first great military intervention of the United States in the Caribbean, to displace Spain once and for all as a hegemonic nation. Cubans, then, time and again throughout the nineteenth century and also the twentieth, saw their yearned-for independence postponed, or frustrated, or relegated to the storehouse of past centuries, or to the remote possibility of hope of a future time.

❧ ❧ ❧

On Saturday, February 24, 1996, a hundred and one years after the start of Cuba's second war of independence, three Cessna 337s were warming up in an isolated hangar at Opa-Locka Airport outside Miami. On the walls of the hangar hung rafts, canteens, and numerous other trophies of the work the group of pilots had been doing for years. The planes belonged to Brothers to the Rescue, an organization that since May 1991 had dedicated itself to the task of rescuing raft people in the Florida Straits. Their mission: to fly over international waters near the western coast of Cuba. Miami reporters who had followed the missionary labor of Brothers to the Rescue estimated at two thousand the number of flights logged in a little less than five years. This would be, then, approximately flight number 2001 and, paradoxically, like in Stanley Kubrick's famous movie from the 1960s, the flight would become *2001: A Space Odyssey.*

José Basulto boarded the N2506 Cessna 337 with Arnaldo Iglesias, who would be his copilot. Arnaldo Iriondo and his wife, Silvia, president of the Mothers' Movement Against Repression in Cuba, got into the back seat. Carlos Costa and Pablo Morales were flying the legendary Spirit of Miami, a blue-and-white plane donated by American Airlines in recognition of the humanitarian work of Brothers to the Rescue. In the third plane, also a blue-and-white Cessna, donated by singer Willie Chirino, traveled pilot Mario de la Peña and observer Armando Alejandre. The Cessna Skymasters planes are 29.9 feet long and 9.2 feet high, with a wing span of 38.2 feet; their cruising speed is 195 miles per hour, and their range is 1,140 miles. José Basulto, the leader of the group, was the last to take off. Flying low over the sea in an intensely blue sky, the three planes proceeded slowly over Miami Beach and headed southeast.

Ten days before the hundred-and-first anniversary of the beginning of Cuba's second war of independence, the Consejo Nacional Coordinador de Concilio Cubano (National Coordinating Board of the Cuban Council), a recently formed Cuban dissident group, ratified the announcement of a national meeting on February 24. The group had met, secretly, for the first time on February 10, and planned the event, despite the fact that they did not have the authorization of the Cuban government. "We aren't defying the government; we are just exercising our rights as citizens."

The council was made up of twenty-eight members from different organizations and regions, twenty-one of whom attended the meeting. Through a direct and secret vote, the delegates elected Leonel Morejón Almagro as national delegate of the council. Also elected as council members of honor were veteran opposition leaders Gustavo Arcos Bergnes, Elizardo Sánchez, and Osvaldo Paya. The council also agreed to contact Pope John Paul II, United Nations Secretary General Boutros Boutros-Ghali, and the Martin Luther King Center, requesting that they intercede before the Cuban government, asking it to provide a place for the meeting.

In late December 1995, the organizers of the council sent a letter to the Council of State requesting permission to hold the national meeting. In early February, just as preparations for the meeting were being completed, Leonel Morejón Almagro received a letter from the Council of State signed by Minerva Valdés Temprana, head of the Department of Attention to the Population, stating: "Just to let you know that we have received your documents at this office."

To many of the dissidents, the late and enigmatic official response—acknowledgment of receipt, according to others—meant assuming as the next step a risky plan of "all or nothing."

Foreign embassy officials in Havana and international journalists who closely followed the development of dissidence in Cuba agreed that, with the creation of the Cuban Council, Castro's opponents had ceased being isolated in fifty separate groups and were now a consistent internal opposition force. According to these same sources, the council's decision to hold the meeting with or without official permission would put the Castro government in the dilemma of either tolerating the meeting and thereby ceding political space to the opposition, or stopping it by force, thereby endangering the cooperation agreement being negotiated with the European Union.

As additional information about the earlier clandestine meeting, a foreign diplomat in Havana stated that the dissidents met under strict discretionary measures "in an apartment with which very few were familiar." Once the participants entered the place, no one could leave until the meeting ended; it lasted from 9 A.M. until 7 P.M. "There was some fear in the air, given the possibility that the police might show up to stop the meeting. It might seem contradictory to be so careful about holding a completely peaceful meeting, but that is the reality of this country," said Julio Martínez, the only reporter from an independent Cuban news agency authorized to attend the meeting.

And the dissident reporter's words rang true when, a few days later, six dissidents were arrested and the homes of other opposition leaders were raided by State Security agents.

Shortly after noon, the three planes were over the Caribbean. The original objective of the mission was to fly to the Bahamas to carry food and supplies to the camp of more than two hundred Cubans stranded in Nassau. But on February 22, the government of the Bahamas had denied permission for the visit. Although the official communiqué did not express it, Brothers to the Rescue knew that the reason for the denial was that there was a Cuban government delegation in the Bahamas, coordinating the details for repatriation of the refugees. Unable to fly to the Bahamas, the group decided to conduct one more reconnaissance mission over the Florida Straits, former scene of the mass exodus of raft people.

The 24th parallel was in sight. Moments before leaving the hangar at Opa-Locka Airport, Basulto had decided to delay his takeoff to wait for a man who had important information to offer him. The man was a mechanic employed by the company that repaired the Brothers to the Rescue planes. The previous day, Basulto had found out that the mechanic had had to make an emergency landing at a military airport in Pinar del Río—in western Cuba—when the plane he was flying from Costa Rica to Miami had engine trouble. Cuban intelligence officers had approached the mechanic and asked him about Basulto and his organization. Basulto asked the mechanic to tell his version of the facts again, and he recorded it, but did not consider it cause for concern. "Nothing out of the ordinary," he told his companions. The departure was further delayed for unknown reasons. Basulto looked around and noticed that fellow pilot Juan Pablo Roque was missing. No one asked about him, but Basulto remembered the conversation they had had two days earlier.

"He called, very worried, saying that he wanted to tell me something, that he wanted an appointment with me," recalled Basulto. "I said 'Fine, come over to the house.' He arrived very early, and seemed a little upset. He told me we were making a mistake by supporting the Cuban Council. I didn't consider the conversation very important, because it seemed that what he was telling me was irrelevant. Roque was there to tell us that we should be very careful because Sebastián Arcos and that whole group were completely infiltrated and that we were taking a risk with that, and that we might be sorry in the future. I responded by thanking him." Basulto believed, although he was not certain, that in this conversation he informed Roque of the overfly operation he would carry out the following Saturday, February 24. Although Roque at times had commented that these operations were very risky, this time he made no comment.

On Tuesday, February 13, Brothers to the Rescue had sent economic aid to the Cuban Council for the financing of the first national meeting on February 24. During a press conference in the Chapel of Charity in Miami, Basulto gave dissident Sebastián Arcos Bergnes a check for an undisclosed amount that would be sent to the Cuban Council. "Cuban Council is a process that could bring change to Cuba, change through nonviolent means. It is our duty to come to the rescue of the process," said Basulto on that occasion. Sebastián Arcos, vice president of the Cuban Human Rights Committee, had left Cuba in late 1995 upon his release from prison and traveled to Miami to undergo cancer surgery. He would be charged with the task of taking the money to Cuba through "safe and discreet channels."

꧁ ꧁ ꧁

The pilots' wristwatches showed that it was 3 P.M.; the day was still blue, beautiful, and brilliant. José Basulto turned on his flight recorder and established contact with Cuban air traffic control. "November Five Four Eight Five Sierra. Good day. Crossing Parallel 24 at this moment. We will be in the area five hours." Havana Center: "Received. Verify responder code."

Three days before Basulto's flight, in Havana, the National Coordinating Board of the Cuban Council had agreed to postpone the February 24 meeting in light of governmental repression against its members. This also occurred one day before the mysterious disappearance of Juan Pablo Roque, a pilot who had deserted the Cuban Air Force and later became a member of Brothers to the Rescue.

On Sunday, February 18, 1996, Lieutenant Colonel Arístides Gómez of the Cuban Interior Ministry had personally informed the dissidents' director Gustavo Arcos Bergnes, secretary general of the Cuban Human Rights Committee, of the Cuban government's decision to prohibit the meeting of the opposition group scheduled for February 24. The government's decision was revealed at a time when most of the opposition coalition leaders had been detained.

The U.S. State Department issued a statement regarding the numerous detentions, stating that "this wave of arrests is among the largest that the regime has carried out in recent years. . . . This latest repressive wave demonstrates dramatically that the regime is incapable of initiating a process of political reforms, and its determination to maintain absolute control over Cuban society." From Cuba, several sources close to the dissidents estimated at eighty to one hundred the number of persons detained.

For its part, the Cuban government, in response to the State Department's statement, accused the U.S. government of organizing and financing the meeting called by the opposition alliance. "Any attempt to interfere in internal matters, any attempt to subjugate the sovereignty of the Cuban people, will not be permitted," stated Foreign Ministry spokesperson Marianela Ferriol. Ferriol, answering reporters' questions during the usual Thursday press conference at the Cuban Ministry of Foreign Affairs, said that the Cuban Council's meeting was "organized, preconceived, sponsored, and financed by the U.S. government. . . . This will never be permitted in our country."

As he always did while flying near Cuba, Basulto scanned the horizon for signs of tiny dots on the wide sea. He could not help but remember the days when the search for raft people began. What drove him to do something was the death of a young raft person, found still alive on a worn and deflated raft; Basulto wanted to prevent similarly tragic endings. Several friends approached him with the idea of doing something to rescue raft people at sea. U.S. pilot Billy Schuss suggested going out with fishing boats from Key West. But that idea was never put into practice. "That would not have worked," said Basulto. At that time, Basulto was assisting with preparations for the Brotherhood Flotilla, a maritime caravan in international waters near Cuba to celebrate May 20, Independence Day. "What better than to conduct a rescue after identifying a problem?" said Basulto. Deciding on the name was easy: Brothers, for the brotherhood they demonstrate, and Rescue, for the task they would carry out. It was also a way of demonstrating to the world how desperate Cubans were to escape from the economic and political calamities of the island. From the moment of its establishment on May 13, 1991, the multinational group of pilots known as Brothers to the Rescue became the wings that would give freedom to the raft people. For their relatives, the organization represented the hope that their loved ones would be found alive at sea.

But early in May 1995, when Brothers to the Rescue was about to celebrate its fourth birthday, the U.S. government signed the migratory accord with Cuba that ended the indefinite detention of Cubans at Guantánamo but also mandated that future raft people be returned to Cuba. As a corollary to the abrupt change in U.S. policy toward the raft people, the Brothers to the Rescue pilots decided to change their role. On May 5, 1995, three days after the announcement of the policy change, José Basulto stated to the press: "Now we have to act as the eyes of our community. Pilots now have instructions to keep an eye on Cuban and U.S. waters with two main goals: (a) to help any raft person sighted; and (b) to document the repatriations announced on Tuesday by Attorney General Janet Reno. We will be the community's eyes. Even if we have to enter Cuban air space. It's optional, but if you want to do so, it's fine . . ." Basulto told the pilots in an emergency meeting on May 4. "We must bring back proof. We want to bring back pictures. Soon our planes will be equipped with cameras and audio and video tape recorders. We will have to learn new techniques. We want all of you to become good photographers," Basulto harangued his pilots.

When the change in U.S. policy was announced on May 2, Brothers to the Rescue had increased their flights and were preparing for "raft people season," that is, the summer months in which the number of clandestine departures usually grew. At that time, the pilots still cooperated with the U.S. Coast Guard, although some opposed it, as it meant sending other Cubans to Guantánamo. But as of May 2, if Brothers to the Rescue located a raft person, they did not call the Coast Guard immediately. First they dropped water and food, along with a note: "If the Coast Guard picks you up, you may be turned over to Cuban authorities." Then, the raft person was asked to choose. If the craft seemed seaworthy and there was no need for medical attention on board—the pilots were asked to judge for themselves—they could decide to allow the travelers to continue their journey on their own.

How many would die? How many would be saved? How many would be forcibly repatriated? It was sad, but no one dared respond.

Such was the state of mind at the Brothers to the Rescue hangar at Opa-Locka Airport. Expressions like "abandoned and betrayed" were heard everywhere. José Basulto, head of the pilots, felt that as long as there were funds, though dwindling, Brothers to the Rescue would continue flying, though probably fewer hours. "From now on, things will be done by surprise. We want to be up there when they're not expecting us. We want to take everyone by surprise. Our missions can be rescue missions again, like before, if another change in U.S. policy occurs. Remember, no one was going to get out of Guantánamo," concluded Basulto.

Between February 5 and 9 of 1996, an extraordinary event was occurring in Cuba: a group of top U.S. Army officers was visiting the island as guests of Cuban Army chief of staff, General Ulises Rosales del Toro. The reason for the invitation to Cuba was to demonstrate the self-defense capabilities of the country and to create an opening at the level of the military in hopes of improving relations. When Soviet troops left the island in 1991, Cuban military leaders realized that it would now be up to them to protect the Revolution, the country, and its independence, and that they would have to do so with a fraction of the enormous budgets they had in the past. Within the global strategy designed by top Cuban military commanders, the United States continued to be clearly identified as the most powerful of all potential enemies. In accord with this strategy, all calculations would be made on the basis of a sudden assault in which the United States would employ the best and most sophisticated technology in its power. The U.S.'s quick strikes in Grenada, Panama, and Kuwait became the various "threat models" in the "possible future war scenarios" that the Cuban military studied conscientiously. According to the words of General Ulises Rosales during the meeting with the U.S. military officers: "Cuba would never make the mistake Saddam Hussein did, of leaving equipment out in the open where it could be destroyed by laser-guided bombs . . . U.S. bombers would never find their targets on the ground. What's more, the war would not be a duel between armed forces, but a 'war of all the people,' in which millions of Cubans would participate . . ."

During the meeting with U.S. officials, Cuban General Rosales stated: "Human intelligence is more powerful than the artificial intelligence of high technology. . . . And in the end, the invaders would have to get out of their planes and boats and fight on land, man to man."

Former Admiral Eugene Carroll, part of the mission of former U.S. military and diplomatic officials who visited the nuclear plant under construction in Juraguá in early February, said that a Cuban general had asked him: "What would happen if we shot down one of the planes that violate our air space?" Carroll told the press that the Cubans' interest in this matter was so noticeable to him that, upon his return to the United States, he informed the appropriate contacts in the Pentagon.

The three Cessna 337s were flying very close to Cuban territorial waters. José Basulto felt euphoric at the excellent weather conditions that allowed him to see the city of Havana in the distance, wrapped in brilliant mid-afternoon clouds. On the planes' radios, the conversation with the Havana Center receiving station had still not ended and was prolonged for several more seconds . . .

PILOT (*possibly Basulto*): Good afternoon, Havana Center. November Two Five Zero Six greets you. Please, we are crossing the 24th Parallel in five minutes, and we will remain in your areas for three or four hours and we are responding One Two Two Two, 500 feet or more.

Havana Center: Received.

Pilot: For your information, Havana Center, our area of operations today is north of Havana. So today we will be in your area and in contact with you. A cordial greeting from Brothers to the Rescue and its president, José Basulto, who is speaking.

Havana Center: Okay. Received, sir. I inform you that the zone north of Havana is activated. You are in danger if you penetrate on side 24 north.

Pilot: We are aware that we are in danger every time we cross the zone south of 24, but we are ready to do so. It is our situation as free Cubans.

Havana Center: Then, your information is copied, sir.

Pilot: Thank you very much. Cordial greetings. We report to you twelve miles north of Havana. We continue our search and rescue mission toward the east at this time . . .

Havana Center: Received, Havana.

Perhaps at that moment in the conversation with the control tower of Havana Center, Basulto and his pilots remembered similar warnings, as when they decided to drop thousands of leaflets containing anti-Castro propaganda—a tactic of political agitation employed by Brothers to the Rescue as a manner of making their support of dissident groups more viable. Flying secretly over Havana, the pilots had dropped thousands of printed sheets on at least two occasions. "Fight for your rights," said one of the leaflets dropped on January 13. Another, dropped that same day, read: "The people own the streets." The proclamations dropped over the city in July 1995 during the commemoration of the first anniversary of the sinking of the *13 de Marzo* tugboat warned the population: "Not *Compañeros,* Brothers."

The Cuban government, for its part, warned that it would not tolerate any more incursions over its territory. It warned that any plane that invaded its air space would be shot down.

The U.S. government, which until then had shown tolerance and even support for the activities of Brothers to the Rescue, criticized the clandestine incursions. It was then that some federal aviation officials began to investigate José Basulto and some of his pilots. The U.S. officials' main threat, reiterated on several occasions, was of revoking their pilots' licenses.

Pilot: Zero One. There's a MiG in the air. Bogie in the air. Where are you?

At that moment, Basulto saw black smoke to the right of his plane; he thought it was a flare, but then realized it was a "marker" used by fighter planes to lock on their targets. "Then, that worried me, because they use that when they're going to fire," Basulto would comment hours later.

Pilot: I know. The bogie is north of us right now, and they shot a flare, apparently to use as a reference.

Pilot: Seagull Charlie, Seagull Mike.

Seconds later, Basulto saw two MiGs. They were flying north on a diagonal, quite close together. Basulto tried to film them with his camera.

Pilot: One, have you heard from Charlie?

Pilot: Negative.

Pilot: What is your position?

Pilot: Seagull Mike is Two Three Three Zero Eight Two Two Nine.

......

Pilot: Seagull Charlie, Seagull Charlie.

Pilot: Charlie, Seagull One.

Pilot: Seagull Mike, are you with us?

......

Pilot: Oh shit . . .

......

Pilot: Do you see smoke under the MiG?

Pilot: I didn't see the MiG. I saw the smoke and a flare.

Pilot: I saw the MiG and I saw smoke. I don't . . . if it was a flare.

......

Pilot: Seagull Charlie, Seagull Charlie, Seagull One . . .

Pilot: Well, it looks like we have to get the hell . . . hear me?

Pilot: Mike, One.

Pilot: Do you have everything turned off?

Pilot: We're next.

Pilot: What?

Pilot: Head to Opa-Locka, to Opa-Locka. To base. To Opa-Locka.

On Friday, February 23, the *Nuevo Herald* had reported that on the previous day, the official press stated that the Cuban government was opening the island's arms and doors to the exiles it had fought for years. In popular Cuban slang, for decades they had been classified as "vile worms that crawl before Yankee imperialism." According to the information, a new document would permit all Cubans residing abroad to travel to Cuba freely as many times as they wished during a two-year period. The measure eliminated the process of applying for an entry visa for each trip to Cuba. This occurred two days before the patriotic celebration of February 24, when the first national meeting of the Cuban Council was to have been held. It had been suspended three days earlier, on Wednesday, February 21, since almost all its members had been detained, one day after pilot Juan Pablo Roque departed for an unknown destination, and two days before he was followed in the same direction by the Cessna 337s commanded by Basulto.

For Cuban Foreign Relations Ministry spokesman Rafael Daussá: "This corroborates the Cuban government's willingness to continue the process of normalization of relations with emigration. It will aid in family reunification." The document took effect on Thursday, and the application would be mailed to anyone who requested it from the Cuban Interests Section in Washington. The travel document would be available to any Cuban eighteen or older residing abroad and possessing a valid Cuban passport or foreign residency. Excluded from the right to travel to Cuba were persons with ties to organizations the Cuban government defined as "terrorist," who had participated in hostile actions against Cuba or had criminal or drug trafficking records. The applicant was required to include a certificate regarding criminal record with the application.

When the news reached the U.S. State Department, its response was: "It is not very exciting. It does not mean much. It is not a fair process. They will select travelers politically."

The implementation of the travel permits came up during the second meeting of Nation and Emigration, held in Havana the previous November. More than three hundred Cuban exiles residing in thirty-six different countries, most of them from the United States, participated in the meeting. On that occasion, Cuban Foreign Minister Roberto Robaina said that his government would not demand "ideological or political agreement to obtain the document, only respect for sovereignty, the country, and the people residing on the island."

Some participants in the Nation and Emigration meeting who were advocating for normalizing trips between Cuba and the United States were partially satisfied with the travel permit. Eloy Gutiérrez Menoyo had commanded the anti-Batista guerrilla group known as the II

National Front of Escambray in 1950 and is currently president of the anti-Castro opposition organization known as Cuban Change. He had repeatedly asked the Castro government to allow Cubans to come and go freely. Gutiérrez saw this document as "a good first step."

"We understand that it is not yet what we are requesting. We see it as positive because it includes many Cubans. But it is still a restrictive and controlled measure because it does not represent everyone. We have to keep fighting," declared Gutiérrez Menoyo.

For Francisco Hernández, a member of the executive board of the Cuban American National Foundation, the measure was "another one of Castro's maneuvers. It's typical of him," said Hernández. "In moments of crisis or when they're arresting dissidents and opponents, he redirects international attention to something that supposedly increases Cubans' rights to visit their country."

The news broke in Miami before the formal announcement was made in Havana and Washington. Starting very early that morning, interested parties began calling the various agencies that arrange trips to Cuba. In 1995, the U.S. Treasury Department had granted only 12,016 humanitarian permits—for reasons of illness—to travel to Cuba. During that same year, some sixty thousand Cubans residing in the United States traveled to the island to visit their relatives. Approximately eighteen thousand made the trip after the lifting of the restrictions imposed in 1994. Meanwhile, another thirty thousand did so going through third countries. In the opinion of Cuban-American economist Antonio Jorge, the Cuban government must have made the decision for purely economic reasons.

Realizing that after several tries he could not establish communication with the other two planes, José Basulto and his three passengers fell deathly silent, watching and waiting in the tiny cockpit. "Then we see a ball of smoke and fire. I think that was the first one they shot down, Carlos's, about eight miles away from us," said Basulto. "That was when I became very concerned. Then I start calling the other Cessna 337 and no one answers. I turn north and head into the clouds," Basulto would relate hours later. In the cockpit of Basulto's plane, there was complete silence. No one wanted to talk, but they all suspected with growing terror what might have happened. Alert for any signal, Basulto turned off the radio to make it more difficult for Cuban radar to detect him. "We knew that something frightful had happened. I felt that at any moment we would be shot down, too," Silvia Iriondo, president of Mothers Against Repression, would remember hours later.

An hour after having first established communication with the control tower in Havana Center to announce the arrival of the planes near Cuban territorial waters, Basulto connected his radio again. But this time the message he sent was not to Cuba, but to radio control operators in Florida. They asked that he make an emergency landing in Key West, but Basulto insisted in continuing on to Opa-Locka Airport. He was barely out of the plane when several FBI and customs officials who were waiting for him in the hangar rushed to meet him. The officials asked Basulto for the video and the tape from his recorder. Basulto insisted that he would not turn over the latter unless they made him a copy immediately. One of the customs officials tried three times to take it from him by force, without success. During the struggle, Basulto's copilot Arnaldo Iglesias reminded him that there was something "of concern." And then he remembered that the wife of Brothers to the Rescue pilot Juan Pablo Roque had said that Roque had left home under "strange circumstances."

On September 4, 1994, a year and a half prior to the downing of the two Cessna 337s, journalist Ana Santiago of the *Nuevo Herald* published a long report about the work of Brothers to the Rescue. Coincidentally, one of her main interviews was with former Cuban Air Force pilot Juan Pablo Roque. Roque began by saying that the enormous number of rafts that appeared every day in the Florida Straits had only one explanation. "As I see it, this all has a logical explanation, the internal situation in Cuba. So, look how that is . . ." Reporter Santiago presented Roque as a young officer, a deserter from the Cuban Armed Forces, who that day was flying his plane more calmly than usual. Roque had received word that his brother and cousin had set sail on a raft ten days earlier from Santa Cruz del Norte, in Havana province. Fortunately they did not die in the attempt; that same week he read their names on the lists of Cubans at Guantánamo. Juan Pablo Roque, former pilot of supersonic MiGs of Soviet manufacture, who, while in the Cuban Armed Forces (FAR), achieved the rank of second in command of San Julián Air Base in Pinar del Río, had swum to Guantánamo on February 18, 1992. "Imagine, and now my brother and cousin are there. On Sunday when I was flying, I thought for sure they were among the hundreds I saw that day. But it's not easy to find someone in that sea of raft people . . ." Roque told the reporter. Four years and two days later, Juan Pablo Roque magically disappeared again. And again, destination unknown . . .

On Sunday, February 25, 1996, just twenty-four hours after the flight of the three Cessna 337s ended in tragedy with the downing of two of them, the United Nations Security Council held an emergency meeting at the request of the United States, after the Cuban government confirmed that its war planes shot down two Brothers to the Rescue planes in an action they termed "necessary to preserve the sacred and inalienable duty to defend national sovereignty."

The lengthy communiqué issued in the early morning hours of Sunday, February 25 by the Cuban Foreign Ministry indicated that "the downing of the two pirate planes should serve as a lesson to those who encourage and carry out similar acts which tend to increase tensions between the U.S. and Cuba." The statement also indicated that the two Cessnas were shot down in international waters and placed blame for the incident on those who "repeatedly disregarded warnings and persisted in their irresponsible ventures."

The emergency meeting of the U.N. Security Council, which began at 8 P.M., was requested by U.S. Ambassador Madeleine Albright following instructions from President Clinton. It was unclear whether the United States would request a mere statement of condemnation against Cuba or seek a stronger resolution. Secretary of State Warren Christopher stated that the action of the Cuban government was a "flagrant violation" of international law and of the norms of civilized behavior. Christopher said that the downing of the planes on instructions from "top Cuban military authorities is a completely unjustified act." The then unspecified options put forth by Christopher were studied on Sunday during a three-hour meeting of the White House National Security Council, with political, military, and intelligence advisers in attendance.

Among those options would be: (1) suspension of commercial flights from Miami to Cuba; (2) interruption of shipments of money to Cuba by relatives in the United States; (3) freezing funds due Cuba for telephone calls to the island.

In search of more information about the procedures employed to shoot down the two Cessnas, the editors of the *Nuevo Herald* contacted Major Orestes Lorenzo, who had deserted from Cuba four years earlier. Lorenzo had managed to get his family out in a spectacular clandestine round trip between Florida and Cuba during which he flew very low over the sea and was thus able to avoid detection by Cuban radar. For Lorenzo, the downing of the planes had "all the characteristics of a lesson, a brutally clear message sent by Castro to the internal opposition and the entire world, that he is not willing to permit even the slightest dissidence nor create any type of political opening on the island."

According to Lorenzo, the Cuban MiGs simply massacred the Cessnas and their crews under orders "that without a doubt could have been issued only by Fidel Castro. Fighter pilots have the ability to intercept planes without shooting them down. That would have been perfectly practicable, but they simply had the order to shoot to kill." There are several usual steps for intercepting a plane:

(1) Moving the wings.
(2) Escorting the planes out of the firing area.
(3) Radio warnings that they will be shot down immediately if they continue on.
(4) Warning shots with tracer bullets in front of the plane to be intercepted.
(5) Warning overflights so that engine turbulence will cause the pilot to desist from continuing his route.

Lorenzo believed that the Cuban fighters went directly to their objectives because they already had their orders. "They were simply hunting them down . . . and they got them."

MiG 29s, such as those used in this attack, use four air-to-air missiles; additionally, the MiG 29 can carry two extra missiles. They are equipped with a double-barrel 23 mm. with two hundred projectiles in each barrel. The MiG 29 uses AA10ER Alamo missiles, which can be shot from any angle once set by radar. It also uses the 11RH. The 10ER system has a range of fifteen kilometers, and the AA11RH has a range of forty kilometers. Once the radar of a MiG 29 has located a target, the target cannot escape even by hiding behind a cloud bank. The pilot of the MiG 29 just has to release the air-to-air missiles, and the launched missiles, through their own radar systems, will take care of fixing the position and correcting it as they fly through space until they reach the fuselage of the enemy plane.

Tim Reilly and his crew were crossing the Florida Straits on a Charleston, South Carolina fishing boat that Saturday afternoon, February 24. They were the only witnesses who saw the Cuban MiGs shoot down the two civilian planes. According to Reilly's statement to the press later that day, "The planes blew up in the air; after the explosion, only fragments fell from the sky . . ."

On Monday, February 26, only forty-eight hours after the Cessnas were shot down, as in soap operas that reserve a bonus of intrigue and postpone the outcome of the plot *ad infinitum,* the audience following the development of the new crisis on both sides of the Florida Straits watched a sensational new chapter: The unexpected presence on the TV screen of the face of disappeared Cuban pilot Juan Pablo Roque! In an interview arranged through official Cuban television, Roque announced that he had returned to Cuba because he wanted to denounce to the world what he now called "the true nature of Brothers to the Rescue." Roque said, "The organization, charged from two thousand to four hundred dollars for locating relatives of people who had called them and passing the information on to the U.S. Coast Guard." Roque also announced that the organization received funds from the Cuban-American National Foundation and from businesses such as Bacardí, and that Brothers to the Rescue president José Basulto was a former CIA agent who had participated actively in terrorist actions in Cuba and Central America in the 1960s. Roque also claimed that he personally received instructions from Basulto to try to assassinate Fidel Castro and that there was nothing humanitarian about the pilots' organization.

※ ※ ※

Listening to Roque's statements on Cuban television, Guillermo Lares, a native of Argentina and chief of pilots of Brothers to the Rescue, stated: "I feel used, and Brothers to the Rescue feels used. This demonstrates that the attack was planned, because he must have been in Cuba when they shot down those two planes. I don't know how he could have worked with us."

Three days after leaving his home near Miami supposedly to carry out a Brothers to the Rescue mission in Key West, the forty-one-year-old Roque still had not returned. He had not called his wife, Ana Roque, nor had he shared the pain of the deaths of his four colleagues. The suspicions were increasing by the hour. By the end of the evening, it was at last clear that what everyone had feared had come true: Roque had returned to Cuba. Roque, who had been a member of the volunteer pilots' group since 1993, surprised his flying companions by disappearing. The fear of possible infiltration was a constant for the members of Brothers to the Rescue, especially after May 1995. That was when a sudden political shift occurred in their actions, as evidenced by the clandestine flights over Havana in July 1995 and January 1996. It seemed impossible to think that Roque, who the previous year had published a book titled *Deserter*, had betrayed them. But the facts, the clues, and their hearts told them it was true. According to Argentinian pilot Lares, Roque was one of those with the greatest knowledge of the organization and its flight plans. "He knew everything. He knew there was a mission on Saturday; he knew who was going to fly. He was aware of everything because he was very involved with Brothers to the Rescue," Lares told reporters.

FBI agents talked to the Roque family for several hours, along with Lares and Guillermo Castilla, a member of the Democracy Movement and close family friend. When they finished, the agents took three bags of evidence and a small box from Roque's home. After his departure, Roque had left a trail of unanswerable questions. He had taken with him his best clothes and jewelry: a Rolex watch, two other watches, and a gold chain with a crucifix. He also took pictures of his children, books, his flight manual and credentials, driver's license, Social Security card, two Bibles, and a permit to re-enter the United States.

Inside the green Jeep Cherokee he drove were his cellular phone, his beeper, his credit cards, and the car keys.

Born and raised in the ranks of the Communist Party, and educated in the Soviet Union, Roque had become a fighter pilot and second in command of an aerial regiment in Pinar del Río. "*Perestroika* caught me in Russia in 1985. There was a great stagnation between Cuba and Russia," Roque stated in an interview with the *Nuevo Herald*.

After arriving in Miami from Guantánamo, Roque joined groups of military deserters. In November 1993 he joined Brothers to the Rescue. He also wanted to send messages of solidarity and peace to the Cuban military, over the radio, cockpit to cockpit. "It will be more effective than any other message because it comes from a former *compañero,* someone they know or identify with. We'll talk, as the pilots' saying goes, on the same wavelength," Roque said then. The book, published by the Cuban Studies Fund of the Cuban American National Foundation, is Roque's autobiography. "*Deserter* is a document that should cause those who favor a dialogue whose result would save Fidel, not the country, to reflect," Roque wrote in his prologue. When Roque deserted, two brothers, also pilots, were left behind. Both were jailed for attempting to leave the country illegally but later escaped to the United States prior to the publication of Roque's book. "This book is a worldwide denunciation. It was my goal ever since I got here, but I couldn't do it until my brothers arrived. Now that they're here with me, here is the book," said Roque in the interview with the *Nuevo Herald*.

Monday, February 26, 1996, was also a day of great agitation on an international political level, particularly in the thirty-five-year-old dispute between Cuba and the United States, aggravated in the extreme by the surprise downing of the Brothers to the Rescue planes. "This attack on civilian aircraft in full flight was a flagrant violation of international law. It is unjust and the United States will not tolerate it," stated President Clinton. After spending the weekend analyzing options presented by the National Security Council and obtaining the opinions of leaders of the Cuba exile community who met in Washington with White House and Congressional officials, Clinton announced five measures to respond to the action of the Castro regime:

(1) Passage of a law to provide economic compensation to the families of the four disappeared pilots through Cuban funds frozen in the United States.

(2) Restricting travel of Cuban officials to the United States.

(3) Working with Congress to pass the Helms-Burton bill, which toughens the U.S. embargo.

(4) Expanding the reach of Radio Martí.

(5) Indefinite suspension of all charter flights to Cuba.

It was the second time in just sixteen months that the Clinton administration had imposed restrictive measures on the Castro regime as a consequence of the periodic crises between the two countries. In essence, the measures announced by Clinton to respond to this crisis were similar to those adopted in September 1994 as a result of the raft people crisis. Those measures were later lifted when an agreement was reached ending illegal immigration and providing for the deportation of Cubans who left the island for the United States.

"We are very pleased. The initial reaction is very favorable," said Jorge Mas Canosa, one of the first to return from Washington after meeting with representatives of the Clinton administration. Among the Cuban exile leaders of various political groups who had traveled to the capital were Ernestino Abreu, president of the Cuban Patriotic Board (Junta Patriótica Cubana); José Miró Torra, president of the 2506 Brigade (Brigada 2506); Ramón Saúl Sánchez, coordinator of the Democracy Movement (Movimiento Democracia); José Basulto, president of Brothers to the Rescue; and Hubert Matos, of Independent and Democratic Cuba (Cuba Independiente y Democrática). Clinton even left open the possibility of new sanctions, stating that he was not ruling out "some additional measure in the future, if necessary."

For his part, Secretary of State Warren Christopher stated in El Salvador, where he was visiting, that Clinton for the moment had not included "any military action among the steps to be taken, but has reserved the possibility of taking measures of this kind in the future."

In the opinion of international political analysts, the Cuban military's action against the civilian aircraft of Brothers to the Rescue put a stop to the discreet unofficial diplomacy that nongovernmental personalities and private U.S. institutions had been carrying out in recent months.

Jorge Domínguez, professor of political science at Harvard University and a specialist in Cuban affairs, said that he had always been in favor of communication with Cuba and in particular of trips by exiles to the island, which in his opinion "contribute more to weakening Castro than to favoring him." Although he admitted that on a political level the United States did not have many options other than the measures announced by Clinton, Domínguez stressed that the suspension of flights to Cuba, approved in 1994, was in his view a mistake. "This is counterproductive," emphasized Domínguez. With regard to the Helms-Burton bill, he suggested, the appropriate procedure was not to approve it or reject it as a consequence of the Cuban government's action. "The bill is good or bad on its own merits, according to the judgment of those who support it or criticize it; I do not see the relationship between this bill and what just happened," concluded Domínguez.

Anticipating Clinton's announcement of the strengthening of measures against Cuba, the Cuban Foreign Ministry on Monday morning issued a strong statement classifying as cynical Christopher's accusations that the planes were shot down outside Cuban territorial limits. "It is extremely shameless to try to justify matters now by alleging that the incident occurred in international waters. The United States is free to make decisions and take whatever steps it deems necessary, but it must be aware that these measures will inevitably have negative consequences for them, too," said the statement. The Cuban government asked the U.N. Security Council to postpone its decision until Tuesday, February 27, to allow time for a statement from Foreign Minister Roberto Robaina. Robaina was on his way to New York from Denmark, where he had arrived the previous day for a scheduled three-day visit.

Also on Monday, February 26, the official Cuban radio station Rebel Radio broadcast an interview with Lieutenant Colonel Francisco Pérez Pérez who, with his brother Alberto, also a lieutenant colonel, as copilot, commanded one of the MiGs that shot down the Brothers to the Rescue planes. Pérez said that another MiG, flown by Emilio Palacios, participated in the action as well; its mission was to cover him.

He added that when he identified the planes he ordered them to abandon Cuban air space and that after they ignored his warning, he received orders to shoot them down. The pilot gave no details of the exact location where the incident occurred.

Also on Monday, independent journalists interviewed the mother of Pablo Morales, one of the victims of the missiles fired at the planes. Mrs. Eva Barba, age seventy, told the reporters: "I feel a great sadness at the death of my son, but I'm sure that he is a patriot, and if he died, he died for his country."

On Wednesday, February 28, international news agencies published the declaration adopted on Tuesday, February 27, by the U.N. Security Council regarding the downing of the two planes by the Cuban Air Force. Among its fundamental paragraphs, the declaration stated:

> The Security Council profoundly laments the downing by the Cuban Air Force of two civilian aircraft on February 24, 1996, which seems to have resulted in the death of four people. The Security Council issues a reminder that, in accord with international law: ". . . States should abstain from using weapons against civilian aircraft in flight and should not endanger the lives of persons aboard nor the safety of the aircraft . . ." States are obligated to respect international law and norms relative to human rights under all circumstances. The Security Council asks that International Civil Aviation investigate the incident thoroughly and urges the governments involved to participate fully in that investigation. The Council asks International Civil Aviation to inform it of its conclusions as soon as possible. The Council will promptly examine that report as well as any new information presented.

New information about the downing of the planes appeared in the press alongside the opposing views of the Cuban and U.S. governments and the Security Council's statement. There were three conflicting positions regarding the scene of the incident.

José Basulto stated that the planes came within fifteen miles of the Havana coast, but never entered Cuban air space, during what he called an "absolutely routine" search and rescue mission. Basulto confirmed that the position of the planes was 23.▓▓, ▓▓.30, and 23.35 degrees of latitude.

U.S. government officials said radar indicated that the plane in which Basulto was traveling was three miles inside Cuban air space when the other two planes were shot down. They also stated that the other two planes did *not* enter the twelve-mile limit imposed by Cuba.

The Cuban Foreign Ministry said that three planes entered Cuban air space on Saturday morning, although Basulto stated that the planes did not leave Opa-Locka until 1:10 P.M. According to Cuba, two planes entered its air space again on Saturday afternoon, but Basulto's plane remained outside the limit.

Further information important for judging the seriousness of the case was the distribution among the representatives of the U.N. member countries of a transcript of the conversations between the Havana control tower and the pilots of the MiG 23 and the MiG 29. Ambassador Albright was the one who circulated the transcripts of the recordings.

MiG-29 (*to Control*): [My] altitude: seventeen hundred.

Control: Are you under the cloud ceiling?

MiG-29: There are no clouds here.

Control: Okay, keep looking under you, to the right . . . Continue on a course of ninety degrees.

MiG-29: We see three planes. Okay, there are three planes moving here. They fly together and then they separate.

MiG-23 (*to Control*): [I'm flying] on a course of seventy [degrees] north of Havana.

Control: What is your altitude?

MiG-23: Two hundred.

MiG-29 (*to Control*): The objective is north of Baracoa. On a course of 270.

MiG-29 (*to MiG-23*)**:** There's a very large boat there.

MiG-23 (*to MiG-29*)**:** I just saw it.

Control (*to MiG-29*)**:** Look for [your objective] under you.

MiG-29: Below, about thirty kilometers from Baracoa Beach.

Control: What is your altitude?

MiG-23: Two hundred.

Control (*to MiG-23*)**:** Climb to one thousand.

MiG-23: Roger. Altitude one thousand.

MiG-29 (*to Control*)**:** [My] altitude is fifteen hundred.

....

Control: Connect the UVD [ultraviolet detector].

MiG-23: Roger. UVD connected.

MiG-29: Connected.

Control (*to MiG-23*)**:** The objective is north of Santa Fé at a distance of twenty-five kilometers.

MiG-23: Roger. Now it's on a course of 180 and an altitude of one thousand.

MiG-29: Okay, the objective is in sight. It's a small plane.

MiG-23: Okay, we have it in sight, we have it in sight. It's a small plane, a small plane.

MiG-29: It's white, white.

MiG-23 (*to MiG-29*)**:** It's white and blue.

MiG-29 (*to Control*)**:** White and blue.

MiG-23 (*to Control*)**:** Give me instructions.

MiG-29 (*to Control*)**:** Instructions [to me, too].

MiG-23 (*to Control*)**:** Listen, authorize me.

MiG-29 (*to Control*): I have it in my sights.

MiG-23 (*to Control*): It's a Cessna 337.

MiG-23 (*to Control*): We have it in our sights. Give us authorization.

MiG-29 (*to Control*): That, that . . . Give us the [expletive].

Control (to MiG-29): Authorized. Authorized to destroy.

MiG-29 (*to Control*): I'm going to shoot.

Control: Authorized. Authorized to destroy.

MiG-29: Roger. I had already received it.

Control (*to MiG-29*): Did you shoot yet?

MiG-29 (*to Control*): First shot. [*He pauses and shouts:*] We blew his balls off! We blew his balls off! [*Original Spanish:* ¡Le partimos los cojones!]

MiG-23 (*to MiG-29*): [*Unintelligible shout.*]

MiG-29: We blew his balls off!

MiG-23 (*to MiG-29*): Wait, wait, look and see where he fell.

MiG-29 (*to MiG-23*): Mark the place where we shot him down. It's [*unintelligible*].

MiG-23 (*to MiG-29*): That one's not going to bother us again!

Interviewed again regarding the downing of the planes, Cuban Aviation Major Orestes Lorenzo identified code 020 as the one that has traditionally belonged to the chief of the Cuban Air Force. "It might be the chief of DAAFAR, General Rubén Martínez Puente," calculated Lorenzo. "This is the 020. You are authorized to destroy it," said a voice from the control tower. The pilots of the MiG-29 that shot down the Cessna 337s were identified as Lieutenant Colonel Francisco Pérez Pérez and his brother, Lieutenant Colonel Alberto Pérez Pérez. Both graduated as MiG-21 pilots in 1975 in the then Soviet Union and participated in the war in Angola. They have served most of their long military career at San Antonio de los Baños Air Base south of Havana province. They had taken off at 3:09 P.M. from that base, accompanied by the MiG-23 piloted by Major Emilio Palacios, which served as cover during the operation.

More chapters remained to be written in the long melodrama starring spy Juan Pablo Roque. Had Jorge Luis Borges, fond of ironies and paradoxes, still been living, he surely would have written a new version of his short story "The Theme of the Traitor and the Hero" inspired by these events. Juan Pablo Roque appeared before the television cameras once again. This time it was in an interview with CNN, transmitted via satellite to the United States. From Havana, Roque calmly stated that the FBI had full knowledge that two Brothers to the Rescue planes would be shot down Saturday, February 24, off the coast of Cuba. He told U.S. reporters that he had tried to dissuade the FBI, alleging that the trip in which four men lost their lives was insane. "They wanted martyrs. They wanted martyrs to continue the marketing, because the anti-Castro ranking was low," said Roque.

The FBI stated on Wednesday, February 28, that it had indeed paid Roque $6,722.40 for information regarding Brothers to the Rescue. But at the same time the FBI denied Roque's assertions that they knew of the attack at least three days before it happened. "I want to make it very clear that the FBI is calling Mr. Roque what he truly is: a liar," declared FBI official Paul Philip. He stated that the motives in paying Roque to inform on Brothers to the Rescue were noble: "This information was used to prevent U.S. citizens from embarking on what is clearly a dangerous mission," said Philip, referring to flights near Cuban territory.

Although he had been in Cuba when the two MiGs downed the two Brothers to the Rescue planes, Roque denied any tie to the incident. "My conscience is clear. I alerted the U.S. government that they were going to shoot them down. I did everything possible to prevent the deaths of my four *compañeros,*" Roque told U.S. reporters.

The climate of intense debate between Cuba and the United States reached a new record that would be hard to surpass on Wednesday, February 28, when Cuban Foreign Minister Roberto Robaina and U.S. Ambassador Madeleine Albright got into a war of epithets in the carpeted hallways and conference rooms of the United Nations.

"What went on here was a crime—the crime of shooting down unarmed planes from the sky," Albright said. The ambassador noted that in reading the transcripts she had been "struck by the joy of these pilots in committing cold-blooded murder and their use of common vulgarity to describe [their actions]. Frankly, this is not *cojones,*" she concluded. "This is *cowardice.*"

Responding to Albright's comments, Robaina defended Cuban *machismo* to reporters: "In language rarely used in diplomatic circles and even ugly for a lady, the U.S. ambassador did not hesitate to assert about my country—and I quote her literally—that this 'was not a problem of balls but of cowardice.' I only wish to say that we have always had more than enough of the former and have never lacked for the latter," declared Robaina.

A new round of hard punches (and possibly also "low blows") occurred between the U.S. and Cuban governments when, suddenly, and to the astonishment of international journalists, six Cuban military officers with ranks of colonel or lieutenant colonel, belonging to Cuban Intelligence, picked up their visas in Mexico to fly to New York. There they would meet with officers from none other than the CIA, to be informed with utmost precision about the details of the downing of the civilian planes. The main objective of the meeting was to demonstrate to the Cuban officers that the two planes were not in Cuban air space when they were shot down. According to U.S. sources, Robaina, who had been telling the United Nations that he had "all the conversations, all the maps . . ." to prove that Cuban air space had been violated, gave in after seeing the proof presented by the CIA.

Meanwhile, at the United Nations, diplomats following the Cuban question closely were astonished at Castro's decision to take action against dissidents just when he seemed to be breaking his diplomatic isolation. This action also occurred on the eve of the U.N. human rights session in Geneva and a vote in the U.S. Congress that could bring about stricter diplomatic sanctions against Cuba. One possible explanation: The Cuban economy was not functioning as well as many foreign observers had been led to believe, and Castro may have felt obligated to send a strong internal message that he would not tolerate any sort of protest. "Castro does that sort of thing when he feels weakest," said a former Latin-American president who follows Cuban affairs closely, remembering that during the crisis in the summer of 1989 Castro had ordered the execution of four top Cuban military officers, including potential rival for power Gen. Arnaldo Ochoa.

The Castro government provided the vote necessary to unite Democrats and Republicans in the U.S. Congress and approve the "Law of Freedom and Democratic Solidarity with Cuba" when it decided to shoot down two unarmed planes, causing the death of four exiles over the Florida Straits. A year after the Helms-Burton bill had been presented, Democrats and Republicans reached a joint agreement on Wednesday, February 28, to pass the law. "The president is happy that we have been able to reach an agreement and find common ground with the Congress," said White House spokesman Mike McCurry. President Clinton announced that he would support the law, over which he had expressed some reservations since it began its long journey through the House and Senate. "The president will enact the law; he wants to sign it. In light of Saturday's incident, he believes that strengthening the embargo is a necessary measure," added McCurry.

The law's main points included:

(1) Authorizing U.S. citizens, including naturalized Cuban exiles, to file claims in U.S. courts against those who conduct business with their property confiscated by the Cuban government since 1959.

(2) Authorizing the president to suspend the effect of that decree for six months in case of a democratic transition in Cuba.

(3) Denying visas to business people and stockholders of foreign companies that buy, rent, or obtain any benefit from property confiscated from U.S. citizens.

(4) Converting all executive decrees and regulations regarding the embargo into law, precluding the possibility of the president lifting it on his own.

(5) Instructing U.S. representatives to organizations such as the International Monetary Fund and the World Bank to oppose Cuba's entry into those institutions unless and until it has a democratic government.

(6) Instructing the president to prepare plans for economic support of a transitional government in Cuba.

(7) Authorizing the president to lift the embargo the moment there is verification that a democratically elected government has come to power on the island.

(8) Conditioning U.S. aid for an eventual transition government in Cuba on the compensation of the claims of U.S. citizens who suffered expropriations.

(9) Conditioning economic aid to the former Soviet republics such as Russia on their doing business with Castro at fair market prices.

(10) Urging the president to ask the U.N. to approve an international embargo against the Cuban government.

(11) Authorizing the president to support initiatives in favor of democracy in Cuba; providing aid to victims of political repression; and facilitating visits of human rights observers to the island.

Representatives of the Cuban government wasted no time in attacking the various points of the Helms-Burton Act. Ricardo Alarcón, president of the Cuban National Assembly, called it "absurd, stupid, and doomed to failure" and, not satisfied with the epithets he had already employed, added that Clinton had joined the "fascists and semi-fascists." Among other things, the sanctions seek to hinder Cuba's plans to attract new investment. According to economic reports by *World Business* in May and June of 1996, the Cuban government had announced a total of $5,132 million in foreign investment on the island. The main promises of investment were from Mexico ($2,256 million), Canada ($741 million), Australia ($500 million), South Africa ($400 million), and Spain ($350 million). In reality, economic experts calculated the amount of foreign investment physically located in Cuba at $736.9 million, including Mexico ($250 million), Spain ($125 million), Canada ($100 million), Italy ($87 million), and Great Britain ($50 million).

The measures resulting from the Helms-Burton Act appeared to affect mainly large companies with close commercial ties to the United States: Sherrit of Canada, which ran the nickel mine in Moa, expropriated by the Cuban government from Freeport Nickel and Sulfur Co. of Louisiana; the Spanish Sol Melia and Tryp hotel chain, which controlled a dozen hotels; another Spanish firm, Tabacalera, S.A., which financed tobacco harvests in the western province of Pinar del Río; Mexican telephone company Domos; the English-Dutch Unilever, which manufactured detergents in association with a Cuban state-run business; British American Tobacco, producing cigarettes through a Brazilian subsidiary; and the British firm EDF-Manha, which prefinanced the sugar harvest in some agro-industrial operations in Villa Clara province.

Javier Alvarez Bolado, president of the Association of Spanish Business People in Cuba, upon learning of the passage of the Helms-Burton Act, immediately declared: "The majority of the hundred and eight Spanish firms located in Cuba are small and medium-sized businesses that do not even have interests in the U.S. nor will they ever . . ."

When Ricardo Alarcón learned of the passage of the Helms-Burton Act, he declared, "If that law did not exist, someday it would have been possible to imagine negotiations which, after all, would have also included the claims against Cuba. Now, the first step toward that goal would have to be to toss the law into the wastepaper basket." Alarcón called the Helms-Burton Act "true insanity" and deemed compliance with its more controversial provisions impossible. According to Alarcón, the total indemnification due U.S. businesses confiscated since 1959 was calculated as approximately six thousand million dollars, but with the extension of the right to indemnification to U.S. citizens of Cuban origin, that figure could go as high as one hundred thousand million dollars. "According to the law, the blockade will remain in effect until there is payment of that amount, which is several times the value of our economy over a period of years," stressed Alarcón. He then pointed out that if President Clinton gave the green light in August, lawsuits against foreign investors would begin three months later, on the eve of elections: "Therefore, it is impossible for them to assume that commitment."

The law provided that foreign businesses that "traffic" in goods confiscated from U.S. citizens had three months to desist from doing business on the island once notified that they are operating with such property. Alarcón also referred to the articles of the law that prohibited firms from doing business with Cuba and prohibited the entry of their relatives into the United States, indicating: "It won't be easy to set up an apparatus to detect if a citizen attempting to enter the U.S. is the mother-in-law or sister-in-law of an investor in Cuba . . . Not even McCarthyism was capable of something like that, because it costs a lot of money," concluded Alarcón.

Until the signing of the Helms-Burton Act, the Clinton administration's strategy of increasing U.S. contacts with the Cuban people had been extremely confusing (Torricelli Law/Tracks I and II). That substantially diminished the possibilities of the United States playing a role in the peaceful transition on the island. Events had strengthened hard-liners on both sides of the Florida Straits, and cast a shadow of suspicion over the slightest contacts that might take place between independent U.S. citizens and Cubans.

"A Stalinist regime like Castro's would never tolerate the sort of political model that existed in Gorbachev's Russia," said Ernesto Betancourt, a Washington political consultant, referring to Track II of the Torricelli Law.

The strong measures against dissidents, the decision to shoot down two unarmed U.S. civilian planes, and a subsequent "Chinese Cultural Revolution"-style speech by army chief Raúl Castro against "ideological penetration" of which foreigners were carriers, were more than precise indicators, according to Cuban analysts, of the bunker mentality that had been unleashed in Cuba. Raúl Castro threatened Cuban academics, filmmakers, journalists, intellectuals, writers, and artists who "avoid patriotic conduct . . . and enter into contact with North Americans." A new era of clashes between "Reformists" and "Conservatives" within the directing apparatus of the Cuban Communist Party had begun shaping up; Raúl Castro's speech apparently attempted to set forth guidelines to follow in the application of the new party line of intransigence toward "any kind of enemy."

"We're back in the days following the Cuban missile crisis in 1962," commented Matías Travieso-Díaz, a Washington attorney who had invited Cuban academics to participate in debates on the future of the Cuban economy.

In the United States, passage of the Helms-Burton Act completely canceled attempts to improve relations with the Cuban regime (Torricelli Law/Tracks I and II). At the same time, it suppressed U.S. promises of a "measured response" to Castro's steps toward liberalization. The attempt to improve relations with Cuba, in the opinion of the experts, had entered a stage of a long and hard freeze.

With Cuban and U.S. officials digging in, and the absence of a credible independent group on the island, the opportunities for reform were being reduced in favor of a revolt. For its part, the climate of extreme tension promoted a new political arena for exiles who sought to provoke a rapid change, as was the case with Brothers to the Rescue, but, it also tied the United States to the possibility of yet another refugee crisis or the need to intervene militarily in Cuba.

"The possibility of peaceful transition in Cuba has been greatly reduced," declared Ed González, a RAND Corporation expert on Cuba who had just completed a study for the Pentagon.

The Helms-Burton Act was signed by President Clinton on Tuesday, March 12, 1996, during a solemn ceremony at the White House. Relatives of the four Brothers to the Rescue pilots killed in the February attack were present, along with Cuban-American legislators and activists from Florida and New Jersey. All stood and applauded when Clinton signed the law. The president gave some of the pens he used for the signing to the relatives of the deceased pilots.

"I sign this law in the name of the four men who died. In memory of them I will continue to do all I can to help the wave of democracy that has swept our hemisphere finally reach the coasts of Cuba." These were the U.S. president's first words to those in attendance at the signing ceremony.

The passage of the Helms-Burton Act by Congress, in response to President Clinton's request, prompted a whole series of questions related to the future of the Cuba-United States dispute. In early 1961, diplomatic relations between the two countries had been severed with the withdrawal of U.S. personnel from Havana and Cuban officials from Washington. Since then, a silent war—not without its true battles—had been waged. The invasion of the Bay of Pigs in 1961, the missile crisis of 1962, and the CIA's Operation Mongoose in the 1960s have been some of the extraordinary episodes of the long conflict between the two governments and between the Castro regime and the anti-Castro exiles in southern Florida.

With the opening of an Interests Office in Havana in the 1970s during the Carter administration, the tension between the two governments had seemed to decrease. But even so, a common opinion among experts was that there was no international legal instrument capable of exerting strong pressure on the Castro government. (At least this was the case while the Soviet Union and Communist bloc still existed.) And since diplomatic relations were broken and the economic embargo established in 1962, nothing could be done beyond that.

The Helms-Burton Act, then, among other things, established that highest point—perhaps the highest of all—in the dispute that had existed between the two countries for more than thirty years. The Helms-Burton Act, in fact, if applied to its full extent, would permit the United States to "run the Cuban economy at a distance," especially at a critical time when the only possible way out of the Cuban economic crisis revolved around the possibility of stimulating foreign investment. Through the law, the U.S. government could, in theory at least, determine in a global sense who can and cannot negotiate with Cuba, and to what extent.

In terms of past Cuban history, application of the Helms-Burton Act calls to mind the Platt Amendment, through which the Republic of Cuba was born back in 1902. It permitted the United States to intervene in Cuba's problems any time its property or economic interests were in jeopardy. (The Platt Amendment Law was repealed in 1934.)

July 1998 was the one-hundredth anniversary of U.S. military intervention in Cuba, that of the legendary Teddy Roosevelt and his Rough Riders, in Cuba's war against Spain. One could not help but wonder if the United States, a century later, was in a very similar position with respect to the island. In future years, any U.S. president could brandish the big stick in one hand, while waving the wad of bills with the other—dollar diplomacy—depending on whether the best interests of the United States were military-interventionist or diplomatic-economic. If this occurred, a hundred years of struggle for the renewed implementation of the Republic of Cuba would have passed in vain.

Although after the collapse of the Eastern European Communist bloc countries, it is not fashionable to quote him, this situation brings to mind the opinion of old Karl Marx—that history at times repeats itself, the first time as tragedy and the second as farce. Or, as U.S. philosopher George Santayana similarly observed in his meditations, "Those who do not learn the lessons of history seem destined to repeat them . . ."

Either of the options for future U.S. administrations—military or economic—would spell a sad ending to the history of a country that on February 24, 1895, began its second war of independence against Spain, a war that ended three years later, coincidentally through the intervention of the United States.

Chapter XI

The Golden Child

IT BEGAN ON THANKSGIVING AND ENDED ON EASTER. On the day before Thanksgiving of 1999, Donato Dalrymple received a call from his life-long friend San Ciancio, inviting him to spend the holiday doing what they enjoyed most: deep-sea fishing. They had not seen each other for a long time. At 7 a.m., Donato Dalrymple, after giving thanks to God as the Baptist pastor that he was, set sail cautiously from the Pompano Beach wharf. His sailing companion warned him to watch for flotsam brought in by the tide, because under those islands of drifting debris, the fish abounded. Off Lighthouse Point, the sea turned rough and the waves grew to a height of five feet. Donato Dalrymple, cautiously gripped the boat's wheel with both hands. At 8:30, amid the endless climbing and sudden descent over the waves, he noticed something strange, dark, and round floating in the middle of the ocean, surround-ed by several other vague dark shapes. Dolphins? Marlins? Gigantic sharks as in the movie Jaws? Sam Ciancio hurried to bait their hooks as the yacht approached the dark shapes. Donato Dalrymple's gaze pierced the foam of the waves, trying to identify the strange object.

Seconds later, Donato Dalrymple had the child on board: a piece of flesh shaken by the cold, and huge open eyes that stared, frightened, at the infinite sky of that Thanksgiving Day morning. Donato Dalrym-ple asked him, "Do you speak English?" The little boy did not answer. Then he asked him, "¿Hablas español?" The boy, with great difficulty, more with a gesture than with words, responded affirmatively. Dal-rymple wrapped him in a blanket and cradled him in his arms, which were covered with tattoos of sea serpents. The little boy sighed, as if relieved of a great burden, and immediately fell asleep. Not five months had passed from the miraculous discovery of the child lost at sea when, at dawn on April 23, 2000, Donato Dalrymple again held the sleeping child tightly in his tattooed arms. This time it was not a pod of protector dolphins watching in astonishment, but a half dozen police and Immigration and Naturalization Service (INS) agents. Armed to the teeth, their faces covered with gas masks, wearing helmets and bullet-proof vests, they went back and forth across the room like robots. One of them deftly handled a terrifying Heckler & Koch 9 mm machine gun capable of firing a round of thirty-two shots in seconds. He pointed it at the young fisherman and ordered him: "Release the boy or I'll blow your head off!"

The child in question was Elián González. He was born six years ago in the city of Cárdenas, Cuba. His innocent face, sometimes sad, sometimes happy, sometimes frightened, sometimes mischievous, sometimes angelic, has gone around the world thousands of times on the pages of newspapers and magazines and on television screens. Not just that. This child has managed, without even trying, to cause a crisis of unforeseen magnitude between the most economically powerful nation on the planet and the island of Cuba, one of the world's last bastions of Communism. This child has been the cause of angry debates in the U.S. House and Senate. He has divided as in a schism the most varied religious sects in the U.S. Fidel Castro has mobilized millions of people who have shouted from every anti-imperialist platform imaginable for Elián to return, willingly or unwillingly, to Cuba. He has occasioned the direct intervention of the U.S. Justice Department and the INS. Dozens of judges, lawyers, prosecutors, and immigration experts have come out for or against his remaining in the United States. In just six months, he went from living in a modest home in the Cuban town of Cárdenas, to floating on an inner tube in the middle of the Atlantic Ocean, to staying in a rented house in the Little Havana district of Miami, to Andrews Air Force Base, to a twenty-six-room fairytale palace outside Washington, D.C., reserved for housing multimillionaire heads of Arab oil states, to a colonial mansion in the historical district in the Washington suburbs very close to Al Gore's home. And Fidel Castro, at the height of his impatience, seeing that the U.S. judicial system was taking too long to award custody of the child to his legitimate father, complained that His Holiness, Pope John Paul II, from his golden throne in the Vatican, had not yet made a pronouncement in support of the boy's return to Cuba.

The history of the boy who previously had none began in the early morning hours of November 21, 1999. In shallow waters off the northern coast of the province of Matanzas, Cuba, some fifteen people were silently pushing out to sea a boat measuring seventeen by twenty feet in which they planned to escape clandestinely to the United States. One of those aboard the ill-fated craft was Elián González. Amidst his mother's pleas for silence, he repeated mischievously, "We're going to the Yuma!" Elián was accompanied by Elizabeth Brotons and Lázaro Munero, who, after having lived in Miami, had returned clandestinely to the island to organize this voyage, on which Lázaro would take his girlfriend, Elizabeth, and her son, Elián. As happened in so many clandestine departures from the island over the last decade, what was the search at all costs for the happiness of the American Dream, turned to tragedy and death in the middle of the Florida Straits. Of a total of fifteen on board, twelve drowned after the boat capsized in the dark sea. The next morning their bloated bodies began to appear, scattered in the waters near Fort Lauderdale, West Palm Beach, Fort Pierce, and Key Biscayne. Two of the survivors, Arianne Horta (aged twenty-two) and Nivaldo Fernández (aged thirty-three), would tell a terrible story of people clinging to inner tubes in the middle of the night, delirious from exhaustion and dehydration and the imminent presence of sharks. Desperate, they begin swimming toward the coast, never to reach it, or they simply slipped their bodies out of the inner tubes and allowed themselves to be swallowed up by the sea. That is what happened to Elián's mother, except that it appears that in one last desperate attempt to save her son she tied him to the inner tube, and destiny, in the person of fisherman Donato Dalrymple, took care of the rest.

Although Elián avoids talking about his mother, and at times says that she will come to get him or that she lives in Miami, one thing is certain: the first images of the little boy, strapped to a stretcher as he was being taken to Joe DiMaggio Children's Hospital, reflect his bewilderment at the tragedy he had experienced. Elián seemed to be asking with his huge open eyes looking sadly into space: For what am I to blame? Why do I, Elián González, have to pay?

The child does not know, but perhaps one day he will know that precisely in the year of his birth, the largest clandestine exodus of raft people in the history of his country occurred. In just five weeks between August 7 and September 14, 1999, approximately thirty-two thousand men, women, and children like him chose to risk crossing the sea and being devoured by the sharks of the Florida Straits rather than suffer deprivation in Cuba. At that time, the island was being terribly affected by the crisis occasioned by the fall of the Eastern European communist bloc. Beginning in the summer of 1994, when the United States, by direct order of President Bill Clinton, stopped the exodus of raft people, the situation changed radically overnight; welcomed as heroes by the Florida Cubans, the raft people became criminals for violating U.S. immigration laws. They could no longer immediately stroll down the busy Miami streets, but instead had to remain in a sort of migratory limbo behind the barbed-wire fences of the U.S. Naval Base on Guantánamo, until the marines finally decided to return them to Cuba. Knowing that this was the fate that awaited young Elián, his great uncle Lázaro González hurried to apply for legal custody when Elián was released from Joe DiMaggio Children's Hospital.

On the second day of Elián's stay in the U.S., the Cuban government, in a diplomatic note entitled "*Un nuevo crimen de Estados Unidos contra el pueblo cubano*" ("A New Crime by the U.S. Against the Cuban People"), blamed the U.S. government for the deaths of the twelve people off the Florida coast. According to the Cuban government, the Cuban Navy telegraphed U.S. Coast Guard units regarding the presence on the open sea of a craft loaded with passengers attempting a clandestine voyage from Cuba to the United States. In conjunction with this complaint, the Cuban government began steps at the U.S. Cuban Interests Section in Havana to have Elián González returned to his father as soon as possible. The response of Elián's Miami relatives was immediate; they answered that they would oppose, by every possible means, the repatriation planned by the Cuban government. The U.S. government, through State Department spokesman James Rubin, called the Cuban accusation "appalling and unwarranted." Thus began, forty-eight hours after he was found floating in the sea on Thanksgiving Day, what the world would come to know in the next six months as "The Battle for Elián."

The Miami Cuban community's displays of solidarity with the González family, in charge of the child's custody for the moment, were not long in coming. On Sunday, local attorneys Spencer Aig and Nelson Rodríguez Varela, aware that the case of the little raft boy might eventually involve even international legal bodies, such as the Court of Justice in the Hague and the United Nations, offered their legal services free of charge. Elián and his relatives also received visits that day from Florida Cuban-American Republican Congresswoman Ileana Ros-Lehtinen and pilot José Basulto, founder of Brothers to the Rescue. Both of these political figures of the Miami Cuban exile community promised the González family economic support and legal and personal counsel.

On Monday, the González family hurried to take Elián to his bedroom so that he would not see or hear on television the words hurled from Cárdenas by his father Juan Miguel González. Juan Miguel accused the Miami Gonzálezes of getting rich through the public exhibition of his son. "If I have to go get my son, I will!" On Tuesday, the INS confirmed that Elián González had just received a permit to stay in the U.S. in the custody of his Miami relatives. From Seattle, where he was participating in the meeting of the World Trade Organization (WTO), Cuban Foreign Relations Minister Felipe Pérez Roque insisted that the child was being forcibly held in the U.S. "His father has custody rights to the child in Cuba; the attitude of the Cuban exiles in Miami is repugnant and offensive, as they are trying to create propaganda, mixing family matters with political ones." On Thursday, in language typical of ultimatums, the Cuban government, in a clear reference to the upcoming round of immigration negotiations that would be held in Havana the next day, December 13, blamed the U.S. for the deterioration that would occur in relations between the two countries if the United States did not send the boy back. The next day, the newspaper *Granma,* official organ of the Cuban Communist Party, on its front page, elevated Elián González to the status of national hero. The editorial stated:

We will free, you Elián, from that hell of selfishness, alienation, abuse and injustice, where they have so brutally and illegally taken you. You will return to the bosom of your family, your town and your country, a symbol and hero who survived clinging for who knows how many endless hours to a piece of rubber. Eleven million Cubans are committed to your freedom!

To reaffirm the content of the editorial, Ricardo Alarcón, president of the Cuban National Assembly and chief political negotiator on immigration matters, went to Cárdenas to visit Juan Miguel González. Before thousands of people who attended the public ceremony, he reiterated:

My recommendation to the U.S. government is that it guarantee Elián's return prior to the next conference, because it is very difficult to imagine that we could have any sort of constructive discussion. This is the fight of Elián's entire family, which is the Cuban people, and we are going to win it.

For its part, *Granma* attacked Ileana Ros-Lehtinen, calling her a "a ferocious wolf" that directs the revolution's enemies in Miami. *Granma* dedicated one of its eight pages to explaining to Cubans just who is "the ferocious wolf disguised as a woman" who two weeks earlier, in front of the television cameras, had wrapped Elián González in a U.S. flag. Since then, the scene of the congresswoman, the child, and the flag was rerun until it became part of a video that was made to ask for Elián's return. After several scenes of wolves, the camera focuses on the head of a wolf, whose face gradually transforms into that of Ileana Ros-Lehtinen. But she was not the only exile figure stigmatized and demonized. In the heat of "The Battle for Elián," the newspaper *Granma,* National Assembly President Ricardo Alarcón, and Fidel Castro himself developed a vocabulary typical of medieval bestiaries. Some of the zoological characterizations of the leaders of the Cuban exile community include Ileana Ros-Lehtinen as a hyena and ferocious wolf, Congressman Lincoln Díaz-Balart as a cross between a jackal and a buffalo, human rights activist Frank Calzón as a dinosaur, attorney Armando Gutiérrez, spokesman for Elián's Miami relatives, as a cross between a vulture and a parrot, and the director of radio station Radio Mambí, Armando Pérez Roura, as a jackal turned chameleon.

Meanwhile, in Miami, unaware of the storm that was beginning to brew above his little head, Elián was celebrating his sixth birthday on U.S. soil. Some fifty people attended the party, held in Barnes Park, where Elián had access to all kinds of entertainment and gifts. He ran around on the grass, went horseback riding through the park, blew out his birthday candles, and competed with the other children for the candy from an airplane-shaped piñata. His greatest joy was tearing the wrapping paper off the endless collection of gifts that he received. In late December and early January, Elián would appear just as happy, raising his fingers in the victory sign as he walked through the Magic Kingdom of Disney World in Orlando, holding Mickey Mouse's hand; being carried on the shoulders of the Miami mayor to watch the Three Kings' Day parade; when he was invited by Mayor Giuliani of New York to attend the New Year's festivities; and laughing happily at the antics of the clowns at the Ringling Bros. Barnum and Bailey Circus as they performed their acrobatics on the floor of the Miami Arena. But while Elián was happy during his birthday party, there was a sadness in the other guests. They were remembering that just a few hours earlier, a collective burial had taken place in which they said goodbye to seven victims of the Thanksgiving Day shipwreck, among them Elián's mother.

In response to the news from Miami, the Cuban government announced that it, too, would officially celebrate Elián's sixth birthday at his school in Cárdenas. At José Martí Airport, an indignant Fidel Castro, welcoming home the delegation that attended the WTO meeting in Seattle, made a statement to the television cameras:

> I hope that what we are doing will be unnecessary, but that they will be sensible and return him within 72 hours, because if they don't, they will see millions of people in the streets demanding the child's freedom. We will move heaven and earth . . . it will be a war, the worldwide battle that will be waged. This is not negotiable, life is not negotiable, a father's right to his son is not negotiable. It is absurd, cruel, and criminal to hold Elián in Florida against the will of his father!

As an immediate response to Fidel Castro's words, two thousand young people ran through the streets of Havana and gathered in front of the U.S. Interests Office. Under the approving eye of the police, who allowed them access, the demonstrators demanded the return of the child and shouted slogans: "Elián, our friend, Cuba is with you!" "We love Elián!" "Long live Fidel!" "Down with Yankee imperialism!"

The demonstrations outside the gray building of the U.S. Interests Office continued throughout the following week. The Cuban government ordered that a 200-meter-long and 50-meter-wide public grandstand be built outside the U.S. diplomatic headquarters. Fifty U.S. diplomats and 250 Cuban employees who worked in the building were virtually besieged by crowds of demonstrators parading and shouting ceaselessly from early in the morning until after midnight. Vicki Huddleston, head of the U.S. mission, assured foreign correspondents, amidst raving shouts of "Cuba yes, Yankees no! Free Elián! Elián, don't worry, the people are with you!" that they would continue working in the building in their usual duties of visa processing and attention to immigration matters. That same afternoon, in the grandstand erected outside the U.S. mission, speeches began, delivered by the leaders of the Federation of Cuban Women, the Union of Communist Youth, the Communist Party, and the Cuban Pioneers. In addition to the political leaders, an endless array of religious personalities also paraded across the platform: evangelical pastors, Hebrew leaders, babalawos of Cuban santería, and members of the Abakuá brotherhood, all of them united in demanding Elián's return to Cuba. Hasan Pérez, president of the University Student Federation, warned the diplomats and employees who at that moment were leaving the diplomatic mission and heading for the parking, "If you do not comply with Comandante Fidel Castro's proposal to bring Elián to Cuba immediately, tomorrow there will be twice this many people and the day after four times this many, until 11 million Cubans march down the Malecón to the Interests Office."

On Monday, December 13, at 7 a.m., a few hours before the opening in Havana of the new round of immigration negotiations between the two governments, two INS officials and one from the Interests Office met with Juan Miguel González. The private meeting of Elián's father with the U.S. delegates took place four days after Fidel Castro publicly proclaimed that Juan Miguel González was not willing to meet with any U.S. official and that Elián's repatriation should take place without any negotiation whatsoever. The news created panic among Elián's Miami relatives. They examined with their attorneys the possible strategies to follow, among which the main option was an application for political asylum for the child. After consulting with the lawyers, the González family, Elián in hand, went to pray at the Ermita de la Caridad. Hundreds of Cuban parishioners had congregated at the popular Miami church to pray for the child to remain in the U.S. "We invite the community to pray for the second half of the Elián miracle," said José Basulto, president of Brothers to the Rescue, in a statement released by the organization. The Democracy Movement put out an urgent call to all Cuban, American, and Latin-American residents of Miami to form a human chain of solidarity around the block where Elián was living, in case U.S. authorities prepared to return him to Cuba without allowing the courts to intervene in his case. "All we ask is that the child not be returned without being allowed to have a court decide his case; that would constitute a terrible concession to Fidel Castro," said Ramón Saúl Sánchez, leader of the Democracy Movement, which since 1995, when Cuba and the U.S. signed the accords that authorized the return of raft people, has led various acts of civil disobedience in Florida.

If it were necessary to judge the psychology of Elián's father during the initial stage of the repatriation process, one would have to call it variable and contradictory. Some images provided of him did not match others. One could assemble a psychological portrait of him as a young Cuban formed within the revolution, who married very young. Juan Miguel González was a member of the Communist Party in Cuba. The couple lived in the city of Cárdenas, very near Varadero Beach, an area almost completely dedicated to international tourism, and they both worked for hotels that paid Cubans part of their salary in dollars. Their relationship with their son, Elián, was perfect. When his wife divorced him and had another boyfriend, Juan Miguel agreed that he would visit her in their home and play with the child. This image of complete harmony showed Juan Miguel as a citizen devoted to the communist system and an exemplary husband. But there was another image that his relatives in Miami and some old friends living in Cuba and the U.S. began to circulate about him. According to this other image, Juan Miguel frequently beat his wife Elizabeth and abused her domestically. And what was even more revealing: on more than one occasion he had privately expressed to relatives his wish to go live in the United States. For that reason, some wondered why Juan Miguel was now so passionately denouncing, on platforms next to Ricardo Alarcón and Fidel Castro, the kidnapping of his son by the Cuban mafia of Florida and Yankee imperialism. It was also stated that, from the moment Juan Miguel González approached the Cuban government for support in the legal procedure of obtaining his son's return, as if by magic, he stopped working, moved to an unknown location, and was put under psychiatric treatment in order to recover from the shock caused by the loss of his son and former wife. But other analysts indicated that all those unknown steps regarding the status and future of Juan Miguel González were nothing more than a screen of disinformation that hid the truth of what was happening: that Juan Miguel González was being prepared by the Cuban Intelligence Services so that at some time he could come to the U.S. to play the fundamental leading role in "The Battle for Elián."

By mid-January 2000, raft child Elián González had left anonymity far behind and was becoming a cover story for Time magazine. Later he would also appear on the cover of *Newsweek,* and his innocent face would again go around the world in another *Time* cover photo, but this time he would appear in the arms of his father. Paradoxically, while Elián was appearing on the cover of *Time,* his father, Juan Miguel González, was avoiding the international press that was requesting interviews with him in Cuba. When U.S. reporters wanted to interview him, they had to arrange an appointment through the Communist Party. Neighbors commented to foreign correspondents who went to interview him in Cárdenas that "Juan Miguel doesn't work anymore; he doesn't live with his family and he has become an important person who has direct access to government and revolutionary leaders, among them Fidel Castro." And as evidence of what they had told the reporters, the neighbors would point to Juan Miguel's house, which previously had faded paint and a dirty appearance, but now was fresh-ly painted blue and brown and displayed clean doors and windows.

In mid-January 2000, Elian's grandmothers from Cuba became involved. It was announced that the two grandmothers would come to the U.S. soon to visit their grandson, in what would be the first direct contact the child had with his family from Cuba after two months of separation. Lázaro González, Elián's great uncle, who from the first had taken charge of the legal demand for custody of the child, said he had no objection to a visit by Raquel Rodríguez, Elián's maternal grandmother, and Mariela Quintana, his paternal grandmother. He warned, however, that if the intention of their trip was to pick up the child and take him back to Cuba, he would only turn him over under a judicial order approved by his attorneys. "This is a country of laws. They can't come to pick him up like someone comes to pick up a suit-case of clothes." Very soon the two grandmothers and the Cuban gov-ernment began to express objections. Mariela Quintana, the paternal grandmother, stated that she would "only be in the U.S. for five min-utes, the time it will take me to pick him up." And all of this was due to the fear that, in their desire to come to the U.S. and pick up their grandson, they would find themselves involved in a legal process in U.S. courts. Finally, the two grandmothers agreed to travel to the U.S. under the sponsorship of the National Council of Churches.

On the afternoon of Thursday, January 20, without notice, the State Department issued visas to the grandmothers, and shortly thereafter a lear jet took off from New York with Bob Edgar and Joan Brown Campbell, representatives of the National Council of Churches, aboard. The plane was to return from Havana that same night with the two grandmothers aboard. But, in fact, it left and returned to New York with no passengers. On Friday, January 21, the lear jet again took off mysteriously, leaving behind a trail of uncertainty about its destination and return. Several hours later, when it landed and the door opened, the two grandmothers appeared for the first time in front of one hundred and thirty reporters and photographers. They appeared disconcerted, never imagining that New York, from the air, would be so big and have so many lights that even at night it seemed bright as day.

From New York, the traveling grandmothers, wearing elegant coats and winter clothes, went to Washington to lobby with Attorney General Janet Reno for Elián's return. The grandmothers appealed to Reno's feminine sensibilities, cried to her, and gave her an emotional letter in which they stated that the possibility of a meeting with their grandson in the coming hours was remote. "We only have Sunday to see Elián, and we would like not only to see him but return with him to Cuba." Janet Reno and Doris Meissner, in a press conference, explained to the grandmothers that Elián's case was pending appeal before a federal court and that they hoped for a resolution as soon as possible. Despite the attorney general's diplomacy, the grandmothers' stay on U.S. soil became aggressively political. The González family, from Miami, see-ing the grandmothers' pitiful request to see their grandson, said pub-licly that the grandmothers were invited to visit their Little Havana home. Jorge Mas Santos, son of the deceased leader of the Cuban-American National Foundation, offered his private jet to rush the grandmothers from New York to Miami. But the response to both con-ciliatory attitudes came quickly from Havana through statements by Ricardo Alarcón. "Miami is the only place in the world where such a meeting is impossible." Nevertheless, through arrangements kept secret even from the press that was covering the grandmothers' trip, on the afternoon of Monday, January 24, they traveled to Miami. In coor-dinated scheduling, the grandmothers boarded the lear jet in Washing-ton at the same instant that the González family, carrying little Elián in their arms, was arriving at the Tamiami Airport outside Miami. But as the journalists were preparing to report on the sensational family reunion, the grandmothers' minds and the lear jet's changed course. At 8:26 p.m. they took off from Miami and returned again to Washington. Robert Edgar, secretary general of the National Council of Churches, felt obligated to appear before the press immediately to explain why the grandmothers had appeared and then disappeared clandestinely from Miami. "We are not confident of the security around the González family home in Miami, and we did not want this to turn into a circus and have them tell the child that it was a party. We do not want a scene with families fighting over a child."

The grandmothers' reunion with their grandson finally took place on Wednesday, January 26. Earlier, in Washington, the grandmothers lobbied for his repatriation with New York Democratic Representative

José Serrano, who, from the first, had come out in favor of the child's quick return to Cuba. The meeting was held in Miami, in the home of Jeanne O'Laughlin, president of Barry University. Despite the secret arrangements for the meeting, police and about two hundred demonstrators surrounded the nun's huge house, carrying Cuban flags and singing patriotic songs.

There were so many versions of the meeting, which only lasted a few minutes, that it would take a long time to get to the truth. The facts are few: the grandmothers showed their grandson photographs of his family and friends in Cuba and played with his stuffed animals. The speculation generated by such simple facts was enormous. The bucolic family image was denied by the hostess, Sister O'Laughlin, who told the press that in order for the grandmothers to get over their fear of being kidnapped, she had them walk through the entire mansion to convince them that there were no doors or secret passageways hidden in the walls; the windows could not be opened from outside; and in the yard, which was very small, there was not enough room for an emergency landing by an artillery helicopter. "I think that people with political interests are using the child as a pawn, and perhaps the grandmothers, too. I understand that the Cuban government has said that we were not nice to the grandmothers and that we spied on them. That is not true."

Nevertheless, the newspaper Granma, which had no reporter or correspondent stationed at O'Laughlin's home, offered a detailed version of everything that occurred behind its walls just one day after the secret meeting:

> Brought by helicopter at 5:15 p.m., they entered the luxurious mansion with great dignity. This was the neutral site that the U.S. Attorney General's Office and the INS, along with Miami authorities, had chosen for the child's meeting with his grandmothers. INS officials, police, nuns associated with the mafia, and Marisleysis herself mingling among them as if she were one more nun, completed the picture. Somewhat macabre. When they were left apparently alone in that room, perhaps full of microphones and even electronic surveillance media,

the silent suffering of the grandmothers began. Suddenly a nun opened the door to the room and told the grandmothers that they could not use the phone. A policeman ordered them to hand over their phones. The conversation was interrupted. Over the cellular phone on which Mariela had been speaking, doubtless still activated, Juan Miguel continued hearing men's voices speaking in English. Deceit, lies, traps, betrayals, humiliations and an inhuman and despotic treatment was the price that the Miami of the mafia charged these grandmothers, as loving as they are heroic, in its hideout in Little Havana, for the successes they had attained before the U.S. people. The image of Elián, like that of Che, regardless of what they do to him, whether they disappear him or destroy him morally and psychologically, will cover the world and remain forever in our minds and in the hearts of young men and women, of adults and the elderly, and of the children who today idolize and fight for him.

In response to the statements in Granma, Sister O'Laughlin stated:

I will advocate for what the child needs right now, and that is freedom. I do not believe that this child will be able to live without fear if he returns to Cuba. Elián needs to be in a safe environment and free of fear as soon as possible. At this time I believe that that place is in the United States.

After the interview with the family, Elián would repeat into the microphones of Miami Cuban radio station Radio Martí: "Tomorrow they're going to make me a citizen." From Havana, his father, Juan Miguel González, stated in interviews with the UNICEF representative and Officer Silma Dimmel of the U.S. Interests Section in Havana, "They called me on Saturday, November 27, and offered me two million, a house, and a car. They also told me that a church had offered Elián four million so that his life would be taken care of."

For its part, the U.S. government reiterated that it was not changing its decision to repatriate Elián, despite the fact that the attorneys of his Miami relatives on Thursday had achieved an extension until March of 2000 to respond to the appeal filed by the attorney general's office asking for dismissal of a lawsuit alleging that the INS had violated the child's rights. Given the openly controversial situation involving not only the two branches of the González family in Cuba and the United States, but also both governments and the various U.S. federal agencies, Richard Nuccio, former adviser to President Bill Clinton on Cuban affairs, considered it appropriate to state that with regard to the Elián González case, political precedents were being established at low levels as well as high ones:

> It will become more and more difficult for the U.S. Coast Guard and the INS to try to separate the decisions they make from the Washington political atmosphere. They will never know if some member of Congress or some congressional hearing will question their decisions, or if government leaders will do the same.

Regarding the upper echelons of political leadership, Nuccio considered that the case was a conflict over who controls U.S. policy toward Cuba:

> And it might be the first time in the country's history that such a small child has been involved in a web of international politics of such magnitude. In a way, Elián is an instrument for both sides, who are using the case for their arguments, since, on the one hand, the Cuban accords are treasonous and against the best interests of the Cuban people. On the other, those who want an end to the embargo and a change in U.S. policy toward Cuba see the matter as an opportunity to cooperate and reduce tensions.

Elián's grandmothers returned to Havana without their grandson. Fidel Castro ordered a great popular welcome for them. The Comandante provided the grandmothers with a Mercedes-Benz, followed by a formal escort of eight cars that traveled the twenty kilometers from the airport to the capital. People shouted crazily "Elián!, Elián!" as the grandmothers, smiling broadly, waved to the crowd from the convertible, like a couple of acclaimed Hollywood actresses. At the brand new Havana Convention Palace, none other than Comandante Fidel Castro, surrounded by an extraordinary praetorian guard of one thousand and eight hundred Pioneer children, anxiously awaited the grandmothers' arrival. That night, the grandmothers appeared before Cuban television cameras and recounted for the people the details of their visit to the United States and the interview at Sister O'Laughlin's home. But there was one detail of the grandmothers' account that immediately angered the Cuban exiles in Miami who saw a rebroadcast of the interview some hours later. Mariela Quintana stated on camera how she had looked at Elián's genital organs during the visit at the nun's home; she had also given him a little bite on his tongue. "Playing with the child, I said: 'Let's see, Patio, stick out your tongue,' and I gave him a little bite on his tongue. And then I opened up his zipper and said: 'Let's see if your little parts have grown'." The grandmothers also stated that when they left the interview, Sister O'Laughlin tried to calm their sadness: "God is very great and will do something so that Elián can go back with you." But grandmother Raquel Rodríguez emphasized, "I was so angry that I told her, 'I don't give a damn about God. I don't believe in God or anyone'." It should be noted that upon their return to New York, the two grandmothers went to mass and prayed with thousands of Protestant worshippers.

Despite the mobilization of the Miami Cuban exile community in Elián's favor, the general U.S. population maintained as its criterion the respect for the right of a father to claim his son under any circumstances, as reported by a Gallup Poll taken in late February 2000, after Elián had been in the United States for three months: 67 percent of Americans approved of the federal government's decision to reunite the child with his father in Cuba.

On Tuesday, March 21, in a fifty-page decision, Judge Kevin Moore denied Elián González the right to apply for political asylum in the United States. Around the same time, it was announced that, at the request of the National Council of Churches, Attorney Gregory B. Craig of the firm Williams & Connolly, the same person who defended President Clinton in the Monica Lewinsky scandal, would handle Juan Miguel González's custody claim. According to the press release from Williams & Connolly, neither the Cuban government nor the U.S. government had influenced the decision to accept the case. The statement did not specify who would pay for the legal services, estimated at $800 per hour. Florida Republican Representative Bill McCollum, sponsor of a bill to grant U.S. citizenship to Elián, stated, "It's a clear message that the Clinton administration is placing its own agenda above what would be in the best interest of the child." Cuban-American Congressman Lincoln Díaz-Balart was much more explicit: "It's difficult to imagine Craig taking a case like this without Clinton asking him to; they're like brothers. It's dramatic to see how this administration has committed itself to the Fidel Castro dictatorship in the return of Elián."

On Thursday, March 23, 2000, U.S. government officials began pressuring Elián's Miami relatives to release him. In a letter to the family's attorneys, the Justice Department gave a deadline of noon on Friday, March 24, for the family quickly to appeal the ruling that the decision to return the child to Cuba be left in the hands of Janet Reno. Thus, the resulting process would be resolved in three weeks, instead of the several months it usually takes. The day after Janet Reno's ultimatum, the silhouette of the Virgin Mary appeared reflected in the glass door of the Total Bank office at 468 27th Avenue in Miami. The bank became a place of pilgrimage for Little Havana residents. Although the bank was closed on Saturdays, a multitude crowded around the entrance to the bank to contemplate the glass door, where appeared what seemed to be a reflection of an oval rainbow surrounded by a white halo, which they identified as the mother of Jesus. "I was moved. I saw a cloak and a crown," stated Armando Sotolongo, a fifty-year-old Cuban for whom, without a doubt, the Virgin's appearance at that moment had to do with Elián. Meanwhile, again unaware of the storm brewing above his little head, on Sunday, March 26, Elián was enjoying the portable swimming pool that his great uncle Lázaro González and his cousin Marisleysis had set up in the yard of their Little Havana home (Elián Park). In the afternoon, still wet and smiling, Elián saw Father Francisco Santana visit his relatives with a message stating, "Elián's fate is in God's hands. Only in God's hands." Early in the morning on Monday, March 27, Marisleysis González, Elián's cousin who, from the time he arrived, had been taking care of him as if she were his second mother, hurriedly stated to the CNN cameras, "The big question that no one has answered yet, and he (Elián's father) has to answer, is very simple: If you love your son so much, why don't you come to see him, why don't you come to get him?"

Many things were beginning to happen with regard to Juan Miguel González's possible trip to pick up his son. On Tuesday, March 28, a federal commission carried out a thorough inspection of Homestead Air Base south of Miami, to organize a possible trip by Elián's father. Miami mayor Joe Carollo, who learned of the presence of federal authorities in his jurisdiction, hurried to declare, "This cannot happen." Certainly, the fact that in 1961 he was one of fourteen thousand young Cubans sent alone by their anti-Communist parents to the United States in Operation Peter Pan, had to do with Carollo's sympathetic statement.

In Havana it was officially announced that on Thursday, March 30, Juan Miguel González, his second wife and their child, and a cousin of Elián would travel to the United States to get Elián. Fidel Castro intervened to request additional visas. He said that Juan Miguel would travel to Washington accompanied by a delegation of thirty people, including National Assembly president and main strategist in Cuba-U.S. negotiations Ricardo Alarcón. Accompanying Alarcón and Juan Miguel González's immediate family would be two of Elián's teachers, a group of psychologists, child psychiatrists, specialized medical personnel, and twelve of Elián's classmates. Fidel Castro added that, if necessary, he would also send by air freight the desks and tables for the children to take classes during their stay in Washington. The question floating in the air after Castro's emphatic statements was, would the U.S. government grant all the visas requested by Comandante Fidel Castro? One day before Fidel Castro's request, U.S. president Bill Clinton himself stated emphatically: "Elián's Miami relatives must respect the decision of the law. If they win in court, the others will have to accept it." This time when Castro and Clinton and the two branches of the González family and the National Council of Churches and the Attorney General and the INS argued, it was not over the presence of Soviet missiles in Cuba or thousands of raft people in the Florida Straits but about a sad, lonely, six-year-old boy. What was happening with the child who was the protagonist of this incredible story?

On Wednesday, March 29, ABC's "Good Morning America" showed several close-ups of Elián González at the moment that host Diane Sawyer asked him if he wished to return to Cuba.

Q. Would you like your father to come visit you here?
A. No.
Q. No? Why not?
A. Because he's going to take me to Cuba and I don't want to go to Cuba.
Q. Would you like him to stay here?
A. He can stay here. I don't want to go.
Q. And if your father comes to live in Miami, and all of you live together in Miami, and everyone stays here in Miami?
A. I would stay, too.

The month of March 2000, was ending with the Miami Cuban exile community ready for war awaiting the arrival of Juan Miguel González. The twenty-two mayors of Miami-Dade County, led by Alex Penelas, announced in front of the Federal Court Building that their police departments would not cooperate with federal authorities if the latter carried out an operation to take Elián from the home of his relatives. Penelas said he held Bill Clinton and Janet Reno responsible for any incidents that might occur in Miami-Dade County if Washington insisted on sending Elián back to Cuba without a court appeal. "We are facing the possibility of riots. Any resulting tragedy will be perceived as their responsibility."

That night, tens of thousands of people armed with flashlights with colored lights formed a grandiose and spectacular shining cross on Calle Ocho in an attempt at further mobilizations to prevent Elián's repatriation. Flags, crucifixes, rosaries, and placards shared space in the two rows of people who formed what they termed the "Cross of Pain" on Calle Ocho. "This is a message of faith," said 42-year-old Ileana Simón, who came from Fort Lauderdale with her husband. "We have to show that they can't trample on our rights. Where man's law ends, God's law begins." Clergy read passages from the Bible, prayed the Lord's Prayer, and the Cuban Chorale sang the hymn "You Will Reign." Although the ceremony had a markedly religious character, the slogans against the White House and in favor of Elián were repeated, especially the best-known ones: "Clinton, you coward, Miami burns with anger" and "Elián, friend, the people are with you."

The month of April 2000, promised to be a month of intense agitation on both sides of the Florida Straits. Would the Clinton administration give in to the pressure of the popular mobilizations in Cuba for Elián's return? Would Fidel Castro triumph again in what he considered another battle against imperialism?

So that no one would question that he would take "The Battle for Elián" to never-dreamed-of limits, Fidel Castro ordered the overnight construction of a three-meter-high bronze sculpture of nineteenth-century Cuban independence leader José Martí in the plaza in front of the U.S. Interests Office in Havana. But this time, Martí, amazingly, was not playing the role of the warrior nor of the apostle of independence, but that of a loving father. In the original version of the sculpture approved by Fidel Castro, Martí would hold in his arms a small boy, a little Elián, which sculptor Andrés González placed on the monument after consulting with Castro; with the index finger of his free left hand, Martí would point menacingly toward the U.S. diplomatic residence. To top it all off, four gigantic iron arches on concrete pedestals would give visitors the sensation of a ceiling and national unity.

In Miami, Elián's relatives were greatly disturbed; on April 3, the boy's residency permit was revoked. The INS informed them that that permit had to be transferred from great uncle Lázaro González to father Juan Miguel González at the moment that the latter arrived from Cuba. Elián's time was running out. The Miami Cubans took to the streets to form human chains, arms linked, in front of the Little Havana home where Elián was living, while others, filled with religious fervor, organized a permanent prayer vigil. During one of these vigils, word reached them that Juan Miguel González had arrived in Washington the morning of April 7. As soon as he got off the plane, he told the press, "I have come to Washington, where I hope to embrace my son for the first time in four months." Juan Miguel was taken by Interests Office officials from the airport to the residence of Fernando Ramírez Estenoz, chief of the Cuban diplomatic mission. In the opinion of political analysts, Elián's father's presence in Washington dramatically tipped the balance in favor of quick repatriation of the child, such that an anonymous government source indicated, "From the moment that Juan Miguel set foot in the Washington airport, our efforts were completely geared toward turning his son over to him." The two psychiatrists and one psychologist appointed by the INS to evaluate the child expressed similar opinions: "Even if he screams and says he doesn't want to go, he should be given to his father."

With the announcement that the U.S. government was giving a twenty-four-hour ultimatum to the González family to turn Elián over, the fervor of the groups in front of the house was renewed. The gigantic multicolored cross formed by thousands of flashlights lighting the sky along Calle Ocho appeared again in the darkness of the night. An emergency motion filed by the González family's attorneys in the Eleventh Circuit Court of Appeals gave the family and the crowd gathered outside the door of their home some breathing room. At the critical hour of 2 p.m., Lázaro González did not go to Opa-Locka Airport with Elián, as the INS had ordered. And despite Attorney Gregory Craig's claims that the family had broken the law, Attorney General Janet Reno announced that she would not send military forces to the González home. In front of the González house, the crowd awaited with growing tension the zero hour for Elián's return. And while the wait was becoming nearly unbearable, some of the best-known figures of Cuban exile culture, such as trumpeter Arturo Sandoval, imposed a respectful silence by masterfully playing the national anthems of Cuba and the United States. Among those in attendance were singer Gloria Estefan and her husband, composer Emilio Estefan, actor Andy García, salsa singer Willie Chirino and his wife, Lissette, and singer Albita Rodríguez. Upon hearing the news that the Miami Gonzálezes had delayed the return of his son for an indefinite period, Juan Miguel González, before hundreds of TV cameras and photographers stationed outside the Cuban diplomatic mission in Washington, raised his middle finger in an obscene gesture that irritated public opinion upon see-ing him so aggressive on the television screens.

The response of the Cuban government was immediate. Alejandro González, spokesman for the Cuban State Department, during the meeting of countries in the Southern Summit, declared to the interna-tional news agencies that were covering the conference, "There were great expectations for today. We are witnessing a new maneuver by the Miami mafia."

On Friday, April 14, 2000, barely twenty-four hours after the Gonzálezes refused to return Elián, INS Commissioner Doris Meissner harshly criticized the family's defiance of the orders she had issued. She sent them a letter repeating that legally they no longer had custody of the minor child: "Our main interest continues to be to reunite Elián with his father." In response to Meissner, the family distributed a letter asking U.S. authorities to allow the child to spend Holy Week with them. "This will be Elián's first Easter in freedom." Upon learning of the new prolonging of his son's stay in the United States, deeply dis-appointed with U.S. authorities and furious with his relatives in Miami, Juan Miguel González attended mass at Washington's National Cathe-dral. After praying, he returned to the Secret Service vehicles that had escorted him wherever he went. He declared to the reporters who were waiting for him at the door to his apartment, "I'm not leaving here without my son; I don't care how long I have to stay."

U.S. pediatrician Irwin Redlener, in support of the most recent statements by Juan Miguel González, sent a letter to the INS in which he warned of the "imminent danger faced by the child Elián González upon remaining in Miami in a psychologically damaging home." Dr. Redlener, who heads the Children's Health Fund, said that he had writ-ten the letter of his own initiative after the airing of a video—taped by Elián's Miami relatives—showing the boy saying that he does not want to return to Cuba. The Cuban government announced the following day, Tuesday, April 18, that it had a mansion ready in Havana to pro-ceed with little Elián's readaptation. Dr. Lesbia Cánovas, director of the Central Institute of Pedagogical Sciences (Instituto Central de Ciencias Pedagógicas), explained on Cuban television, "This transition is necessary; our goal is that he become fully integrated into his school group, his school, not just the classroom but also his environment." An old white mansion located at the intersection of 1st and 34th streets in the Miramar neighborhood was hurriedly prepared as an active spiritual retreat for Elián. The mansion was fitted out as a house and school for Elián, his father, Juan Miguel, his stepmother and his brother, his maternal and paternal grandparents, twelve of his classmates, his preschool and first-grade teachers, psychologists, pediatricians, and medical personnel.

That same afternoon, at five, what people began calling "The Elián Show" was beginning in Cuba: two commercial-free hours on the only state channel, dedicated entirely to the retransmission of news about the case of the most famous shipwrecked child in the world. Fidel Castro, who at 5 p.m. was serving as moderator of a panel at one of the meetings of the summit of seventy-seven developing nations that was being held in the Havana Convention Palace, left in the middle of an address by United Nations Secretary General Kofi Annan to be present in the television studio for the "The Elián Show."

On April 21, *The Washington Post* stated that Janet Reno had decided to remove Elián from his great uncle's home in Miami and had ordered police officials to determine the best time to do so. *The New York Times,* quoting unidentified government officials, said that the operation to remove Elián from the home of his relatives would be carried out by immigration agents and federal marshals who had been arriving in Miami during the past few days. According to *The Times,* Reno "is under strong pressure from inside and outside the government to put an end to the embarrassing South Florida soap opera." According to independent reporter Matt Drudge, Reno told a group of collaborators the previous day, "The President wants the child out of the house."

"We aren't afraid! We aren't afraid!" shouted the demonstrators surrounding the Gonzálezes' house in Miami, foreshadowing a possible confrontation with law enforcement officers. And over the microphone they had used every day to express their opinions, several of those in attendance stated that they were willing "to die" to prevent Elián from leaving Little Havana. Ramón Saúl Sánchez, president of the Democracy Movement, said that they had "many suspicions" that the government would act over the weekend, but he insisted that any act of opposition would be peaceful. "We will respond to violence with nonviolence." Women dressed in mourning sang a hymn, "Protect This Child, Lord."

Rui Ferreira, a Nuevo Herald reporter of Portuguese origin who resided in Havana as a correspondent until authorities expelled him from Cuba in early 1998, was reading news dispatches on the computer, when he heard a CNN correspondent say to his cameraman, "They'll be here in ten minutes." He knew very well what that meant. The zero hour, the moment of truth, had arrived. He ran as fast as he could to the stairs opposite Lázaro González's home. Positioned there, some two meters above the ground, he was able to see, second by second as in an action film, the arrival of the INS and border patrol agents who took Elián before dawn.

It was 5:07 a.m. when, suddenly, to his right, Rui Ferreira saw that the metal barricades sealing off the street were being opened by two police officers, and four unmarked white vans with dark polarized windows penetrated rapidly. Agents armed with batons and machine guns, wearing bulletproof vests and helmets, jumped from the vehicles. In a well-coordinated action, those who got out on the side where the reporters were, began to shout in English and Spanish, "Don't move, don't move!" while they unleashed pepper spray all around them with no regard for who was hit. On the other side of the street, four agents headed for the fence of the González home, cut through it, and ran the few meters to the stairs leading up to the door of the house. "Open up, open the door!" they shouted in unison, pounding on the door with a sledgehammer. With the fourth or fifth blow, the door gave way and was finally knocked down with a kick. The agents were now inside the house. Some thirty Cuban exiles who managed to recover from the surprise and the pepper spray that the federal agents had used on them, managed to leap over the metal barricade that was holding them back and run toward the house. From inside a nearby home, several women of the group Mothers Against Repression (MAR) emerged; they had maintained a constant vigil for days. Behind them appeared two agents who had entered the area from the other side of the block. Silvia Iriondo, leader of the group, seemed to have suffered from the pepper spray. The group of women advanced, with great difficulty, to the González yard. The agents out in the street were trying to contain the groups of reporters and demonstrators, who shouted at them "Murderers, murderers!"

How much time had passed since the CNN reporter sounded the alarm to his companion and Rui Ferreira ran to a nearby stairway and saw the vans arrive? He looked at his watch and calculated that it had been less than a minute, barely 45 or 50 seconds, and at that precise instant he saw Elián appear in the doorway, where the door had been kicked in. First a very fleeting glimpse: the child, very small, lost amid so many uniformed troops and almost completely wrapped in a blanket. As he approached the van, his image grew larger. A woman was carrying him on the run. Elián was screaming and screaming, surrounded by police agents who were armed to the teeth. Elián was screaming and thrashing his arms and legs. "No, no, no!" Elián screamed, but no one paid any heed to his cries.

Inside the van, Elián continued screaming, but someone abruptly closed the door, and no more screams were heard nor were there any more glimpses of the child, who disappeared into the darkness of that early morning. Suddenly, when the agents were beginning to withdraw toward the remaining vans, the demonstrators, who had advanced half a block, hurled a volley of bottles, rocks, sticks, pieces of metal, chairs, and tables, all of which bounced violently against the metal shells of the vans. At that moment, a terrible cry of pain, or perhaps of horror, was heard from inside the house through the open doors. It was Elián's great uncle, Lázaro González, who despite the effects of the gas, found the strength to exclaim, "Cowards, cowards, cowards!" Behind him, through the doorway, came Donato Dalrymple and Elián's other great uncle, Delfín González. Lázaro was sobbing profusely. Delfín, more composed, began to shout at the Miami police, who were still there: "Traitors! There is no more democracy in this country!"

Elián was immediately taken to Watson Island and, from there, by helicopter to Homestead Air Base. There, he was transferred to an Air Force plane for a direct flight to Andrews Air Force Base in Washington, D.C. Upon his arrival at Andrews, his father, Juan Miguel González, boarded the plane and spent some time with his son inside the cabin. Later, photos provided to the press by Attorney Gregory Craig showed Elián smiling in the arms of the father he had not seen in more than five months. These photos of Elián, smiling with his father, contrasted with others taken by a reporter during the police operation, which showed the child frightened at the close proximity of the soldier armed with the horrific Heckler & Koch 9-mm machine gun. From Andrews Air Force Base, Elián was taken with the rest of his family to a luxurious country mansion at Wye Plantation, one hundred miles east of Washington. Under strict legal decrees pronounced by the Court of Appeals, he had a hearing scheduled for May 11. From the moment that he was taken to the country mansion, Elián was visited continuously by more than two dozen Cuban diplomats, their wives, children, and assistants, which gave rise to accusations that communist agents were using the child's tranquil stay to "deprogram" him on U.S. soil. At some moment during his stay, Elián, along with other Cuban children sent from the island, was dressed in the uniform of the Pioneers Organization; they all shouted the Pioneers' slogan: "For communism we will be like Che!" Congressman Lincoln Díaz-Balart declared bitterly, "When I think about the unlimited access those Castroite agents have to the child, while his relatives and the rest of the world, including the press, are denied access, it gives me chills. They're brainwashing him, it's that simple."

Elián and his family moved again on Thursday, May 25, to live in a Cleveland Park neighborhood in northwest Washington, D.C., in a building that belonged to the youth exchange organization Youth For Understanding. They had barely moved into their new residence when a team of workers from Long Fence Company arrived and in less than three hours put up a ten-foot-high fence to prevent curious onlookers, reporters, and photographers from seeing in.

⚜   ⚜   ⚜

Back in Miami an hour after the crowd had thrown rocks, garbage cans, and chairs at the agents, groups of demonstrators blocked traffic on Highway 836 and 27th Avenue. Ramón Saúl Sánchez called for a work stoppage, but begged the crowd gathered in front of the house to avoid violence. Anti-riot police occupied the main street corners in Little Havana and chased groups of demonstrators. Twelve hours later, at 6:15 p.m., the Miami police reported that 184 people had been arrested. "Murderers, sellouts, you've betrayed us again," were some of the most heated words heard during the early hours of the morning. "Just like they crucified Christ 2000 years ago, today they did it to this innocent child," said others. A boy about thirteen years of age was thrown to the ground and beaten violently by police on the corner of Flagler Street and 33rd Avenue, his face bloodied. A man in a blue Nissan Sentra burst onto the scene and got out of his vehicle armed with an aluminum baseball bat and landed several blows that left three agents wounded. A swarm of police officers attacked the man and beat him with his own bat. Groups of masked young men threw stones and burned garbage cans along streets and avenues. At noon, more than one hundred demonstrators proceeded to Miami International Airport, and a human barrier prevented the exit and entry of cars along 42nd Street. Miami Fire Department spokesman Captain Joe Fernández reported that as of 4:30 p.m., they had responded to 128 incidents related to burning tires, garbage cans, and buildings. The wave of protests finally culminated in a gigantic patriotic march on Saturday, April 29, along Calle Ocho. About 100,000 people expressed their rejection of the federal government's action and demanded freedom for Cuba. Mayor Carollo's reaction to the news that city police officers, despite his orders to the contrary, had participated in the abduction of the child, was furious. He demanded the resignation of Miami Police Chief William O'Brien, who was forced to retire after 25 years of service.

In Havana, Fidel Castro, learning of the successful abduction of Elián, decreed a day of truce in the long struggle fought by the Cuban people for more than forty years against what he calls U.S. imperialism. Coincidentally, Castro made this announcement during the 39th anniversary (1961 - 2000) of the defeat of the invasion by Cuban exiles at the Bay of Pigs, very near the place from which he had directed the final battle against the invaders. Despite his jubilation, Castro did not approve of Juan Miguel and Elián having to remain in the U.S. until a hearing by the federal court in Atlanta. He, therefore, took advantage of Cuba's May Day (International Workers' Day) celebration to accuse the United States of attempting to convince Elián's father to remain there.

Once Elián had been turned over by the U.S. to his father, what for five months had been "The Battle for Elián" began to turn into Elián Mania on both shores of the Florida Straits. In addition to the mobilizations of thousands of people shouting "Return Elián!" and the daily two-hour "The Elián Show" devoted exclusively to news about the child kidnapped in the United States, Fidel Castro ordered the printing of thousands of sets of eight postcards, each bearing photos of the reunion of Elián and his father. The postcards were sent to all the primary schools in the country through the Pioneers organization. Parallel to Fidel Castro's campaigns on the island, the U.S. government was forced to pay about $120,000 per week in expenses for the special twenty-four-hour security service surrounding every movement of Elián González in his successive places of residence at Andrews Air Force Base, the mansion in Maryland, and finally, the building in the suburban Washington neighborhood. The security mechanism normally assigned to taking care of this six-year-old child was made up of fifty federal agents and twenty INS agents. The federal service spent approximately $81,000 on its protection team, including the cost of gasoline, vehicles, telephone calls, and computer software. The INS spent another $40,000. According to The New York Post, the total cost of security and surveillance of Elián totaled $1.4 million. According to the Post, housing was provided to Elián and his family through private organizations such as the National Council of Churches. Their meals and supplies were covered by the Cuban government.

A California businessman of Iranian origin, Max Zadeh, began advertising and selling 16.9-ounce bottled water under the name "Elián Water." The idea of selling bottled water associated with Elián had immediate repercussions within the Cuban exile community in Miami. In addition to the traditional and folkloric little bottles of "holy water" said to have been touched by Elián and blessed by a Little Havana priest, someone had the idea of bottling "the air and the aroma" of the neighborhood where the boy lived in Miami; when auctioned, the bottles brought in $14,999. A clever merchant put on sale for $15,000 over the Internet the raft on which, supposedly, Elián had arrived in the United States. Another businessperson put up for sale on the Internet for the price of four million dollars one of the dolphins that allegedly had saved the shipwrecked child. And there was one even bolder individual who offered Elián himself for sale for the sum of $10 million. Another entity that participated fervently in "The Battle for Elián" and Elián Mania was the powerful anti-Castro organization the Cuban-American National Foundation. Jorge Mas Santos, foundation president, estimated that the organization invested approximately $10,000 in the trips that Elián's Miami relatives made to lobby in Washington. Other expenses of the Foundation included the stay of its security chief, Mario Miranda, at the González family home in Little Havana during the entire duration of the legal battle over the child. Finally, the Foundation's security chief was detained at gunpoint outside the home in the early morning of April 23, when the federal troops raided the González residence. The Foundation also gave money to Elián's great uncle Lázaro González and provided jobs for him and the survivors of the shipwreck in which Elián's mother, Elizabeth Brotons, had lost her life.

On Thursday, June 1, 2000, the Appeals Court in Atlanta ruled that Elián González could not seek political asylum in the United States. Upon hearing the result on radio and television, some women on vigil in front of the González home fainted; others sobbed loudly. The men did not hide their emotions either. But there was no violence. The unanimous reaction of the hundreds of people gathered in front of the Little Havana home was one of pain, powerlessness, and frustration. Their spirits calmed a little when they learned that Elián could still remain in the United States for three more weeks while the family's attorneys exhausted the ultimate legal recourse: an appeal to the U.S. Supreme Court.

Exile leaders called for moderation. Jorge Mas Santos made a plea for calm. "A massive demonstration now would be counterproductive." Olga Nidia García, aged seventeen, tearful, cried to everyone who would listen, "My faith is crushed. How is it possible that Fidel Castro rules here, too?"

From Washington, in a press conference in which Attorney Gregory Craig also participated, Juan Miguel González said that he was very satisfied with the court's decision. For the first time he dared to pronounce a word in English before cameras and microphones: "Thanks." In Havana, Fidel Castro interpreted the decision in military terms: "We have won a battle, but there are still some skirmishes to win." He immediately convoked a sensational women's demonstration of patriotic reaffirmation outside the U.S. Interests Office: a half million women—married, single, divorced, widows, mothers, grandmothers, daughters, and granddaughters—shouted anti-imperialist slogans, having as their chorus, "Return Elián! Return Elián!" At the end of the rally, there was a reading of a communiqué issued by the Revolutionary Leadership:

> Our people have the right to demand the liberation and return of all of them to Cuba. Holding them in the United States is not only the fruit of a cruel and unjustifiable revenge on the part of the mafia and their allies, but also of the despicable purpose and the ridiculous hope, on the part of the highest governmental and political authorities of that country, of buying a Cuban father whom they have consistently humiliated and offended.

In its Friday, June 9, 2000, edition, *El Nuevo Herald,* the most widely circulated newspaper in the city of Miami, provided previously unpublished information about alleged collaboration between the Havana and Washington governments in the final actions that led to the military assault by 151 armed officers on the González family home in Little Havana. According to the *Nuevo Herald*'s information, documents requested from the court by Judicial Watch, a nongovernmental organization headquartered in Washington, revealed, among other things, that: (1) the State Department, along with other government agencies, worked with the Cubans to handle the information provided to the U.S. media about the Elián case; (2) the head of the INS, Doris Meissner, had participated in the conversations to arrange Elián's grandmothers' trip, considering that the trip "could facilitate Elián's return to Cuba"; (3) the INS decided that "it would not be involved" directly in the grandmothers' trip and agenda and therefore suggested arranging for the participation of the Miami Catholic Church through Cardinal Jaime Ortega, archbishop of Havana. El Nuevo Herald also noted that a few hours after Elián was forcibly taken from his Miami residence on April 23, Fidel Castro acknowledged in a speech given in Jagüey Grande, Matanzas, that he and Ricardo Alarcón were in direct telephone contact with Attorney Gregory Craig, who in turn was negotiating at the same time, also by phone, with Janet Reno and the negotiators appointed by Elián's Miami relatives. These statements by Castro, which were recorded and immediately published by El Nuevo Herald, were never reproduced by the official press in Cuba. The Havana government also acknowledged that it had sent intelligence information to the State Department, warning of the presence of alleged armed men whose mission would be to prevent any action by federal agents to take Elián in Miami. "All these documents and information demonstrate that, from the beginning, there was voluntary coordination by Clinton with Castro," stated Cuban-American Congressman Lincoln Díaz-Balart. "Sooner or later the true story of all this collaboration will come to light," the Florida Republican lawmaker stressed.

Events happened fast again during the second half of June, 2000. On Wednesday, June 28, around noon, the Cuban government exhorted the population to keep calm following the news that the U.S. Supreme Court had refused to accept the case of Elián González, thus removing the final obstacle to the child's return to Cuba.

After a total of two hundred and sixteen days of "The Battle for Elián," the shipwrecked child returned to his place of origin, the island of Cuba, on Wednesday afternoon, June 28, 2000. Of him one could say, as in an old Castilian lyric poem, "He came by sea, lived on land, lit fires, became smoke in the air." Forty-one minutes after the Supreme Court issued its decision, two jets of the Airline Brokers Company of Miami were taking off for Havana from a Washington airport. The metal door of the plane that took him to José Martí Airport in Havana had barely opened when Elián found himself surrounded by shouts, hugs, and tears from his grandparents, more than 800 Pioneer children, and teachers from the Marcelo Salado Elementary that he had attended in Cárdenas. He was greeted by Fidel Castro and Ricardo Alarcón.

The González family of Miami that fought for his custody for the first two hundred and fifteen days was not able to see him or talk to him again in the last fifty days of his stay in the United States; at every moment, Juan Miguel González flatly refused to grant them even the opportunity to say goodbye to the child. The González home in Miami, where Elián had lived for five months, looked like a tightly closed cemetery. Two flags, one Cuban and the other American, languished in the middle of the yard "Elián Park." Around them, wilted by the summer heat, lay several floral offerings dried by time and the sun. Behind them, motionless, were the slide and swing where little Elián had played so many times. Inside, half sleepwalkers and half ghosts, resided great uncle and aunt Lázaro and Angela González. Marisleysis, Elián's cousin who had cared for him like a second mother, had not wanted to return to the Little Havana house since the morning of April 23 when the military forces had snatched the child from her arms. "They are very sad; it's very sad to be there," said Armando Gutiérrez, the family's official spokesman.

Among the politicians who had dealt directly with the Elián case, the opinions could not be more conflicting. President Bill Clinton stated that he had recently discussed with German authorities in that country the reunification of American and German families. "Those problems have reaffirmed for me that we did the right thing." Attorney General Janet Reno showed her satisfaction with the decision of the highest court in the land: "The law has permitted a legal process to be carried out, and this child now knows that he may remain with his father." Republican Congressman Lincoln Díaz-Balart was especially harsh in his criticism of the Clinton administration because of the methods employed to return Elián to his father: "This day of infamy will be remembered with the emblematic date of the presidency of a coward, who sent the 'Clinton commandos' against a defenseless child while he slept to return him to a tyrant; his mother gave her life to save him." Florida Governor Jeb Bush also expressed his disappointment: "Despite the emotional feelings in South Florida, it is my firm desire that the unfortunate divisions that this case caused in the community begin to disappear."

The Cuban government issued a brief communiqué when it learned of Elián's return: "We have achieved the objective of the child's return to live in his country after an arduous and unprecedented battle of ideas and masses. This is no time for bragging, conceit, or boasting, which is incompatible with our revolutionary habits and norms."

As soon as he left customs at the Cuban airport, Elián González was taken to a big, luxurious house in the exclusive Miramar area that the Cuban government had reserved for him and his family as a temporary home. From the moment he entered the mansion, it was as if the night had swallowed him up. From comments that have filtered out, it is known that living in the house were Elián, his immediate family, other children who, along with him, attended the school created inside the residence, teachers, psychologists, and psychiatric specialists. Outside, all the blocks around the mansion were patrolled by armed police, who prevented vehicle traffic and removed possible onlookers from the residence facilities. In a front-page note the same day Elián arrived back in Cuba, Wednesday, June 28, Granma indicated that Elián's family was in complete agreement with the model plan being carried out with the child to reintegrate him into Cuban reality. "Our selfless teachers and pedagogues will carry out the master work of turning him into a model child, worthy of his history and his friendliness and his talent so that he may forever be at once a normal citizen, a symbol, an example, and a glory for all the children of our country, and a source of pride for the educators of Cuba."

⚓ ⚓ ⚓

Ten or twelve years from now, will Elián González return to the United States manning his own raft? Will the international press and public opinion, which experienced his incredible odyssey day after day, forget him? Will he endure? Will he survive? Will he adapt?